University of Northern Iowa

The Summer Nights Never End
...Until They Do

Life, Liberty, and the Lure of the Short-Run

Robert James Waller

The Summer Nights Never End
...Until They Do

Life, Liberty, and the Lure of the Short-Run

Robert James Waller

W&A PUBLISHING

TRADERS PRESS

One Peregrine Way, Cedar Falls, Iowa 50613
www.w-apublishing.com | www.traderspress.com

This book is printed on acid-free paper.

Copyright © 2011 by Robert James Waller. All rights reserved.

Published by W&A Publishing, Cedar Falls, Iowa www.w-apublishing.com.

No part of this book may be reproduced or transmitted in any form or by any means, electronic or mechanical, including photocopying, recording, or by any information storage and retrieval system, except as permitted under Section 107 or 108 of the 1976 United States Copyright Act, without permission in writing from the publisher and the copyright holder. Requests to the publisher for permission should be addressed to One Peregrine Way, Cedar Falls, IA 50613.

In the publication of this book, every effort has been made to offer the most current, correct, and clearly expressed information possible. Nonetheless, inadvertent errors can occur, and rules and regulations governing personal finance and investing often change. Any advice and strategies contained herein may not be suitable for your situation, and there is a risk of loss in financial investing and/or trading stocks, commodity futures, options, and foreign exchange products.

Neither the publisher nor author shall be liable for any loss of profit or any other commercial damages, including but not limited to special, incidental, consequential, or other damages that are incurred as a consequence of the use and application, directly or indirectly, of any information presented in this book. If legal, tax advice, or other expert assistance is required, the services of a professional should be sought.

Library of Congress Control Number: 2011943274
ISBN: 978-1-934354-25-4
ISBN-10: 1-934354-25-2
Printed in the United States of America
10 9 8 7 6 5 4 3 2 1

Other Books by Robert James Waller

The Bridges of Madison County

Border Music

High Plains Tango

Slow Waltz in Cedar Bend

Puerto Vallarta Squeeze

A Thousand Country Roads

The Long Night of Winchell Dear

Old Songs in a New Café

Just Beyond the Firelight

One Good Road Is Enough

Iowa: Today and Tomorrow

DEDICATION

To all those who helped me through the years, including the rivers.
To old dogs and sleepy cats—my writing companions.
And especially to Linda, who long has suffered my mumblings and impromptu lectures as I make coffee and fix morning oatmeal.

Contents

Preface i

Part I: **The Blueprint**

Chapter 1   Weight Gain, Infidelity, and Retirement Savings Are the Same. 1
Chapter 2   Love, Money, and the Paths We Take. 9
Chapter 3   The Value of the Small Increment 21
Chapter 4   Getting Trapped. 29
Chapter 5   Social Traps 35
Chapter 6   Vicious Circles, Beneficent Spirals, and the Power of Feedback 45
Chapter 7   Getting Out of Trouble: Conventional Approaches 55
Chapter 8   Getting Out of Trouble: Incentives 67
Chapter 9   Avoiding Problems 85
Chapter 10   A Tsunami Trap: The Case of Public Pension Funds. 109
Chapter 11   Democracy and Its Saboteurs (Intentional and Otherwise) 115

Part II   **Matters Personal and General**

Chapter 12   Views of Humans. 133
Chapter 13   Political Economy 141
Chapter 14   Miscellaneous Topics. 173

Part III   **Loose Ends and Recapitulation**

Chapter 15   Synthesis 199

Epilogue   An Essay: What the Rivers Taught Me 209
Appendix   Financial Versus Personal Discounting (Optional Reading) .. 2217
References 221

Student: *Professor, I truly enjoyed your class last semester, but now I have a problem.*

Professor: *Thank you and congratulations on your grade; those scores are not easily won. What is your problem?*

Student: *After learning to think your way, I no longer can think any other way.*

Professor (smiling): *Perhaps you will find release, but recovery may be slow and the recidivism rate is high.*

—Conversation in an academic hallway, circa 1990

Preface

Life is a goulash—or can be. The cacophony of our daily lives, the buzz and discordance of events around us, the pressures of job and family, all of these easily lead to muddled thinking—frequently to a drifting and formless existence. Philosopher and psychologist William James called this mélange "unstructured states of confusion." In my teaching, consulting, and daily living I have long been interested in bringing form to the formless, in making sense of the confusion, in making the meaningless take on meaning. Synthesis is the term I like, and synthesis is the source of wisdom and happiness, of art and artful living. Money, too. And synthesis is something few do well or do not at all.

My purpose here is designed to accomplish one objective: To lay out a way of thinking—a paradigm if you will—for quickly making sense of the great buzzing confusion that surrounds us on a daily basis. Concomitantly, I will demonstrate how to move smoothly from the macro problems of society down to the personal level and back again, or start at the personal level and reverse the process. One man's portable theory, you could call it, since, like the economics theory of supply and demand, it transitions with ease from situation to situation—the problems change, the framework holds. The paradigm has served me well in my managerial, consulting, teaching, writing, music, and personal lives; I trust it will do the same for you. I emphasize: This is not armchair ruminating, but rather the result of practical experience augmented by my training in various academic fields.

Consider for a moment the following dilemmas:

- Maintaining a healthy body weight.
- The decline of the black rhinoceros.
- Marital infidelity.
- Failure by the federal government to secure the borders of the United States.
- The credit and housing crisis.
- The fiscal difficulties of local, state, and federal governments, in the U. S. and abroad.
- Saving for retirement.
- Traffic jams.
- The inherent shortcomings of democracy as a way of societal organization and why political decision-making appears so irrational.
- The possibility of climate change.
- Drug addiction.
- Bernard Madoff's infamous Ponzi scheme.
- The apparent inability to prevent Iran from achieving nuclear weapons.
- The potential human costs of athletics.
- My daughter refusing to learn the multiplication tables.
- Avoiding dental care.
- Contraction of sexually transmitted diseases.
- Air pollution.
- The decline of ocean fisheries.
- Failure by college students to study for examinations.
- The overuse of antibiotics to the point they become ineffective.
- The overuse of pesticides to the point they become ineffective.

- Excessive credit card debt.

At bottom, these are all the same problem. I emphasize: They are all the same problem at their roots. So if you had a way to understand one of the problems, you would understand the central features of all of them. That is what this book is about, a systematic way of thinking, contributing to intellectual efficiency, a paradigm, if you will. What, then, are the central features of those problems?

- They are the products of human decision-making, not of forces beyond our control, natural disasters excepted.
- The decisions were and are guided by incentives, by competing road signs causing the wrong paths to be taken.
- Nearly all the problems are built of small increments accruing over time.
- Some of the problems listed have both micro and macro aspects, others are individual problems, though a large number of individual problems metastasize into society's problems, e.g., obesity, drug addiction, lack of retirement saving.
- They involve trade-offs between happiness now and happiness in the future.
- The seductiveness of incentives entices people and societies into traps, resulting in the constant growth of inefficient and ineffective government programs designed to control human behavior, with a consequent loss of freedom.
- Some of the traps ensnare future generations, raising serious moral issues for us as individuals and as a society, though such morality concerns are shouted down by current demands for this or that.
- The traps and conventional solutions to them limit what can be accomplished in the future, e.g., increasing governmental debt constrains options when new problems involving government finance arise. The same is true of credit card debt constraining future choices for an individual.
- The problems entail feedback cycles, sometimes colloquially labeled vicious circles, virtuous circles, and bubbles. For example, the housing and credit crunch of 2008-2010, Ponzi schemes, stock market escalations or declines, and inattention to physical health. Presently

Preface

the United States is undergoing a government debt bubble—a Ponzi scheme—at all levels, as debt is used to finance more debt.

- Non-governmental solutions to the problems and avoidance of the problems can be devised, whether the problems are personal or social.

I promise this, firmly I do promise: With a small investment of time, careful readers will be provided with a synthesized way of understanding both personal and societal problems, along with basic approaches to solving such problems. I will provide a conceptual framework for (almost) instantly grasping the central features of problems, whether personal or societal, including issues surrounding democracy and freedom. Furthermore, I will demonstrate clearly how social problems are the result of individual problems and, conversely, how individual problems can flow from social problems, and how to effortlessly move back and forth between the macro and micro views.

This is the only work I know of that synthesizes the set of ideas into a unified and useful whole. It took me years of thinking, study, and practical experience to construct the paradigm, but now I can listen to a newscast or read a newspaper or watch television news and rapidly assimilate into an organized form what comes at me as mostly disorganized data and information. The same holds true for personal matters when I am momentarily befuddled by a problem in my everyday existence or in thinking about long-term personal goals.

This book is a distillation of an 800-page manuscript full of equations, economic theory, cognitive psychology, and tutorials involving various branches of mathematics. Here, the technical demands on the reader are light—a few diagrams, nothing more. But, and however, the diagrams are not casual doodling; they have a rigorous mathematical basis even though no knowledge of mathematics is needed to understand them. The diagrams are a key component of the book and also have their roots in the science of human cognition.

The numerous examples I use are familiar to almost everyone. But the examples are merely vehicles; the key to the book is mastery of the paradigm so that it travels with the reader. And the conceptual baggage for such travels is modest: Decision-making, incentives, small increments, cycles, traps, and solutions to or avoidance of traps (problems). Early readers of the manuscript tell me the ideas have greatly enhanced their self-awareness and helped them understand the outcomes of the decisions they have made or will make; in some cases, I am told behavioral changes already have occurred.

In sum, the book describes a singular intellectual technology that is of great practical use, one that also leads to wisdom and understanding. While people are eager to acquire the newest automobile or communications devices, such as mapping systems or an iPad, they are slow to grasp the need for similar tools in the arena of conceptualization—something to do with overconfidence in the human brain, I posit. As a result, so-called unintended consequences permeate our lives. This book provides such an intellectual technology and presents it in accessible form.

My wife Linda calls me a sensible wild man. A few years after we "started up," which I take to be some sort of Linda-Texan, at times a language entirely its own, she looked at me and said in her mild drawl, "Robert, you know what you are? Ya'all are a sensible wild man." I am not certain of the context in which she offered that description and, as a matter of good taste, probably wouldn't mention it if I did. In any case, I liked it when she said it, still like it, and my friends tell me it stands as an apt description.

You will find the sensible wild man roaming throughout these pages, mostly sensible I think, but perhaps wild to some who think conventionally or are of a lazy mind or are encumbered with brassbound ideology and are fatally constrained by that thinking. Ideologies are tortoise shells of the mind, difficult to change once formed, and linked intimately not only to self-perception but also to lifestyles and social milieus. I trust you, as an intelligent reader, will remove the shell and examine it for dents and breaches as the book moves along.

As I build the paradigm, concept by concept, some of the examples will seem trivial, but eventually I will extend these all the way to large dilemmas, such as whether or not democracy is a sustainable form of societal organization. Here and there I will suggest you take out paper and pencil to actively engage in thinking with me. Though not difficult conceptually, this is a book that demands thoughtful participation by the reader and is not designed for a breezy read. Please try and sketch some of your own thoughts where I ask for them, since the rewards will be great. Cognitive effort has a cost, I understand, and I urge you to pay that cost, at least in minimal outlays.

Book Organization and References
The organization of the book is simple. In Part I, encompassing Chapters 1-11, I lay out a powerful framework for thinking, a blueprint, and apply it to many and varied problems, both personal and societal. If you proceed no farther than Part I plus Chapter 15, the book will be worth your while. Part II is somewhat more personal where I deal with my political philosophy and how I arrived at that point of view, as well as matters involving political economy and miscellaneous topics, still using the blueprint laid out in the first 11 chapters. Part III contains only one chapter comprising a brief summary of what has gone before. The epilogue is a gentle ending to what has come before.

Keeping the text uncluttered, I will use footnotes at the bottom of pages where I think a little extra explanation is needed or to provide a slightly extraneous comment. References will be of the form (Smith and Jones 1990, 378), indicating the year of publication and the pertinent page number, and can be found at the end of the book. At times when the reference is common knowledge, I will assume no formal attribution is necessary. If a work has been cited nearby, I will repeat the author's name followed by only the page number, e.g., (Smith and Jones, 379) or sometimes just the page number when the attribution is clear. If I only wish to cite a work in general terms, it will appear as (Smith and Jones 1990).

So we begin. Thank you in advance for traveling with me through 40 years of thinking and practice.

ACKNOWLEDGEMENTS

Thanks to those who read various editions of this book, some of whom offered useful suggestions and comment. Namely: Linda Bow, Bob Bachler, Abbey Daniels, Scott Cawelti, Robert and Laurie Gentry, Carol French Johnson, Tom Reuschling, Kent Rylander, Jim Levine, and Troy Henkels. Perhaps the most interesting comment came from Laurie Gentry who, having finished the book, said this: "My life is ruined for the better," a comment that somehow captures the essence of the book.

PART I: THE BLUEPRINT

Chapter 1

WEIGHT GAIN, INFIDELITY, AND RETIREMENT SAVINGS ARE THE SAME

Distant Voices, Good Intentions
The present bellows and blusters, pounds its fist and demands attention: "*Choose me now!*" But the future speaks only in a faint and distant voice, waving a slender hand and begging for at least some consideration. Alas, like the allure of a transient lover, the seductiveness of the present usually wins out—for a time, that is—until the future becomes the present and regret emerges at having ignored its earlier cries, along with astonishment at how soon it arrived. Youth covers many sins, but age removes the veil, and the 54 percent of American workers who have less than $25,000 in retirement savings (27 percent have less than $1,000) are going to discover just that in a time span shorter than they imagine.

This partially can be explained by something called *discounting*, a term used frequently in finance and economics. Here's a simple example. You deposit $1,000 in a savings account earning a glorious 20 percent. At the end of one year the account will have $1,200 in it (for this book, I assume all interest is computed annually). Suppose you are offered the following two options: You can have $1,000 now or a risk-free $1,200 a year from now.

Most people will choose to receive the $1,000 immediately. However, if the same people are asked to choose between $1,000 in five years or $1,200 in six years, they will choose to wait for the $1,200.

Time passes and you find yourself at year five where you are offered the same options: $1,000 now or $1,200 in one year. Again you probably choose the $1,000. Yet in year zero you were willing to wait for the $1,200 in year six when compared to $1,000 in year five. Curious, eh? Yes, but typical of all but the most disciplined, rational folks.

This sort of decision-making has been studied extensively in a field called behavioral economics. What's going on? It has to do with *impatience* and more generally what I call the *lure of the short-run*.

Imagine the $1,000 received in the present is left in the savings account, earning 20 percent each year for 15 years. At year 15, you would have $15,407. This is called *compounding* or *compound interest*, an idea that seems to elude most people when it comes to thinking about the future.

Suppose the options of $1,000 now or $1,200 in a year are offered over and over again, year after year, e.g., a yearly bonus. Jimmy cannot resist buying the newest styles and opts to spend the $1,000 each time it is offered. Julia, on the other hand, is a disciplined, highly rational person who adds the yearly $1,000 to the 20 percent savings account. In 15 years, Jimmy will have a closet full of last year's clothing, Julia will have $101,849.

Ralphie, who is 5' 9", weighed 160 pounds at age 20. He is a busy fellow, has a breakfast burrito then grabs a double cheeseburger, fries, and a soda for lunch, and believes he has no time for exercise, though he *knows* he should take better care of himself and *intends* to improve. He notices a weight gain of 2 pounds a year, which seems insignificant. In 30 years he weighs 220 pounds and has a Body Mass Index (BMI) of 32.6—Ralphie is obese (a BMI of 30 or greater). Even with a hardly noticeable gain of one pound per year his BMI at 50 would be 28 and classed as overweight approaching obesity.

Something is going on in these examples and it has to do with discounting, among other things. When someone says, "I don't trust most politicians and apply a hefty discount to anything they have to say," they are lowering the value of political statements. In roughly the same fashion, discounting devalues the future. Jimmy prefers consuming *now* rather than saving, whereas Julia prefers to save for the future; Julia values anticipated future happiness more than present consumption, or at least balances the two. Ralphie is valuing future health less than current pleasure and convenience. When someone devalues the future relative to the present, here's what is occurring:

1. The person is impatient. As the old Queen song goes, "I want it all and I want it right now." The lure of the short-run is operating.

2. Money in the future is worth less than money in hand. Consider the following choice: You can have $100 today and invest it at 5 percent, resulting in $105 in one year, or you can have $100 a year from now. At 5 percent, $100 received in one year is worth only $95 in today's terms because $95 at 5 percent will bring in $100 after a year. So receiving the $100 today is preferred, naturally. These sorts of calculations I will label *financial discounting*, involving the time value of money. If the interest rate were 10 percent, $100 in a year would be worth only $91 today because $91 invested at 10 percent returns $100 after one year. When an interest rate is used to compute the present worth of a future sum of money, it is often called the *discount rate*, i.e., the future is being discounted to a present value.

3. A high *personal discount rate* is being applied to the future. This interpretation allows a transition from financial discounting to personal discounting. In most cases it is a matter of current satisfactions overriding good intentions.

4. The person has no concept of the future, no vision of what he/she might prefer life to look like in the future. Unfortunately, this disability affects many people, as well as governments and some business firms.

How about Ralphie heading toward obesity or becoming seriously overweight? Let's take another example with Ralphie going out for lunch. His physician has advised him to lose weight or to not gain additional weight. Ralphie enters the restaurant with good intentions to eat a salad dressed with vinegar and oil. But the diner at the next table is served pasta with cream sauce and Ralphie succumbs, promising to do better tomorrow.

The following day at lunch, Ralphie is with a friend who suggests they share a pizza with four toppings. When Ralphie demurs in favor of a salad, the friend chortles and says, "Ralphie, old boy, trying to make me look bad? C'mon, you only live once." Ralphie says, "Oh, what the heck" and agrees to the pizza and also to share a pitcher of beer with his friend. Meanwhile, good intentions have been told to wait in the parking lot. In choosing the pasta instead of the salad, then pizza the following day, each time Ralphie has assigned a momentarily high discount rate to the future.

Now, suppose Ralphie is asked about his intentions for the following week. He responds that salad surely will be the choice next week. But when next week arrives, it becomes the present and the temptations are there once again. In short, there is a divergence between long-term goals—good intentions—and short-run behavior. Such behavior is common to almost everyone in various circumstances. It seems we are two different people with two different minds inhabiting the same body: The short-run person and the long-term person. And therein rests a concise summary of just about every problem on earth—short-run gratification versus long-term good.

It is useful to think of the human brain as being comprised of two distinct but contradictory ways of thinking. Thaler and Sunstein (2008, 19) capture this polarity simply and well: A distinction can be made "...between two kinds of thinking, one that is intuitive and automatic, and another that is reflective and rational." The battle is constant: We want to do/consume x right now, but somewhere deep down we know y is the salutary path because it is the right thing to do in terms of our future well-being. Incidentally, rats and pigeons show similar preferences for the short-run versus the long-run (I leave it to the reader to interpret those results).

Notice how the following all relate to discounting the future relative to the present.

- If we had the self-control to save over time, retirement would be a much better place.[1]

---

[1] Nature provided squirrels with an instinct to save nuts for the winter. Humans seem to lack in that regard.

- If we had the discipline to eat a nutritious diet and exercise regularly, obesity would not be epidemic.
- If people could control credit card use, average credit card debt per household of those households using credit cards would not have been $15,788 in 2010.
- If self-control in the form of abstinence, selective abstinence, or condom use were present, the rate of sexually transmitted diseases would be lower.
- If people would save for routine medical expenses while carrying an inexpensive medical-catastrophe insurance policy, medical costs in America would be far lower. Enlightened business firms such as Whole Foods have had great success with this approach.
- If congresses and administrations could exert self-control to enhance national well-being, the United States government would not be so deep in debt, amounting to over $45,000 per person, more than $130,000 for a three-person household, or around $127,000 *per person* if only taxpayers are used in the calculation (January 4, 2011 figures). Governments have behaved exactly like Ralphie, e.g., the United States, Greece, Spain, Ireland, Great Britain.

Figure 1.1 is a diagram showing a rudimentary portrait of the weight-gain problem. I will be using such diagrams often in this book, grounded in rigorous mathematics but requiring no mathematical knowledge and simple to understand. Does it show all the variables influencing body weight? No, of course not, but exercise and nutrition account for most body-weight issues, with other factors being subcomponents of exercise and nutrition.

The type of diagram in Figure 1.1 is a powerful thinking device; I use them constantly. Note the legend at the bottom of the diagram, which indicates the meaning of the lines with arrowheads. Start with exercise. As the quantity of exercise increases, body weight decreases; hence, the minus sign on the line. It is an inverse relationship, in other words. The same is true for nutrition—the better the nutrition, the less body weight. At the left of the diagram, the higher the discounted long-term value of exercise, the less you will exercise. The same for the discounting attached to nutrition. Thus, the more the future is discounted, the less exercise will be undertaken, and the less the amount of exercise, the greater the BMI.

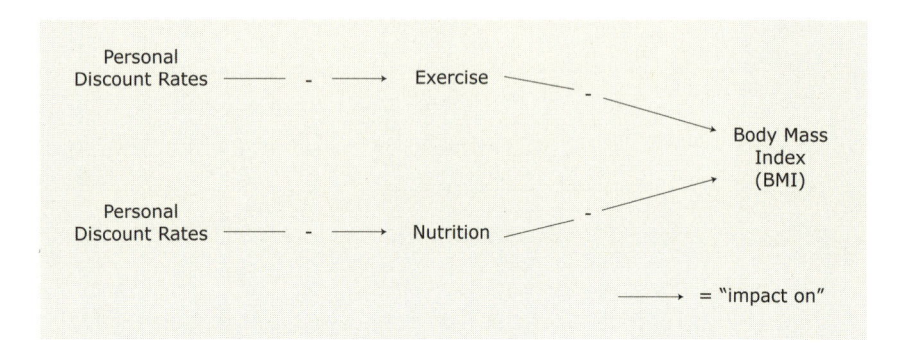

```
Personal
Discount Rates  ──── - ───▶ Exercise ────────╲
                                              ╲
                                               ▶ Body Mass
                                                 Index
                                               ▶ (BMI)
                                              ╱
Personal                                     ╱
Discount Rates  ──── - ───▶ Nutrition ──────╱

                         ────▶ = "impact on"
```

Figure 1.1 Basic BMI Diagram

Since I will have much to say about such relationships, let's review them for a moment. Ralphie believes he does not have time for exercise and therefore is discounting the value of exercise in terms of future health to the point he never gets it done. The lack of exercise impacts on his body weight. It is no more complicated than that. No time for exercise is a common excuse. The real reason may be indolence, a preference for watching television rather than getting up and moving about. Having dealt with the struggle for many years, I am sympathetic toward those with demanding jobs and families, both of which constrain the time available for anything else, but those factors contribute to assigning a high discount rate to the future and, hence, exercise. A paradox: We ask our bodies to carry us through 24 hours a day, year after year, and yet have no time for daily maintenance, but we take our vehicles to the shop for periodic maintenance because the ultimate cost of no maintenance is well-known, severe, and relatively close at hand.

Infidelity is not to be treated lightly. Why does it occur? Ralphie succumbed to temptations of the moment in his food choices, discounting the future and ignoring the later consequences of his decisions. Likewise, infidelity is a matter of discounting the future. For example, Governor Mark Sanford of South Carolina discounted the future heavily when he took up with an Argentinean woman; the affair cost him his marriage and a promising career in politics. I'm certain his long-run intentions were good, given the career and family possibilities before him, but his good intentions were overwhelmed by the lure of the short-run.

The Blindfold Effect

The *Blindfold Effect* is how I label all of the examples in this chapter, from Jimmy's clothes purchases to Ralphie's eating habits to infidelity. We all are subject to the lure of the short-run, though some exhibit more self-control than others, which is another way of saying a low discount rate is attached to the future, just like Julia investing rather than spending.

That's enough for now on discounting; it is incredibly important in understanding your own behavior as well as large social problems, We'll get to the latter in short-order. The appendix at the end of the book provides a brief tutorial that more fully explains discounting. Next, I will embed discounting into a larger context: Decision-making.

Chapter 2

LOVE, MONEY, AND THE PATHS WE TAKE

Choices and Consequences

Alarm clock rings: Get up, stay in bed. If get up, turn on coffee, don't turn on coffee. Into the bathroom: Brush teeth, don't brush teeth. Open closet: Red tie, blue tie or (author ever alert to gender sensitivity) red dress, blue dress. After work: Exercise, don't exercise. Dinner: Eat dessert, don't eat dessert. After dinner, sit by the phone: Call X for Saturday date, call Y for Saturday date, stay home on Saturday night and do neglected reallocation of investment assets or prepare for Monday morning meeting. In a small room somewhere: Decide to become a suicide bomber, take a different life path.

Aside from breathing and the quiet beating of your heart, nothing is more fundamental to human existence than decision-making. Nothing. Wait, what about religion, your beliefs, spirituality of all kinds? All of those are inputs to decisions, as I explain further on.

Choices have consequences, and the consequences have a way of becoming the genesis of more decisions. Sometimes it's good stuff, making decisions. The Caribbean or the Pacific? An island or a cruise? A formal candlelight dinner on Saturday or a weekend at the beach? Sometimes decision-making wrenches the gut and drives people to desperate measures involving consequences from which there is no return, e.g., abortion, committing murder, launching a missile with a nuclear warhead at another country, suicide by Indian farmers who cannot repay their debts, robbing the local convenience store to make a mortgage payment, posting nude photos of yourself on social media. In impoverished circumstances, feed your child or feed yourself.

If economics is the study of scarcity, which it is, then all decisions are economic decisions. Two activities requiring the same scarce resources, such as time or money, cannot be executed at once, choices must be made, billionaires excluded. Still, the very rich confront a scarcity of time and other resources such as not being in two places at once, perhaps even intelligence if the money was inherited.

The Core of Decision-making

Decisions have the following key components, and I will deal with each of them before we are finished.

- Alternatives, the options you confront, such as what car to purchase, whether to eat pasta with cream sauce or a salad, whether to save or spend, whether to commit infidelity or remain faithful.
- Outcomes. These are the expected results of a decision, though uncertainty about the exact outcome may be present.
- Criteria, the standards you use in evaluating your alternatives.
- Incentives, which I will explain shortly.
- Discounting (see Chapter 1).
- Risk and risk tolerance.

Alternatives and Outcomes

In Chapter 1, our friend Jimmy made a decision to spend his annual bonus, while Julie chose to invest hers. See Figure 2.1. The same alternatives confronted each of them:

1. Spend the entire bonus.
2. Save the entire bonus.
3. Save part of the bonus, spend the remainder.

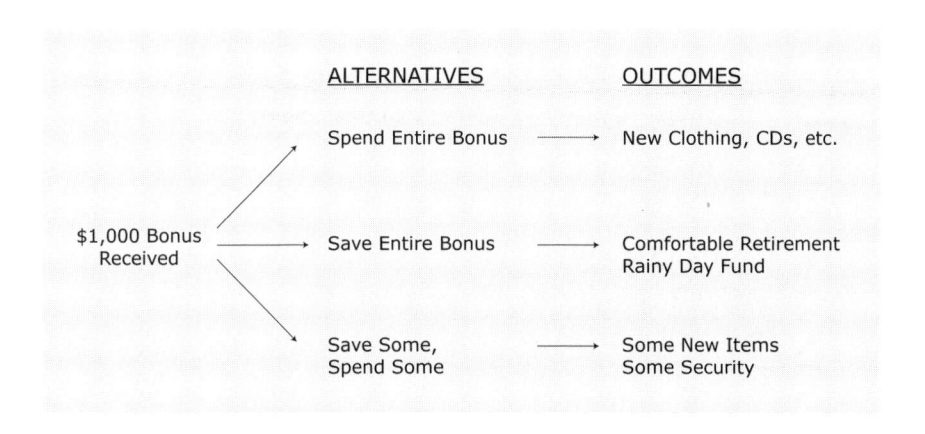

```
                    ALTERNATIVES              OUTCOMES

                    Spend Entire Bonus  ──→   New Clothing, CDs, etc.

  $1,000 Bonus ──→  Save Entire Bonus   ──→   Comfortable Retirement
    Received                                  Rainy Day Fund

                    Save Some,          ──→   Some New Items
                    Spend Some                Some Security
```

Figure 2.1 The Bonus Decision

In Figure 2.1, the alternatives and outcomes are easy to see. Select "Spend the entire bonus" and, as an outcome, fun stuff flows into your life. Save the bonus and look forward to a bright future including fun stuff later on. Alternative 3 could be broken down into multiple alternatives. The expected outcomes are shown at the end of the little tree diagram.

Criteria

Criteria are the mental yardsticks used to evaluate and compare alternatives, enabling a choice to be made. Here's a concrete example. Because I have enough assets to carry me through the rest of my life with some left over for charitable and family giving, my dominant investment criterion is preservation of assets. Since inflation can eat away at the purchasing power of assets, I restate the dominant criterion as, "Preservation of assets consistent with keeping pace with inflation" (no, those two goals are not contradictory, as a clueless investment "advisor" once tried to convince me). I use that criterion, along with some others, in ranking investment alternatives—if it came down to a speculative stock offering the possibility of an extremely high return versus a high-quality but pedestrian stock, I would choose the latter because of my dominant criterion.

Politicians have "maximize electability" as a criterion, usually the dominant one when they are voting on major issues. A typical criteria list for the purchase of a point-and-shoot cameras might be: Easy to use, good results in automatic mode, fits in purse or pocket, boots up quickly, manual override of auto exposure, price less than $250, image stabilizer. For an acoustic guitar: Size, sound quality, appearance, price. For a car: Purchase price, appearance, projected cost of operation, cargo capacity, and so forth. *U.S. News* annually ranks colleges using seven criteria such as student selectivity, faculty resources, and graduation and retention rates.

Few people think clearly about their criteria set in any given decision, allowing the criteria to remain vague and to shift in importance relative to one another during the actual decision process. You start out car shopping with cargo capacity as your overriding criterion and the Toyota SUV seems the best choice, but across the highway at a Ford dealership is an attractive red coupe and suddenly appearance ranks first in your criteria set. Shopping for a house, you have listed three baths as absolutely necessary, but the bright new kitchen in another house with only one-and-a-half baths captures your heart and a decision is made to purchase the home with the bright new kitchen in spite of your earlier dominant criterion. Allowing criteria to change in relative importance to one another is just fine, as long as you are aware of the shifts and the impact on alternative selection.

When outcomes are stated in words, as they are in Figure 2.1, they can appear to be duplicates of criteria. Julia saves her bonus. What does that say about her criteria set? For example, "Comfortable Retirement" might be her top-ranked criterion, which also happens to be how one of the outcomes is stated. Perhaps her second-ranked criterion is to have sufficient money set aside for emergencies, including job loss. If the rainy-day fund is top-ranked, Julia might invest in shorter-term assets for her emergency reserve as opposed to long-term investments for retirement. If I place Julia's retirement savings (see Chapter 1) of $101,849 at the end of the tree branch instead of "Comfortable Retirement," then the difference between outcomes and criteria becomes clear. $101,849 is the outcome, a comfortable retirement is a criterion used to evaluate the alternatives.

Differences involving criteria are an important source of conflict between and among humans, as well as between and among nations and in all labor negotiations. The conflict arises because of disagreement over the content of the criteria set or disagreement about how criteria should be ranked. He wants a sports car, she wants cargo capacity; she wants a romantic dinner out, he wants to spend the money on attending a professional football game (I apologize for the stereotypes). Progressives have criteria sets favoring large government, *classical* liberals prefer small government.

Parenthetical Note: Visualizing Alternatives, Criteria, and Outcomes
Here I present a simple method for visualizing decision concepts as I discuss them. Multiple-criteria problems are difficult, e.g., buying a home, allocating investment assets, voting, where more than one criterion is present and these criteria are in conflict with one another. For example, alternative A_1 scores higher than A_2 on criterion C_2 but A_2 scores higher than A_1 on criterion C_1. Considerable scholarly work has gone into methods for handling such problems, material far too technical for this book. But I quickly can help you to understand what I am referring to as I discuss alternatives, criteria, and outcomes.

Imagine you are trying to choose between two cars—the alternatives—and you have listed price, safety, and gas mileage as your main criteria. These criteria will be used to measure the relative attractiveness to you of Car 1 versus Car 2. See Figure 2.2. In simple terms, view the entries in the table cells as scores in terms of how well, for example, each car scores or rates on the criterion of safety; these scores are the expected outcomes. An aggregation of the ratings for each alternative by methods not explained here helps the decision-maker to select an alternative.

		Criteria		
		Price	Safety	Gas
Alternatives	Car 1	Rating of Car 1 on Price Criteria	Rating of Car 1 on Safety	Rating of Car 1 on Gas Mileage
	Car 2	Rating of Car 2 on Price Criteria	Rating of Car 2 on Safety	Rating of Car 2 on Gas Mileage

Figure 2.2 Visualizing Alternatives, Outcomes, and Criteria

Now imagine you are a politician and instead of cars you are trying to decide on whether to choose Policy 1 or Policy 2. Suppose you have two criteria:

"Maximize Electability" and "Maximize National Well-Being." If electability is your dominant criterion by a wide margin (higher rating) and Policy 2 scores high on this criterion but low on national well-being, a majority of politicians will choose Policy 2, e.g., pork-barrel spending for your district while adding to the national debt, which reduces national well-being.

See Figure 2.3 for an example of political decision-making. The politician in this case has two criteria: Electability and national well-being. The criteria are ranked on a scale of 0-10, with electability assigned a 10 and national well-being a 6. Then, employing a *second* 0-10 scale, the policies in question—the alternatives—are scored in terms of how well the expected outcomes of those alternatives satisfy the criteria. For example, Policy 2 scores a 9 on electability but only a score of 2 on national well-being, producing an overall score of (9 x 10) + (2 x 6) = 90 + 12 = 102 for that alternative. Do most people use such devices in making decisions? No, but the process models what happens in the human mind even if formal procedures are not used; however, the thought process ordinarily is muddled in such a way that it's difficult to see it occurring, but the results imply the process. I use this simple approach in automobile purchases and home buying, along with other decisions.

		Criterion Electability (10)	Criterion National Well-Being	Scores
Alternatives	Policy 1	Rating of Policy 1 on Electability (3)	Rating of Policy 1 on National Well-Being (8)	(3x10) + (8x6) =78
	Policy 2	Rating of Policy 2 on Electability (9)	Rating of Policy 2 on National Well-Being (2)	(9x10) + (2x6) =102

Figure 2.3 A Political Decision

Decision-tree diagrams are more troublesome to use for multiple criteria, with the criteria either implicit or listed to one side, though there are ways to circumvent this trouble. The tabular (matrix) approach makes it easy to explicitly include multiple criteria but cannot show multiple stages of decision-making as easy as a tree diagram. So, use either means of visualizing decision problems, depending on the problem at hand and your preference. For this book, when I am discussing conflicting multiple criteria, I suggest the tabular approach.

Incentives

— Personal Vignette —

When Linda and I first took up residence in an old hunting lodge, deep in the mountains of southwest Texas, the place was infested with vermin, namely rats and mice along with a few squirrels. All day and night they scampered back and forth in the ceiling, ran down the walls into the living area, and generally presented unsavory living conditions. Those behaviors were annoying, but also had other more deleterious effects: Snakes. Almost every day a rattlesnake would be crawling near the building, a threat to both us and our four dogs, though the dogs seemed to have a better-than-human sense of where the snakes were and the good common sense to avoid them.

So I thought about incentives. Why were the snakes consistently close to the building? Incentives were at work: The snakes were drawn to the rodents; the snakes had an incentive to approach the building. I said to Linda, "We need cats." Second, there was a lot of trash stacked around outside—woodpiles and such—another good home for rodents and rattlesnakes. The debris provided a double incentive for the snakes, in the form of food and shelter.

Linda adopted two feral cats, soft and furry little creatures but wise to high-desert ways, and tamed them down. We cleaned up the trash and moved woodpiles a long way from the building, while the cats either killed the rodents or drove them out. The snakes no longer had their former incentives and decamped to areas offering better food supplies. It was pure economic thinking applied to a pressing problem: Cats + trash removal = no rodents = no snake incentives = no more snakes = back to the romantic life instead of hip-hopping around and over rattlesnakes. Happy ending.

— End of Personal Vignette —

Mother Theresa had her own incentives, of that I am certain. Gandhi, too. Similarly for the oft-commended Dali Lama, as well as Einstein. And the same for: Smokers, welfare recipients, politicians, automobile drivers, obese people, athletes, those who work in office cubicles, thieves, miners, people ruled by cruel dictators, bureaucrats, college professors, scientists, fly fishers, experts of all kinds, real estate agents, surgeons, and...you...and me... and everyone. People in so-called humanistic organizations or environment groups or heads of labor unions also have personal incentives, though usually those are cloaked in lofty rhetoric of doing good for others, all the while pushing for increases in their own salaries and fringe benefits. If the last sentence seems too cynical, I will temper it by admitting that often these people have genuinely honorable motives intertwined with their personal incentives.

A bonus program in a business firm is an example of incentives being used to guide behavior (Wall Street loves bonuses as incentives). The same holds for incentive pay on top of ordinary salary for a professional athlete if he or she achieves some high goal. The typical dictionary definition of incentive will have a phrase such as "something that motivates action or effort." That definition sort of lies there and snaps at you without saying much. In the language of this book, I define an incentive as follows: In decision-making, an incentive is the expected outcome or range of possible outcomes if a particular course of action is taken. Of course, an outcome can be unpleasant, in which case the persnickety can use "disincentive." In short, incentives are the expected or hoped-for outcomes flowing from the selection of a given alternative. Labeling outcomes and incentives as being identical can be slightly confusing, and it becomes clearer if I say outcomes act as incentives. Please focus on that last clause: Outcomes *act* as incentives.

Incentives are pervasive. They are everywhere, for good and for bad. Why bother brushing your teeth in the morning? Think about the incentives, the inducements to do so or abstain. Mouth feels cleaner? A good-morning kiss in the offing? Regular dental maintenance? All of these? Levitt and Dubner (2005, 13) are succinct: "*Incentives are the cornerstone of modern life.*" And understanding incentives—or sometimes ferreting them out—is the key to identifying and solving just about any personal or social riddle, from retirement saving to sports cheating to online dating to government waste. I would omit the modifier "modern" in the above quote and suggest that incentives have always been the cornerstone of life. Plus, I would change the quote even further: Decision-making, in conjunction with expected outcomes acting as incentives and embedded in decision-making, is the cornerstone of life.

Curiously, in the discussions of incentives I have seen, the exact positioning of incentives in the mosaic of life is omitted. The word is bandied about and most of us have an intuitive idea of what it means, but it floats out there in a vague and imprecise fashion. Of course, an "incentive-based compensation package" seems clear enough. So does touching a hot stove when you are young and the ensuing incentive not to touch it thereafter. Yet, the exact location of where incentives and behavior marry-up is not specified. My definition works: Expected outcomes act as incentives. Period.

Discounting and Incentives

A mildly subtle point concerns the relationship between discounting and incentives. Jimmy and Julia confront the same decision. If each receives a $1,000 first-time bonus, after one year Jimmy will have no additional money in a savings account, as was seen in Chapter 1. Julia will have an additional $1,200 based on her decision to invest the money. They have revealed *different personal discount rates* regarding what to do with the $1,000. Intuitively speaking, Jimmy values satisfaction in the present greater than $1,200 in the future; he is attaching a high *personal discount rate to the future*. How high? Something greater than 20 percent. For example, if he discounts the outcome of $1,200 at 45 percent, the worth of $1,200 in one year is only $828 versus the joy of spending $1,000 immediately.

On the other hand, Julia is revealing a personal discount rate less than 20 percent. For example, if her personal discount rate is 5 percent, she is attaching a present value of $1,143 to the $1,200. Since $1,143 is greater than the $1,000 in hand, she invests the money (a present sum of $1,143 invested for one year at 5 percent equals $1,200). A personal discount rate of 20 percent for both Jimmy and Julia would make them both indifferent between spending or saving the $1,000, since the discounted value of $1,200 received in one year at 20 percent is exactly $1,000. Thus, because Jimmy and Julia assign different discount rates to the future, Jimmy elects to spend his $1,000, while Julia invests her $1,000[2]. Thus, *differences in the personal discount rate influence how expected outcomes are valued and those values act as incentives.*

If this all seems like twiddle-twaddle, like nerdish folderol, it is not. Incentives and discounting drill right to the core of why things go awry and how to fix the problems. I will make extensive use of the ideas in this chapter as we move along.

Risk and the Classic Decision Problem
There is what I call the "Classic Decision Problem." We all confront it but handle it differently, depending on our psychological makeup and life circumstances, age being a critical factor. Figure 2.4 is an illustration of the classic problem. It works like this. You are confronted with a choice between "Do Nothing" (i.e., stay on the tried and true course of whatever it might be) and some other alternative that has at least two outcomes: A state of affairs making you worse off than you are now or making you better off. I have shown only two outcomes for "Make a Change," though there may be a number of possibilities. The probabilities for the separate alternatives of the decision tree must total to 1.0 for each alternative. Also, doing nothing often has more than one outcome, e.g., staying in a job and suffering a cut in salary when hard times descend. But the central idea persists.

In general, people are averse to losses and prefer clinging to present circumstances rather than stepping out and taking risks offering the possibility of substantial rewards but also the chance of loss. The data show that people are about twice as unhappy with a loss as they are happy with a gain of the same magnitude. Plus, there is comfort in the status quo, imparting a high degree of inertia to all human behavior. Some hypothesize this sense of caution is located in the amygdala portion of the brain, though it does

---

[2] If you haven't done any work with discounting, this kind of thinking can seem strange, almost counter-intuitive. Computer spreadsheet programs have computational aids for future and present value, and an internet search for "present value calculator" will return all sorts of calculators you can play with. Please go to the internet and spend a few minutes playing with future values and present values.

not explain why certain people are more prone to take risks than others. Another reason for clinging to the status quo is fear of making the wrong decision, but that stance has its own possibility of error, as buggy whip manufacturers discovered.

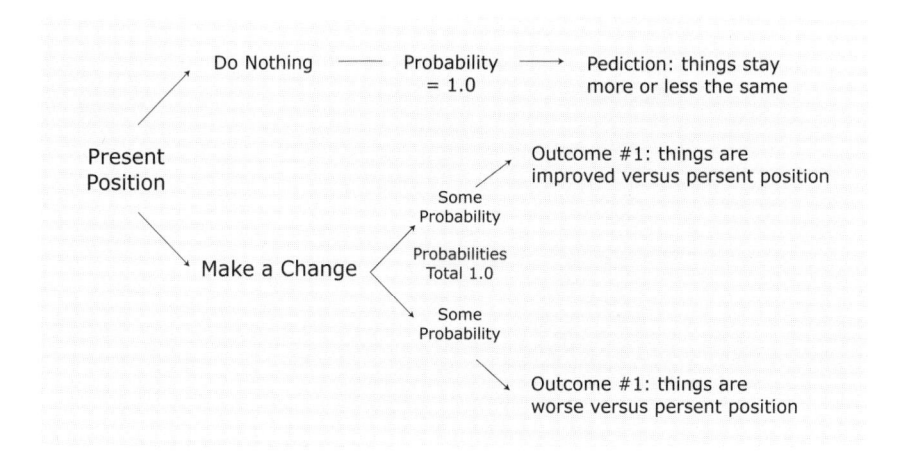

```
                  Do Nothing ———— Probability ——→ Pediction: things stay
                 ╱                = 1.0             more or less the same
                ╱
    Present                            ╱→ Outcome #1: things are
    Position                          ╱   improved versus persent position
                ╲                 Some
                 ╲              Probability
                  ╲           Probabilities
                   ╲ Make a Change <  Total 1.0
                                  Some
                                Probability
                                      ╲→ Outcome #1: things are
                                         worse versus persent position
```

Figure 2.4 The Classic Decision Problem, Generalized View

Moreover, decision-making requires cognitive effort, an unpleasant chore for many, leading to selection of the default (Do-Nothing) option. In financial decisions, information-gathering along with monetary costs of legal advice and filling out forms can be powerful negative incentives and result in attachment to the status quo. And if there is a strong desire to conform to the expectations of others, that also is a push to choose the default option (it's why artists are considered weird and untrustworthy, if not a little dangerous, but yet fascinating to more ordinary folks, because they do not conform).

Some examples of the Classic Decision Problem are:
- Stay in a marriage, get a divorce.
- Leave assets in government-backed bonds, invest in the stock market.
- In my novel, *The Bridges of Madison County*, Francesca faced a decision concerning whether to stay on an Iowa farm with her husband or to leave with Robert Kincaid.

- Socialize national health care, leave as is (Democrats clearly have preferred the former).
- Privatize all or part of Social Security, leave as is.
- Well-known professional football player Plaxico Burress was indicted in 2009 on two counts of criminal possession of a weapon and one count of reckless endangerment. He was offered a plea bargain of two years in jail (think of it as the Do-Nothing option) or submitting to a jury trial where the minimum sentence would be three-and-a-half years, if convicted. He selected the plea-bargain alternative. What does his choice imply about his probability estimates? Or, maybe he and his lawyer were unable to estimate probabilities, given the erratic behavior of juries.

Personal recommendation: In matters of the heart, too much rationality can be destructive. *Animus non integritatem sed facinus cupit*: "The heart wills not purity but adventure." At the extremes, however, that dictum can quickly lead to a rocky and formless life, ultimately an unhappy state of affairs. Sigh. As Mark Twain said, all things in moderation, including moderation.

Closing this chapter, I offer you a personal conjecture, something I believe is worth considering and it fits perfectly with The Classic Decision Problem. One of the main attractions of a socialist or statist economy has to do with risk tolerance. People, in general, but fortunately not all of us, have an aversion to losses; they value loss avoidance greater than possible gains, as noted earlier. In terms of a society's economic arrangements, the statist economy seems to promise security versus the risks involved in a market-based economy. Government employees—including teachers and state university professors (along with those in well-endowed private universities)—have almost ironclad job security, guaranteed pensions, and decent salaries, even though they may feel differently about the latter. Entrepreneurs and capitalists in general prefer a world of possible high payoffs coupled with the possibility of great loss, especially when they are young. Thus, the choice between a government-run economy and the market system involves the Classic Decision Problem. I will return to this conjecture later in the book.

Chapter 3

THE VALUE OF THE SMALL INCREMENT

Small Steps, Large Outcomes

From the age of 12 or so the central feature of my life has been a progression of small changes, both upward in the sense of beneficial and downward in the reverse.[1] In the large, and fortunately, up-trending has dominated, frequently the changes being small enough as to be imperceptible or nearly so. Thirty years ago I gave this insight a proper label: *The value of the small increment* (VSI). As I mentioned earlier, VSI and its profound ramifications amount unequivocally to the most important insight I have ever generated and winds its way through much of this book.

Without being especially smart or clever, but with the lift of small increments, I have managed a decent life, mostly happy, mostly productive. No counterfeit, unvirtuous foot-shuffling here, only honest self-appraisal as best I can manage that dicey task.[2] If you lack in some areas, or even if you

---

[1] Of course there were many small changes occurring mentally and physically before age 12, but I am speaking here of the those salient changes of which I was and am conscious.

[2] I once said that if I were to have an epitaph, which I hope I do not, it would read, "He was fairly good."

The Blueprint

don't, there is a good chance you can improve your lot by utilizing the value of the small increment.

Jimmy, Julia, and Ralphie from earlier examples were all engaged in small increments. And each small increment involved discounting and decision-making. Each time Jimmy decides to spend his bonus on new consumer goods, assigning a high discount rate to the future, he is making a decision, a small increment relative to his entire life. The same is true for Julia, except her incremental decisions entail saving. Ralphie is making food choices one meal at a time—small increments.

The catch is this Small increments add to large sums over time. The sum may be positive and substantial, exemplified by Julia's savings account, or negative and substantial as Ralphie continues to gain weight with a consequent decline in health status.

Whether we label it discipline or self-control, or lack thereof, small increments can be sequentially stacked to eventually form a future state of being more desirable than a present state or a state far worse than might have been. The VSIs are all around us, occurring as you read this book, occurring as I type the words. Creationist theory pretty much deals with one large increment while Darwinian evolution is a prime example of the value of the small increment, negative or positive as you appraise our species. You can argue about the results of evolution, but not about the size of the increments; the Galapagos finches of Darwin evolved in tiny increments over thousands of years.

People surely understand the VSI, don't they? Don't we? It's an intuitive notion, more or less, and probably was hinted at by teachers or parents or grandparents. Self-help books instruct using the old saw, "Every journey requires a first step, yah-dah, etc." or parrot a favorite expression from decades ago, "Every day I'm getting better in every way," that aspiration being a tallish order. Just about everyone can take a first step, but real journeys require many steps, many small increments, e.g., it is one thing to join a health club (a first step), quite another to be faithful to an exercise routine, which is why such clubs charge a high membership fee at the outset and a low or even negative marginal cost (to the club) per visit.

I posit VSI is one of those things people sense but don't necessarily practice. Quitting smoking, learning to play a musical instrument, being successful in a career, losing weight or preventing weight gain, saving money for retirement, writing a book, or practicing a long-range jump shot are all examples of employing the small increment now for some future benefit. And people probably do apply the small increment when forced to by school or parents, but then let it go once they are on their own. They hold their breaths for a while, waiting until authority is removed from their lives, and that's it.

The trick, you see, particularly for individuals, is to provide incentives for ourselves such that what seem to be present sacrifices have their own small rewards. These immediate rewards can help offset the current pain of sacrifice on the way to even better things later on. In sum, what we normally think of as discipline or self-control is nothing more than a matter of understanding the value of the small increment and *acting on that understanding*. Also, instead of small rewards, the incentives could be relative punishments, causing small suffering now to avoid severe, perhaps deadly, punishments in the future. Saving for retirement might be viewed as a punishment for some, since they are giving up immediate pleasures in return for a more prosperous future. Others, however, may find saving a reward in itself. I use the terms punishment, sacrifice, negative incentives, and disincentives interchangeably.

Distant goals can seem so large as to be unobtainable, if all the small increments are summed and only the total is contemplated. The seemingly vast sum required overwhelms the moment, and submission to the present becomes the default option, the future disregarded. I would have liked some of my books to be finished in two hours instead of three years, but as a student of the VSI, one day I begin and continue minute by minute, hour after hour, day after day for all the days and years that follow until a book leaves my hands.

For 20 years I had an old Zen expression pasted above my desk: "To obtain a thing you must first stop wanting it." That apparent contradiction contains within it a major truth about small increments. The Buddha believed in small increments upward, while savoring the process, and the Buddha's curve was of gentle slope. The Buddha, I think, would not have approved of Mao Zedong's "Great Leap Forward" or radical changes in American health care. Gentle slopes allow for gentle retreats if things go wrong.

Addiction to cigarette smoking is a matter of small increments and breaking the habit requires attention to small increments. Most addictions are like that. Pollution of a river ordinarily is done in small increments. Traffic jams are a result of small increments, as I will explain in the next chapter. Failing to prepare for an examination involves small increments, decisions exactly the same as Jimmy's lack of prudence and Ralphie's surrender to temptation meal after meal, and want of attention to the small increments of study leads to "pulling an all-nighter," usually a futile attempt at substituting one big increment for failing to accumulate small increments. When I taught an advanced course in decision theory at the college level, I experimented with the technique of any class meeting being fair game for a comprehensive exam, the exam dates determined randomly by drawing dates from a paper bag. I had the best prepared classes in the university, of that I am confident. As I told the students, every day in the real world of living might call for a comprehensive examination of one sort or another and you never know when it is coming.

In the following chapter, a synthesis of discounting, decision-making, and small increments will be presented, illustrating how the result of many small increments can lead us to places we would rather not be. For now, understand and underscore this: *Such incremental values can be negative or positive, having the power to either build or destroy.* People usually think of increments as positive, in the American Heritage Dictionary sense: A slight, often barely perceptible augmentation. But small changes can just as easily be *decrements*, hence, *the value of the small decrement* (VSD). We shall observe many examples of VSDs as the book progresses, though I use the term "small increments" in a broad sense, allowing it to be either positive or negative.

One of the best examples of small increments is compound interest. Small deposits accumulate over time, almost unnoticed, but result in large future sums. Einstein supposedly said something to the effect that "compound interest is the most powerful force in the universe," though no evidence can be found he actually said that. But whoever said it was close to a major truth. The value of the small increment is a generalized statement that includes compound interest as a specific example of such increments.

How did the United States federal government become so large and so strapped financially? Mostly through small increments. For example, a General Accounting Office study released on March 1, 2011, detailed hundreds of duplicative offices and programs within the federal bureaucracy. Examples: 82 programs to improve teacher quality and 56 to help people achieve financial literacy. Each of these was instituted based on some congressional incentive at various times, with the summation amounting to, well, ludicrous proportions. Even what seem to be large increments, such as Medicaid, were built person by person, year by year, as rules were relaxed to permit more participants.

— *Personal Vignettes* —

Here are two examples of discounting and the value of the small increment. In my doctoral studies I had to pass five different written "field examinations" on five different subjects before moving on to a general oral examination encompassing all those fields, after which came the dissertation stage and yet another oral exam dealing with my dissertation. A student was allowed a total of only one re-take on any one of the five written examinations, after which expulsion from the program occurred.

Everybody feared the written economics exam, a four-hour, alleged horror one had to pass, but which ended in failure for more than a few. Adding to the fear was the fact that three different examinations on different subjects were given during a ten-day period in August, with the additional two occurring the following January (why I do not have ulcers is a stroke of good fortune). It was understood that all of economics was open to questioning, from one's first economics course through the material covered in the doctoral studies. The December before the August trial of terror, I purchased a large three-ring notebook and began to fill it with handwritten pages of notes, graphs, and mathematics, starting with the simplest concepts in supply and demand, then on through the advanced material.

Instead of playing my guitar for a while each day or going to the rare movie or drinking beer at Nick's English Hut on Saturday nights, I continued to fill the notebook (I was investing instead of consuming, assigning a low discount rate to the future). By March, there were several hundred pages between the covers. Then, grabbing time whenever I could in addition to my regular class studies, I began to work through the notebook, summarizing, refining, and studying, all of which expended the small increments of time I could spare. It required several weeks to get completely through the material the first time. During the early summer, I intensified my study, referring often to my books and class notes for clarification and understanding. By exam time in August, I could run through the huge notebook in an hour or two, simply flipping the pages and glancing at them, so familiar were the concepts.

Two other doctoral students came to me for tutoring, and I helped them as best I could. The night before the examination, I went to a movie, turned in early, and the following morning at 5 a.m. made one last pass through the notebook before quietly shutting my apartment door and walking across the campus. Slowly I walked, simultaneously feeling both trepidation and confidence, my pockets filled with pens and, for drawing graphs, colored pencils, a protractor, and a compass (the kind used for drawing and measuring, not to find my way to the examination room).

It was hot in the examination room, a warm Indiana breeze blowing through open windows in a building without air conditioning. A fellow student sitting opposite me at the long table, and who had failed the examination on his first try, fainted from the tension he suffered, tipped backwards in his chair, and had to be hospitalized. I found the exam almost enjoyable, so thoroughly had I prepared. I passed the test, as did the two fellow doctoral students I tutored. Do you see the discounting at work in all of this?

When I needed a new roof on an old metal building, my home for years in a remote mountainous area of southwest Texas, the roofing contractor said he could install a 20-year roof or a 50-year roof. I said to him, "Look, I am getting old; do you have a five-year roof?" Think about this bit of joshing in terms of discounting and why elderly people vote against school bonds and changes in Social Security.

— End of Personal Vignettes —

Chapter 4

GETTING TRAPPED

If We Are so Smart, How Come . . .

- There is an obesity epidemic?
- It is possible we are fishing the seas down to the level of species extinction?
- Teenagers listen to very loud music when it is demonstrable that it will cause hearing problems later on?
- People have huge credit card debts?
- We in the U. S. cannot fix the forthcoming insolvency of the American Social Security system? Or Medicare?
- People cannot quit smoking or taking drugs that destroy their bodies? And how did they get to that point in the first place?
- The illegal immigration problem both in Europe and the U. S. seems to be unfixable?
- The United States continues to pile up government debt even though it will eventually weaken or destroy the entire economic system?
- Many Americans will not have a comfortable retirement, but college professors and government employees will?

- There are traffic jams?
- We pollute the bays and ocean fronts where we fish and swim, and the streams and aquifers from where we obtain our drinking water? Why are we draining the aquifers much faster than they can be recharged, using the water for washing our cars or growing certain crops in climates unsuited for them?
- People buy more house than they can afford? Why do financial institutions lend them the money to make those purchases?
- Students party or play computer games or watch television instead of studying, resulting in "all-nighters" cramming for examinations.
- Squirrels save by storing nuts for the approaching winter, but humans do not save for retirement?
- We overuse antibiotics to the point they become ineffective?
- We overuse pesticides to the point they become ineffective?

And, and, and...the problems are, it seems, of diluvian proportions in their occurrence, size, scope, and omnipresence. There is a single answer to the above questions: Decision-making. Bringing along decision-making, discounting, criteria, incentives, and VSIs from the first three chapters, I now investigate the idea of dark and wicked things called traps.[1] You will quickly see them in your own life, in your friends' lives, and in society.

The Dentist Trap

It is a man's own mind, not his enemy or foe, that lures him to evil ways.

—Buddha

I begin with a simple example that explains much. Someone, you perhaps, avoids going to the dentist because of imagined discomfort or anticipated cost, or because you simply don't like anyone fussing around inside one of your orifices, particularly with tools that poke, buzz, grind, probe, and chip. Figure 4.1 shows the dentist decision tree. Of course,

---

[1] I originally encountered the idea of traps 30 years ago in a little book by Cross and Guyer (1980).

daily maintenance also is important and genetics play some role, but I am keeping it basic here.

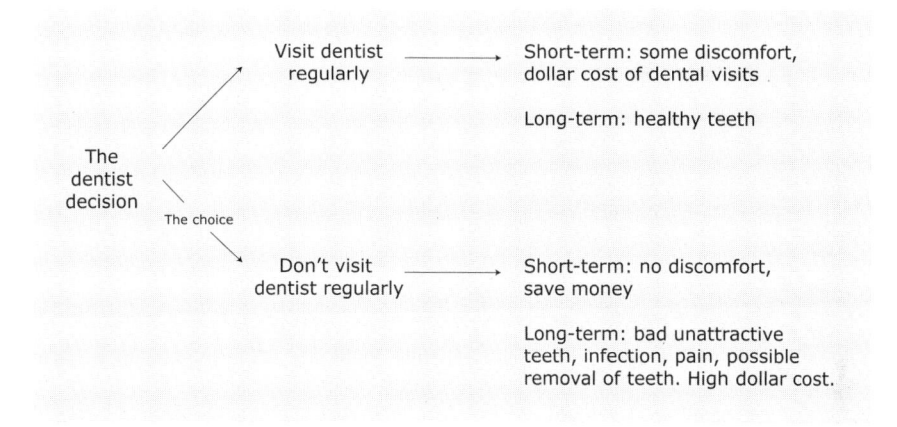

```
                        Visit dentist  ──────▶  Short-term: some discomfort,
                        regularly                dollar cost of dental visits
                    ╱
                   ╱                             Long-term: healthy teeth
     The
   dentist
   decision    ╲
              ╲ The choice
                   ╲
                    ▶   Don't visit   ──────▶  Short-term: no discomfort,
                        dentist regularly       save money

                                                Long-term: bad unattractive
                                                teeth, infection, pain, possible
                                                removal of teeth. High dollar cost.
```

Figure 4.1 The Dentist Decision

Time passes and the decision is made over and over again to avoid the dentist—small increments (Chapter 3). Discounting (Chapter 1) is occurring: Future benefits are being heavily discounted and are traded off against immediate rewards in the form of dollar costs not incurred and present discomfort not suffered by avoiding the dentist. This trade-off is made each time a visit to the dentist is contemplated and each time the discounted future benefits of dental care evidently are less than the present rewards from not visiting the dentist. In the end, however, the cumulative short-term rewards of avoiding the dentist are far less than the ultimate cost of the avoidance. Or, for example, you could say the cumulative rewards over 20 years from avoidance are less than the healthy-teeth reward at year 20. In either event, a trap is sprung.

Notice the consequences flowing from the value of the small increment (VSI) and the decision-making that drives the small increments. Each time you consider a visit to the dentist, that is a decision based on incentives (expected outcomes act as incentives, as explained in Chapter 2).[2] At first, damage to adult teeth may not be particularly noticeable, but subsequent small

---

[2] Along with outcomes, decision criteria play an important role. I will get to that in a while.

incremental decisions not to take care of the teeth result in more damage. The more damage, the more cost and discomfort accrue in thinking about going to the dentist, providing even greater incentives not to make that choice. At some point, in spite of advances in dentistry, there is no alternative but to have all of one's teeth extracted and to be fitted with dentures. In addition, tooth and gum infections are sure to happen, especially with smoking added on, and can lead to other problems such as heart trouble; therefore, you may not make it to extraction or expensive periodontal surgery likely will be required. Cross and Guyer (1980) appropriately call this a *time-delay trap*, and the label should be self-explanatory.

Moreover, in addition to the time delay, this trap incorporates sliding reinforcers, a particularly insidious form of incentives. As time passes and the teeth degenerate, the anticipated costs of dental care rise, providing even more incentive to avoid the dentist. In short, the negative incentives increase over time because of the earlier negative incentives that caused previous choices to be made—think of the escalating disincentives as stair steps. Avoidance of daily study by college students is exactly the same kind of trap, as are many of those listed at the beginning of this chapter. Cleaning up your office has similar characteristics; the longer it is delayed, the more difficult it is to get started. Think of such traps this way: They are akin to reverse savings accounts, compounding in a negative direction.

More Individual Traps

The National Football League provides a perfect example of a one-person trap, deriving from both the culture and economics of professional football. Try to visualize a simple decision tree as I describe the situation. A player suffers a concussion in game n. If he chooses to remain out of action for the recommended period of recovery time, say n + 4, a three-part outcome presents itself: He incurs the displeasure of his teammates for letting them down, he worries his substitute may perform so brilliantly that he with the concussion loses his job, and he foregoes the enjoyment of playing. Yet, if he suffers one or more additional concussions by returning too soon or continuing to play after several concussions, he risks permanent disability in a few years. The decision is to return immediately or wait the prescribed amount of time and undergo continuous testing. In terms of future health, most return to the field too soon or return when their careers should be over. The trap is obvious, and the example extends to other severe injuries, as well. Painkillers are administered to mask discomfort, enabling a player to continue participation, even when the body is sending signals indicating rest and rehabilitation are needed. An extremely high discount rate is being applied to the future, with most players admitting the future does not even enter their decision-making.

Remark. Notice in the dentist decision, the rewards are immediate (avoidance of cost and discomfort), while the higher costs are farther out in time, as is true of the football example. The negative reinforcers, in other words, do not occur soon enough to alter behavior. You already know enough about discounting to grasp this idea in a general way. Costs that do not occur until time has passed are discounted heavily in the present or completely ignored. Thalso is relates to feedback cycles, which I take up in Chapter 6.

Colonoscopies are one of the great indignities in our lives. Let's spare ourselves the visual images and concentrate on decision-making. The costs, monetary and psychological, cause people to avoid colonoscopies. Approximately 112,000 Americans are afflicted with colon cancer each year, though with regular screenings it is largely preventable. Risking the greater ultimate indignity and monetary cost is playing the colon-cancer lottery, avoiding colonoscopies, and developing cancer—a trap, and a very nasty one.

A warm summer night, the car radio plays softly, it is dark along a country road. Desire increases, temptation is amplified, and a short time later one of the following occurs: A sexually transmitted disease (STD), an unwanted pregnancy, contraction of the HIV virus, possible guilt or other emotional distress. A trap has formed. The summer nights never end ... until they do, and the main title of this book has just appeared.

Jimmy continues to spend all his discretionary income—decision-making, discounting, incentives, VSIs—and suddenly he is 65 and discovers he is consigned to live a grim existence with Social Security as his sole source of income. The one-time dreams of travel, golf, sailing, fly fishing fast mountain streams, and other anticipated pleasures are gone. Jimmy is trapped.

Summary

By now, I hope it is becoming clear how decision-making, discounting, incentives, VSIs, and traps all fit together. One-person traps, however, often have consequences beyond the individual, such as a family member's smoking that results in huge medical bills for the entire family and for society beyond the family. Furthermore, many individuals acting on their own can each contribute to traps ensnaring everybody. These are called social traps or societal traps and I take them up next.

Herewith I present the perfect and infinitely succinct summary to this chapter. Reflecting upon her past behavior, my wife said this about her unexpected pregnancy when she was a young woman: "Getting there was fun, got there was not." Linda has a knack for moving directly to the heart of things, and I have a fierce admiration for her honesty.

Chapter 5

SOCIAL TRAPS

Big to Small, Small to Big

From macro to micro and back to macro, or the converse, is how I approach problems. Example: Obesity is a general problem afflicting societies (macro level) and imposing huge costs on everyone, but ultimately is caused by individuals making decisions (micro level). If a solution can be found to change human behavior, to lessen the obesity problem, the effects will move beyond the single person back to a healthier society (macro level), physically and economically. The decline in the attractiveness of a neighborhood (macro level) can often be traced to the decisions of one or a few individual homeowners not to maintain their properties (micro level), eventually leading to an overall decline as other homeowners have little incentive to take care of their properties, and blight sets in.

You like to head home at exactly 4:30 in the afternoon when your workday is finished, as do many other people, occasioning a traffic jam affecting all drivers but ultimately caused by the decisions of individual drivers. Individuals who made bad decisions in buying more home than they could afford default on their loans, foreclosure signs are fastened on doors, and property values in the entire neighborhood begin to decline due to vandalism and other factors, leading to financial troubles for the remaining residents. A business firm or government entity finds it profitable to dump pollutants into a stream, thereby destroying the beauty and recreational opportunities of those living downstream, along with contaminants in the drinking water, resulting in a trap for all but the perpetrator. Quaint towns become known for their charming qualities, which act as incentives for people to move there; many arrive, the town becomes congested and loses the charm that caused people to move there in the first place.

Social traps arise from individual decisions, where the actions of separately acting persons or a single person or a business or government, responding to incentives, enmesh others in a trap, perhaps an entire society or world. Thus, individual decisions, discounting and the lure of the short-run, incentives, VSIs, traps. Notice how the same general structure can be applied through all the problems we have looked at thus far in the book. Understanding these similarities is an efficiency device, a time-saver in thinking, a powerful intellectual technology that can easily be carried from problem to problem.

In *Leviathan*, the great political philosopher Thomas Hobbes famously spoke of a war of every man against every man and in a different work of "a war of all against all." Hobbes was referring to an imagined "state of nature" where no government was present and where chaos reigned. It is only a mild stretch to understand that certain social traps are a Hobbesian form of all doing damage to all, though the harm may be an unintentional byproduct of individual decision-making.

The Tragedy of the Commons
Biologist Garrett Hardin wrote a simple, brilliant, and influential article titled "The Tragedy of the Commons" (Hardin 1968), which beautifully illustrates social traps. The elements of Hardin's example occur so frequently that an entire category of problems can be labeled "commons traps." In case you are unfamiliar with the concept, here is the nub of it, in my words. An early New England village has a common pasture—the commons—open to all who wish to graze cattle. One of the herdsmen,

let us call him Choiceman, grazes a single cow but knows he could better himself by sending one extra cow to pasture, so he adds an additional cow since it costs him nothing in the way of grazing fees or land acquisition. If the pasture is large and the population of herdsmen low, the effect of one more animal is negligible on the pasture's health and beneficial to Choiceman. But every herdsman has the same incentive as Choiceman. If all bring an extra cow, the quality of the grazing slightly declines (VSI). As the number of cows or herdsmen increases, the pasture eventually becomes overgrazed and barren, a situation in which each individual making perfectly rational decisions leads to suffering for all. A trap, that's for sure. The decisions are rational for the individual, but not for the larger group and eventually appear irrational for each herdsman when the trap is sprung.

The Ogallala aquifer is the prime source of water for a large section of the American high plains. In my novel, *High Plains Tango*, various characters ruminate on and dismiss the possibility of draining the Ogallala aquifer through overuse and wasteful use of the water therein by farmers, ranchers, and communities. I wrote the original draft of that book in 1993, and now the trap is closing as wells cease to produce and towns whither away.

In the words of Milton and Rose Friedman (1980), "When everybody owns something, nobody owns it, and nobody has a direct interest in maintaining or improving its condition." If you doubt those words, look at the state of public housing in the United States, litter along highways, polluted air, and old refrigerators and tires dumped into public streams.

Consider unlimited immigration as some open-borders advocates favor. Immigrants want to come to the U. S. for the opportunities and benefits it provides. When all can enter, the opportunities are diluted, potentially to zero. The United States is a commons of opportunities and benefits that can be exhausted, just like Hardin's pasture.

Patents and copyrights are designed to protect a "winner" lest his invention be completely made worthless by everyone entering the "commons" provided by the invention's opportunities. If all could enter, profits would be reduced to zero, and society would be deprived of the invention's benefits since no incentive would be present to produce the device or service.

Hardin draws his definition of tragedy from the writings of philosopher Alfred North Whitehead and the definition is apt for our purposes here: "The essence of dramatic tragedy is not unhappiness. It resides in the solemnity of the remorseless working of things." That is wonderful language, read it again simply for the ring of it: "...The solemnity of the remorseless working of things."

The conclusion is that each person behaving in what appears to be a perfectly rational manner in the short-term, eventually creates destruction for larger society, including himself in the long-term. Hardin (1995): "...If a pasture is run as a commons open to all, the right of each to use it is not matched by an operational responsibility to take care of it. It is no use asking independent herdsmen in a commons to act responsibly, for they dare not. The considerate herdsman who refrains from overloading the commons suffers more than a selfish one... "

Hardin continues (the italics are his), "If *everyone* would only restrain himself, all would be well; but it takes *only one less than everyone* to ruin a system of voluntary restraint. In a crowded world of less than perfect human beings—and we will never know any other—mutual ruin is inevitable in the commons. This is the core of the tragedy of the commons." Well said and dead-on accurate. It is a short step to seeing the relation of Hardin's simple model to obesity as a societal problem along with other dilemmas such as air pollution, rising population, traffic jams, overfishing the seas, Wall Street shenanigans involving complex derivatives, and so forth.

Though I am adamant about the importance of private property and individual freedom, you have just witnessed why the cries for government intervention of one kind or another are ever-mounting. In sum, if something desirable is free or vastly under-priced—air, water, national parks, medical care—it will be exploited until nothing is left for anyone.[1]

Traps Involving Costs to Both the Individual and Others
Back to the obesity issue. The badly overweight or obese person is caught

---

[1] Compare the commons situation to how a herdsman would behave if he owned the pasture rather than operating as one of many using the free commons. Private property has unmatched advantages for the conduct of a society and conservation of resources, natural resources included.

in a personal trap while putting an additional load on the medical system, raising costs for everyone. As larger ambulances, special gurneys and stretchers, reinforced and expanded hospital beds, and plus-size MRI machines are required, the social costs run beyond the more obvious costs of increased doctor visits and surgeries that raise overall health insurance premiums.[2] An extremely overweight person in the airplane seat beside you and causing you discomfort is another social cost. Figure 5.1 illustrates how obesity or simply excessive body weight generates both a personal trap and social trap.

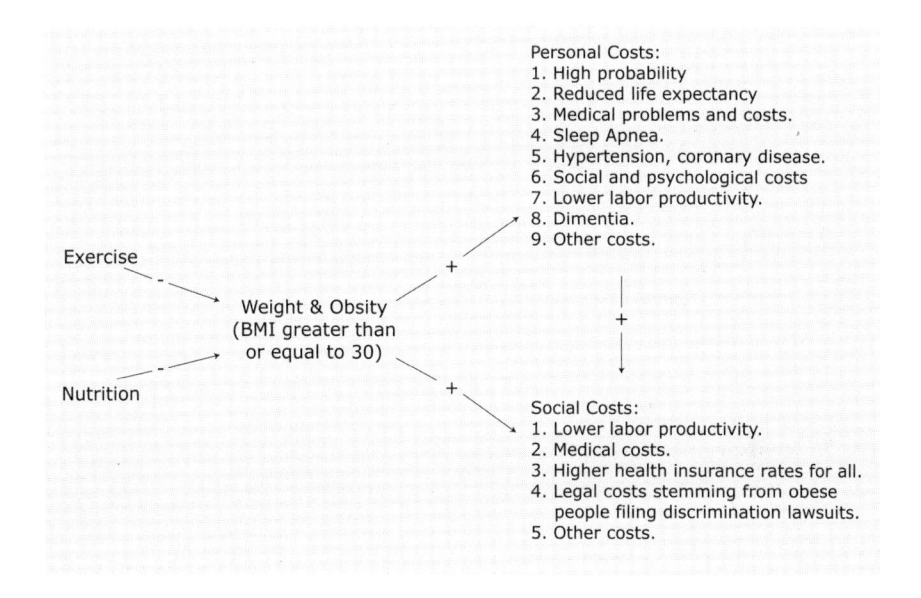

```
                                    Personal Costs:
                                    1. High probability
                                    2. Reduced life expectancy
                                    3. Medical problems and costs.
                                    4. Sleep Apnea.
                                    5. Hypertension, coronary disease.
                                    6. Social and psychological costs
                                    7. Lower labor productivity.
                                    8. Dimentia.
                                    9. Other costs.
  Exercise
           ↘                    +
              Weight & Obesity
              (BMI greater than          +
              or equal to 30)
           ↗                    
  Nutrition                   +
                                    Social Costs:
                                    1. Lower labor productivity.
                                    2. Medical costs.
                                    3. Higher health insurance rates for all.
                                    4. Legal costs stemming from obese
                                       people filing discrimination lawsuits.
                                    5. Other costs.
```

Figure 5.1 The Obesity Trap

More examples:

- As mentioned earlier, a single resident of a nice neighborhood shuns property maintenance and upkeep lowering his or her own property values. But those living nearby also discover the value of their homes declining because no potential buyers want to put up with the unsightly neighbor.

---

[2] Britain spends over $80 million per year on specialized equipment just to accommodate obese patients, including—heaven help us all—winches for hospitals and emergency vehicles.

The Blueprint

- Decimation of the Atlantic cod fisheries has occurred because each individual fisherman and each nation have an incentive to maximize their short-run catch at the expense of preserving the fisheries.
- A shortage of landing and takeoff slots at busy airports during peak travel times along with flight delays and other costs of congestion.
- The AIDS epidemic.
- Failure to save for retirement or not accumulating a rainy-day fund for difficult times, resulting in taxpayer subsidies via the government.
- Smoking or drug addiction imposing costs on society as a whole.
- Overuse of pesticides by individual farmers, resulting in less productive land over time, resulting in higher food costs. India presently is suffering this.
- Stripping of hillsides for firewood or building materials resulting in erosion and mudslides.
- Failure to wear seatbelts, causing more severe injuries to drivers and passengers, costs partially borne by everyone in terms of medical and insurance costs.

Traps Involving Personal Behavior Where The Costs Are Paid Solely by Others

Economists say that when someone else pays the costs of your behavior, you have *externalized* the costs, ladled them off onto others. You have created an *externality*. Classic examples are a manufacturing firm or a city unwilling to install pollutant recovery devices or change its core technology, causing downstream dwellers to contend with polluted water. Crime is an attempt by criminals to benefit entirely at a cost to others. The federal government, using a tactic to make its budget appear more reasonable, shoves costs such as Medicaid onto the states.

Not many would identify the following as a trap but it is: Failure to have a will, physician directives, and appropriate powers-of-attorney, imposing pre- and post-mortem personal and monetary costs on relatives, plus tying up the judicial system. The cost of instituting such documents is minimal (it can be done online), so the motivation must have something to do with either sloth or denial of the ultimate end we all face. It also involves choosing the do-nothing alternative (Chapter 2) because of the cognitive decision-making cost involved and I suspect fear of offending heirs, i.e., let the kids fight it out after I'm gone.

More Examples of Social Traps
- Overuse of and over-prescribing of antibiotics, resulting in bacteria mutating in self-defense to the point the antibiotics are no longer effective.
- Careless drivers who by their actions cause accidents, injuring or killing not only themselves but others.
- A driver traveling 40 miles per hour on a 70 miles per hour crowded highway; those behind the driver are trapped.
- If the number of livestock owned is a sign of wealth, there is an incentive to acquire more livestock. Even if plots of land are privately owned, if all landowners continue to expand, desertification results. See the southward movement of the Sahara for an example of this.
- Having children you cannot afford and letting society foot the bill through various welfare programs. This is the same as an upstream polluter.
- People who file chancy or outright frivolous lawsuits resulting in substantial court costs all of us pay for.
- Academic department heads distributing merit pay equally across all faculty members because that is the "fair" way to do it. Can you see a trap forming? I have been there. It also is a maneuver to avoid hard decisions, equivalent to the do-nothing option. Good academics seldom make good managers.
- At a grocery or video store, ten people stuck behind a person in a check-out line who first has to find a check to write out for $2.89 and then get it approved by the supervisor.
- Living not far from me is a man who is troubled by coyotes and puts out poisoned chicken bones along the roadsides to eradicate them. The bones are picked up by various critters, dispersed into neighbors' yards

and pastures, and pets die from chewing on the bones. Examine this in terms of a social trap, pollution, and externalities.

- A regional brownout or blackout due to an overload of electrical use on a hot afternoon is a good example of a social trap and closely resembles the tragedy of the commons.
- Those of us who did not take out subprime mortgages were caught in a more general financial trap of economic decline by those who made the loans or took out the loans.
- Inter-generational traps. Huge deficits due to government profligacy create traps, as current behavior ensnares future generations. Other examples: Non-reversible pollution, stripping of forests to the point they cannot recover, building dams for present electricity needs that deny the pleasure of wild rivers for future generations.
- Careless drivers or those who purposely create auto accidents to collect liability/injury payments create a trap that snares honest policyholders in the form of higher premiums.
- Passing on an STD to a previously uninfected partner.

A very good example is avoiding maintenance and replacement of infrastructure. It can be viewed as a variation on both the dentist and commons trap. People do not want their taxes raised to take care of something they cannot see (bad roadways excepted), since much of our infrastructure such as sewer and water lines is underground or hidden in complex edifices such as bridges. Politicians would rather spend money on programs having more flair and vote-buying power. Infrastructure seems boring, expensive, and its future condition seems like, well, something that will get fixed sometime but not now. Then a bridge collapses, a water line breaks, a sewer system clogs, and a trap is sprung.

Social traps are everywhere. All of them are the result of decisions, discounting, incentives, small increments, and the lure of the short-run. There seems to be no answer to resolving or preventing traps other than a centralized guiding authority, one with police power—a parental government—or is there another way? I will address that sticky question later.

Along with government, religions attempt to solve both trap avoidance and getting out of traps. Think about what a typical religion tries to accomplish. First, it constrains your set of choices, the alternatives to be considered, e.g., the Ten Commandments. Second, it attempts to influence discount rates by assigning a low rate to heavenly delights in the future versus short-run pleasures. Third, and related to the second, religions vividly paint outcomes as happiness or hell to inflate incentives. Confessions in the Catholic Church allow for backsliding but with the possibility of clearance if you make it to the confessional before dying. I am not being irreligious here; if religion did not exist we might have to invent it just to keep things under some semblance of control.

Next I need to build one more idea into the conceptual framework being developed in this book, the notion of feedback systems and how feedback relates to everything we have examined thus far.

Chapter 6

VICIOUS CIRCLES, BENEFICENT SPIRALS, AND THE POWER OF FEEDBACK

A brief study of feedback will add the final implement to the basic toolbox for this book. Two types of feedback systems are of interest: Positive and negative.

Positive Feedback

In practical terms, a positive feedback system always moves in the same direction. Such feedback systems are all around us, e.g., increases in the stock market causing more increases in the stock market as new investors enter or existing investors add to their investments to avoid missing the run-up. The reverse: People exit the market in fear of losing money, causing even more of a sell-off, causing further declines in the market, which also is a positive feedback system even though it is moving downward. Lack of exercise contributes to obesity, which contributes to lack of exercise, which contributes to obesity.

   The dentist decision in Chapter 4 implicitly contained feedback loops. Check out Figure 6.1 where the loops are made explicit and dashed lines are used to show the passage of time. Follow the logic through the diagram,

The Blueprint

```
           +---------------------------------------+
           ↓                    +                  |
         Cost                                      |
            \                                      |
             +                                     |
              \                                    |
               →                          Problems
             Avoid Dentist  --- + ---- →   with teeth
              →                                    |
             +                                     |
            /                                      |
   Anticipated                                     |
   Discomfort                                      |
      ↑                                            |
      |_____ + _____|

                                    ──→  = "leads to"
```

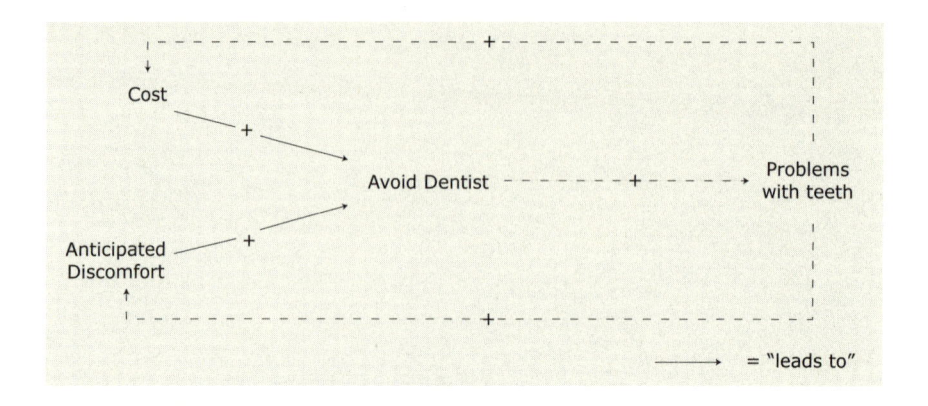

Figure 6.1 The Dentist Decision Incorporating Feedback Loops

starting with "Avoid Dentist." The plus sign on the line means the greater the dentist avoidance, the greater the problems with teeth. The line contains two pieces of information: The arrow direction meaning "leads to" and the sign indicating in which direction the effect occurs, up or down.

Continue along from "Problems with Teeth" to "Cost" (the monetary cost of dental visits) and the opposite loop leading to "Anticipated Discomfort," which is a type of expected cost. As time passes, increasing cost and anticipated discomfort both lead to a greater incentive to avoid the dentist, the cycle continues until a trap is formed, as explained in Chapter 4.

Next I integrate a simple decision tree into the dentist diagram. See Figure 6.2. The double slash on the line to "Visit Dentist" indicates a rejected alternative. In addition, I have added the trap at the right side of the diagram. This example and its portrayal in Figure 6.2 incorporates feedback into decision-making, incentives, discounting, VSIs, and traps. In a simple diagram, therefore, a skeletal portrayal of many of the world's personal and societal problems is captured when other problems are substituted for the dentist problems, with only minor modifications to the structure. Think about neglect of infrastructure repair and replacement. Consider why politicians "kick the can" down the road in reforming Medicare or Social Security, maximizing electability while sacrificing national well-being. Try sketching your own decision tree-feedback diagram to illustrate why politicians hesitate to reform Medicare.

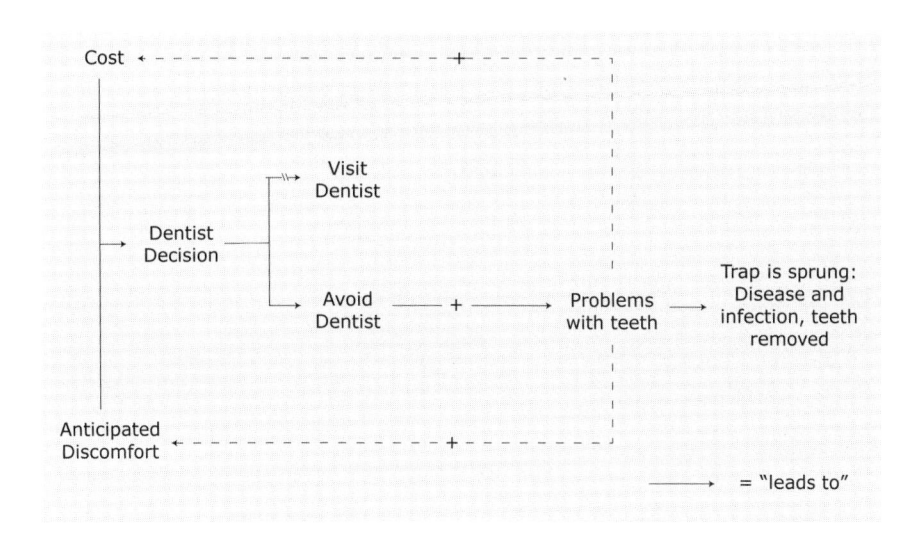

```
        Cost ←--------------+--------¬
                                     |
                                     |
              ┌──→ Visit             |
              |    Dentist           |
              |                      |
      Dentist─┤                      |
   →  Decision|                      |
              |                      |         Trap is sprung:
              |                      |         Disease and
              └──→ Avoid ────+────→ Problems ──→ infection, teeth
                   Dentist            with teeth   removed
                                     |
                                     |
   Anticipated                       |
   Discomfort  ←-----------+---------┘

                                      ───────→ = "leads to"
```

Figure 6.2 The Dentist Decision, Loops and Decision Tree

Oh so gently, allow me to suggest people are not used to thinking in rigorous, precise terms when contemplating problems. The diagrams I am using tend to require such precision, both in their construction and in their interpretation, particularly in assigning or understanding the plus and minus signs. A general rule: If there is an even number of minus signs in a feedback loop, regardless of how many elements and lines are involved, it is a *positive feedback system*, i.e., it will keep moving in the same direction, up or down. The same is true if it contains all plus signs, since zero minus signs is treated here as an even number.

"Positive" in the way I am using it does not mean "good" from a moral or policymaking perspective; it is a description, not a judgment. The computation is merely a matter of multiplying the signs on a feedback loop. Example: + * - * - = + is a positive feedback system. So is + * + * + = +. As with discounting, this requires a bit, just a small amount, of cognitive effort to keep straight.

The decimation of the black rhinoceros population provides an example with a different texture from other problems we have looked at. The horn of the black rhinoceros is prized in the Middle East and Asia for everything from dagger handles (especially North Yemen) to doubtful, if not laughable,

The Blueprint

use as an aphrodisiac (tiger-penis soup allegedly has similar stimulative powers), and a curative for AIDS (South Korea). Taiwanese medical practitioners routinely stock the horn. So do purveyors in San Francisco's Chinatown. Old traditions are difficult to kill, though animals are not.

See Figure 6.3, which is only a portion of a larger analysis I have done but not included in this book. My purpose here is to illustrate how the plus and minus signs operate in positive feedback systems. By now, the diagram should be largely self-explanatory. Start anywhere in this cycle and use the following logic as an example: As the price of rhino horn increases, poaching increases because of the incentives; as poaching increases, so do kills per year; more kills, less rhinos; less rhinos, the less the availability of horn; less availability lessens the supply of horn; and we end where we started with a smaller supply resulting in a higher price for the horn, which leads to more poaching. The number of minus signs is two, an even number, indicating a positive feedback system. Round and round goes the sad song, in a minor key with lyrics grim. Compare this to overfishing a particular species or to the commons example.

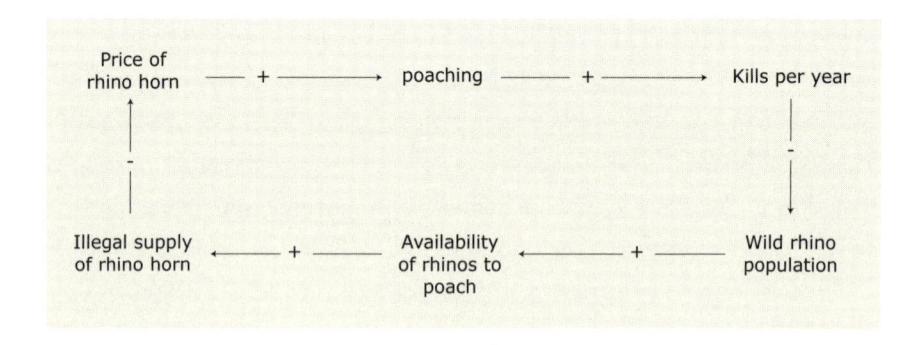

```
Price of
rhino horn  ——— + ———→  poaching  ——— + ———→  Kills per year
    ↑                                              │
    │                                              │
    −                                              −
    │                                              │
    │                                              ↓
Illegal supply  ←— + ——  Availability  ←— + ——  Wild rhino
of rhino horn            of rhinos to            population
                         poach
```

Figure 6.3 Decline of the Black Rhino—the Cycle

Cycles, the proper term rather than circles or spirals, are found in many interesting problems. But cycles are not always sinister, things are not always heading up or spiraling down causing grief and sorrow; sometimes the reverse is true and are popularly called "virtuous circles."

Here is a "bad" cycle: Rice becomes in short supply, people hurry out and buy lots of rice so they can hoard it, rice becomes in even shorter supply—that sort of behavior falls into the vicious-circle category. (Always remember this: It is important to get there and stock up before the hoarders arrive.)

Good cycle: Early academic achievement leads to praise and *honestly* acquired self-esteem, leading to further academic achievement, leading to more rewards, and so forth—nothing vicious here, except the possibility of being labeled a nerd (but nerds tend to win in the long term at a higher frequency rate than quarterbacks, and you are reading the words of a former college basketball player). Bad cycle: Poor academic achievement may lead to disruptive behavior in class as a way of attracting attention, leading to problems in school, leading to poor academic achievement, leading to more dysfunctional behavior—a vicious circle. Bad cycle: Excessive household spending leads to credit card debt, which leads to high interest charges, which leads to more credit card debt, which leads to higher accrued interest leading to more debt.

Bad cycle: American consumers become overleveraged (too much debt) and reduce spending, resulting in less sales for companies, so companies stop hiring or lay people off, which leads to less consumer spending, and the cycle continues.

Practicing basketball leads to proficiency, leading to rewards, leading to more practice, and on and on. Too much basketball, however, can shift the cycle in a downward direction because of lack of attention to schoolwork. Inflation: Higher prices cause people to buy ahead of prices rising farther, with the increased demand causing even higher prices, and before long you have to trundle down to the market pushing a wheelbarrow full of cash to purchase a loaf of bread. Occasionally the adjective "runaway" is used to indicate a positive feedback cycle. For instance, it is said that sheet ice in Greenland and portions of Antarctica are in a "runaway melt mode," meaning the more melt the more ice is exposed to water causing more melt and so forth. Disharmonies in a marriage can lead to escalating feelings leading to more disharmonies.

Try sketching some of the cycle examples I listed. Add plus or minus signs. Add or subtract elements and observe what happens.

Can a positive feedback system continue indefinitely? Usually not, since a breaking point occurs somewhere—morbid obesity leads to an early death, avoiding the dentist leads to all sorts of problems and not just with teeth. Speculation plus poor lending practices and financially illiterate borrowers lead to higher and higher housing prices, sometimes called a "bubble." But such "irrational exuberance" (in economist Allen Greenspan's phrase) can eventually cause a system to run out of steam as one or more of the elements becomes exhausted or an outside authority intervenes, causing the system to pull back or crash. The disharmonic marriage may culminate in divorce. There are many examples of positive feedback cycles imploding. In 1637 Holland, a frenzy of tulip-bulb buying—yes, tulip bulbs—led to a runaway speculation cycle until the government finally passed a statute curbing the cycle. A more recent one is the infamous housing bubble in the first decade of the present century. But love and affection in a relationship can be part of a good cycle lasting for a long time.

Negative Feedback

Positive feedback cycles are the type of cycles most often found in headline-grabbing problems, such as obesity, inflation, rising home prices, drug use leading to more drug use, violence leading to more violence, and over-fishing a species leading to more over-fishing of the species as attempts to maintain catch levels are instituted. And, I note, media people using the overworked rubric of "crisis" do not have the slightest idea they are often talking about positive feedback systems and ordinarily only talk about part of the problem, to boot.

Yet negative feedback cycles are just as interesting, for they lead to equilibriums. "Equilibrium" has a nice sound to it, makes one conjure up a picture of things being in a pleasant state of balance with no tendency toward change, which is why such cycles usually do not make the headlines; when all is in relative balance, there is no news as contemporary news organizations interpret it. But value judgments of "good" should not be attached to equilibriums, for systems can establish equilibriums at undesirable levels and may need a kick to get them moving, which amounts to changing a negative feedback cycle to a positive feedback cycle, at least for a while, a major argument made for government fiscal and monetary policy. When the United States economy enters a recession and appears stuck there, the economic system has reached equilibrium at a level lower than desired and cries for government intervention follow. One such intervention could be cutting taxes rather than so-called fiscal stimulus via government spending, though politicians favoring larger government prefer the latter (incentives at work).

The body has negative feedback systems striving for equilibrium in many ways. It tries to maintain a constant body temperature at or about 98.6 degrees F. In hot conditions, you perspire, which is the body's way of keeping you at or moving you back toward the equilibrium temperature. When you are cold, muscles involuntarily contract, causing you to shiver and generate heat.

If your residence is too cold, the sensor in your thermostat sends a message to the heating system to crank up. When the heat begins to exceed the set-point, the sensor tells the system to shut down, thereby maintaining equilibrium. The float valve is an ancient device and we still use it to regulate the level of tank water in flush toilets. Inventory control systems adjust restocking or de-stocking (a sale or discounts) as inventory levels trend down or up beyond a desired level, respectively.

Negative feedback systems frequently have automatic control devices built into them to regulate the output of the system and keep it from going out of control, e.g., the thermostat. Modern airplanes have automatic pilots. If you become inebriated and then drive an automobile, you, as the regulating device, fail. Various technological contrivances have been fashioned to prevent you from starting the vehicle if you are drunk, which amount to devices keeping a system under control. Or, some outside intervention periodically is used to bring a system back into equilibrium.[1] Diet pills are supposed to do that, though evidence shows they are minimally effective and may be dangerous. A film called *The China Syndrome* dealt with the failure of feedback and control systems in a nuclear power plant until

---

[1] The science of control systems spans many fields, especially engineering. The way in which I am using positive and negative feedback in this chapter is similar to engineering concepts, but somewhat less rigorous.

heroic human intervention occurred; the Chernobyl nuclear disaster in the Soviet Union was an example of negative feedback systems failing to hold the plant within specified bounds.

Timing of Feedback and Lack of Feedback
Somewhere in the growing years you toddled too near something hot, touching a stove burner or the equivalent. The feedback was instantaneous, sending a message, "This behavioral alternative is not a good one to select!" The feedback loops connected with most traps tend to be long in duration, too long to make timely corrections. If an obese person, with two heart attacks, failing knees, and a bad back, who now is lying in a hospital bed awaiting amputation of a foot due to Type 2 diabetes, could return to an earlier time and start over, previous behavior might have been altered. If somehow a particular future could be brought back to a specified present where people could instantly experience the disabilities arising from obesity—similar to touching a hot stove burner—they likely would not become obese in the first place. Think diligently about that example, for it lies at the core of many of our dilemmas, not just obesity, e.g., drug addiction, alcoholism, soil erosion, deforestation, over-fishing a species, smoking, retirement planning, pollution, government spending that leads to accumulated debt, credit card debt, and a whole lot of other situations.

Suppose Jimmy, our friend who lives a skyrocket life with his bonus money, could experience at age 25 the grim reality of living on a meager income at 70. Jimmy understandably would be inclined to change his personal discounting and choose the alternative of saving at least part of his bonus. If a person yet unborn could somehow be transported back to the present and vociferously confront her elected representatives, even threaten them with bodily harm, perhaps even cast a vote, it is probable the representatives would rethink their profligate spending that loads government debt onto the backs of future generations.

In short, the trick is bringing the future back to the present; please hold that phrase in your mind. When feedback is of long duration, the future speaks only with a faint and distant voice and heavy discounting occurs. Some are able to construct concrete visions of the future and also hear that future speaking with a much louder voice, henceforth accounting for the future, while others who are unable to envision futures attach high discount rates to what is yet to come. Religion and governments both attempt to constrain human choices such that the future is accounted for, but loss of freedom always results. It is a conundrum I turn to in the next chapter.

And, for those familiar with Dickens's A Christmas Carol, recall that in Ebenezer Scrooge's third dream the ghost of Christmases yet to come foretells the great unhappiness that will befall Scrooge in the future if he does not change his penurious, cranky behavior. From time to time, it seems we all could use a ghost of pleasures or punishments yet to come.[2]

---

[2] I owe a debt to Tom Reuschling, my long-time friend and colleague, for suggesting the Dickens tale as apropos to bringing the future back to the present.

Chapter 7

GETTING OUT OF TROUBLE: CONVENTIONAL APPROACHES

A Quick Review

Understand this: My dominant decision criterion in socio-economic matters is freedom; call it liberty if you like. Freedom slips away in small increments, almost unnoticed—a law here, a regulation there, a rule somewhere else. Eventually freedom is severely constrained, a trap has formed.

Jimmy spends, Julia saves. In the end, Jimmy will need assistance, some of Julia's savings is taken to support Jimmy in the name of something called "distributive justice," a devolution of Julia's freedom and the creation of an injustice to Julia while supposedly fostering justice for Jimmy. Jimmy is caught in a trap, the policing power of the government subsequently and indirectly includes Julia as a victim of Jimmy's trap. Julia is punished for good behavior, Jimmy is rewarded for bad behavior; welcome to modern government philosophy and Julia suffering "distributive injustice." Politicians like to speak of socially beneficent "sacrifice" on Julia's part, but Julia *has already sacrificed by foregoing immediate pleasures in favor of future happiness.*

A quick review. Decisions are at the heart of things. People select an alternative from a set of alternatives, from a choice set. The choice is made by applying criteria to the alternatives' expected outcomes, where the outcomes serve as incentives. Outcomes are discounted according to personal valuations of the future versus the present, hence affecting incentives. The lure of the short-run tilts alternative selection toward the present. In many cases, feedback loops linking outcomes to choices tend to be long, resulting in the formation of traps. So what do we do? Here is the conventional stuff.

Fixing Things: Lugubrious Sermons, Ineffective Education, Endless Regulations

How do we as a society typically behave when traps are apparent (this is true of most or all societies, as far as I can tell)? First, we get people up behind podiums to instruct other people that they should behave differently, to select a more salutary alternative than the one selected at present. Thus, "Don't eat so much, eat better food, exercise; if you don't follow my advice, here's what will happen." "Don't smoke, it's not good for you, you'll get lung cancer and/or arteriostenosis or arteriosclerosis in 30 years." Don't pollute, don't drive large vehicles, don't have unprotected sex, don't use illegal drugs. Just say no. Don't, don't, don't ..." In essence, this is an attempt to change behavior by changing criteria (including time preference), or to limit the set of alternatives that will be considered, because the nasty outcomes still lie at the end of the decision tree if alternatives remain unchanged.

The moral exhortation tactic provides speakers with the cozy self-satisfaction (an incentive) they have done something to solve the problem at hand, and if other people ignore the wisdom presented and fail to act on it, that is not the speaker's problem. The same dictums are droned about premarital sex and other trap-inducing behavior, but the summer nights never end. Occasionally, moral exhortation to change behavior works, but only when it is thunderous, enduring, and insisted on by a charismatic figure. Or, when things are in such bad shape, the populace is willing to try anything. Adolf Hitler mastered that. However, most often the behavior change is temporary and recidivation occurs when the tutelary moves on to the next town, e.g., various rallies held to extol the virtues of responsible fatherhood or to re-energize a particular religious or social ideology. Ever wonder why certain religious sects have summer camp meetings? Because exhortations need constant renewal, having worn thin with time, which is why such meetings are called "revivals."

My position is that reason is not an effective device for changing people's minds or behavior, in spite of Western civilization's veneration of logic and sound argument. If well-reasoned moral exhortation worked, nobody would smoke, illegal drug use would be zero, students would behave in school and be high achievers within their capabilities, there would be no obesity, and the seas would not be over-fished. You get the point.

When moral exhortation doesn't work, which it hardly ever does, a second approach is to call for more education. What kind of education? I have only slightly more faith in cries for additional education in solving decision-based problems than I do in moral exhortation, meaning not a whole lot.[1] As Cross and Guyer (1980, 3) state, "It is surprising that the popular faith in simple education can be so persistent in the face of repeated demonstrations that it may not be effective at all." I would reply to Cross and Guyer that it is not surprising, since faith in this case is a cheap way of kicking the can down the road for someone else to deal with, rather than at least meliorating the problem, and the failure of education attempts do not surface for a long time (feedback loop), by which time people cannot remember who called for more education.

The inadequacy of both sermons and education is this: Mere understanding of a problem does not necessarily lead to behavioral change. I smoked cigarettes for many years even though I knew it was not good for me, but that didn't stop me from smoking. Why? Simple: I smoked because the lure of the short-run and immediate outcomes dominated long-term health, resulting in the assignment of a high discount rate to the future for this particular activity.

---

[1] I am not denigrating the power of education, in general, just the ineffectual, spasmodic calls for education as a way of avoiding hard solutions to hard problems. And evidence exists indicating a relationship between educational levels and self-control.

If large automobiles are harmful to the environment, why not educate people about the deleterious effects of gas-guzzlers while promoting the purchase of smaller, fuel-efficient vehicles? That has been done for decades. Why doesn't it work? Simple: Other criteria such as comfort, image, cargo capacity, towing power, and safety are dominating the criterion of a better but conceptually distant environment. University and high school parking lots are full of large vehicles while students are supposedly being educated in atmospheric pollution, and the last time I looked, Styrofoam cups were ubiquitous in faculty lounges. Employee counseling on financial decision-making and so-called benefit fairs to foster wise investing exhibit little permanent improvement in decision-making about retirement savings (Thaler and Sunstein 2006, 112). As of 2011, the federal government has—yes, it has—56 programs to help people better understand their finances, yet financial troubles abound.

Stage three rolls up when sermons and education don't do the job: Appoint a study group or a committee or commission or the militant-sounding "task force" to have a look at the problem. If those folks gin up solutions, usually their report calls for changing behavior because it is good to change the behavior causing the problem, along with—you guessed it—calls for more education. "More education" thus becomes a large closet into which problems are shunted so we temporarily can forget about them and go on to other things, leaving the problem to yet another study group in the future.

Am I saying people have a misplaced faith in sermons and/or education? Yes, I am. But allow me to be a little more cynical for a moment. Solving hard problems is hard, and the solutions are almost always unpopular with certain groups, whereas everybody applauds the idea of more education; therefore, advocate more education and receive praise from all rather than suggest solutions angering some or many.

Plus, I am less than sanguine about the capacity of humans to change behavior or their willingness to change based on what somebody else recommends. Physicians tell me over and over again about their frustrations in dealing with overweight patients who have or will contract diabetes, heart disease, bad knees, painful back conditions, and all the other maladies flowing from lack of exercise and unsound diets. The physicians also say that patients often get very angry when told they are destroying themselves due to weight gains and seek different, more sympathetic and less forthright medical care. Most doctors have given up on the behavioral aspects leading to excessive body fat and just treat the problems caused by it.

Beyond moral exhortation and calls for education, the final stage of our usual problem-solving strategies, when all else has failed, is to pass laws, regulations, and ordinances restricting behavior. Legislation of one kind or another increasingly seems to be the preferred approach, a societal reflex and also because many of our political leaders are lawyers who like to legislate. Curiously, politicians tout the passage of new laws as proof of administrative success, while I consider every new law a potential constraint on choice. This is where matters become serious if you value personal freedom, as I do. In short, constrain the choice set and punish those who insist on not observing the constraint while simultaneously imposing constraints on those not exhibiting the detrimental behavior. Sometimes those remedies are necessary if people are directly harming others by their actions, such as criminals and people who are curiously attached to the junk cars in their yards or insist on keeping 23 dogs on their property. But it is expensive, requiring enforcement and eventual legal wrangling, along with the creation of new, costly bureaucracies at the federal or state or local level. People are ingenious at discovering ways to evade laws, and, when unsuccessful, hire attorneys to help them find new tactics or to justify their evasion using the now-prevalent notion of "rights."

Ban smoking in bars and restaurants? Why? Second-hand smoke has been the provided answer. But why not let bars and restaurants decide whether to allow smoking and then give patrons and employees the option of being or not being in a smoky room? Let incentives and the market sort it out. Each time we invoke the nanny solution, freedom declines a little more, choices are more constrained, and it becomes reflexively easier to fashion another nanny solution to the next fashionable problem. The loss of freedom occurs in small increments, as choice sets are forcibly shrunk via governments' police power.

Understand, there is the likelihood of a new trap inherent in laws and regulations intended to solve a different trap. Each time a problem arises and laws are passed followed by regulations providing details to the laws—small increments—it becomes more difficult to do anything, even lawful and reasonable behavior. Eventually, governments, businesses, and ordinary citizens become entangled in a morass of paperwork and constrained behavior to the point that frustration becomes overwhelming, even though they may not have been snared in the trap at the outset (ask any small business person about regulations and paperwork). However, government bureaucrats applaud this complexity since it provides justification for government jobs and empire-building.

Legislators, prodded by constituents or interest groups, enact more and more laws producing seemingly endless regulations such that we all become trapped in the legal web, even if the enactments seem small at the time. The United States Internal Revenue Code is thousands of pages in length, the majority of the provisions brought forth in small increments. Most people in congress, if they do not know that, probably don't care because they do not compute their own taxes. And if you want to see incentives and disincentives at work, the tax code contains some of the best examples anywhere, including the promotion of marriage and contrary incentives to not being married, large families, purchasing hybrid cars, weatherizing your house, not earning income beyond a certain level, hiring temporary workers instead of full-time employees, and home buying. A knotty question: Should it be the job of the tax code to influence behavior or to redistribute income or purely to generate revenue for the government? In the United States, we mix the three objectives into an inedible stew, along with tax benefits for favored constituencies, such benefits being one of the major impediments to a simplified tax system (notice the incentives at work).

Escapes, Releases, and Mends

There are various ways to be extricated from a trap. Apply the following tangible example to the various traps I have presented. Walking through the woods, you step into an animal trap. You can pry apart the jaws of the trap and get out or scream for help and lie around in misery waiting for someone else to extricate you. Compare a healthy, muscular person caught in the trap with the predicament of a person who has been undergoing chemotherapy, is in a weakened condition, and has been caught in the trap. Some can escape, some need a release. Some do not deserve releases and should be left to devise escapes for themselves, the incentive of continued pain providing such motivation.

Escapes. Escapes are for the able and self-reliant. Example: Quitting smoking by going cold turkey—the incentives for quitting are many. Example: Rearranging your finances to pay off credit card debt or convincing your mortgage holder to renegotiate the loan or taking a second job to pay off credit balances. Emerging from my nine-and-a-half years of university studies, the backlog of wants and needs was huge, beyond what my teaching salary would support, e.g., extensive dental care for the family (remember the dentist trap?). The result was mounting debt. At one point I threw all the credit cards into a kitchen drawer and did not use them until my finances had stabilized, thereafter always paying the entire balance each month; the incentive here was weariness from troublesome debt and paying high interest rates on unpaid balances. I also took a second job playing guitar in a local club to help pay off the debts.

Example: Looking in the mirror and being appalled at what you see, thence deciding to institute an exercise and nutrition program; the incentives are health and beneficent vanity. There are more, but each involves a personal *decision*, in fact a series of decisions, a series of small increments. Each time the desire to smoke appears, a decision is made not to smoke, until there no longer a desire to do so. Each time there is a temptation to consume a pizza, a salad dressed with vinegar and oil is chosen instead. Each time excuses not to exercise come to mind, they are put aside in favor of exercise. Each time the temptation arises to buy on credit something not absolutely needed, the choice is made to save the money for retirement. These are the VSIs (value of the small increment) I have promoted, though VSIs can work both ways, for good and for bad. They are escapes when used in a good way.

In the above situations, the basic structure of the decision has not changed. What *has changed* is that a lower discount rate is being applied to the future (see Chapter 1); the future now is speaking with a louder, more insistent voice, overriding the lurch toward immediate pleasure. Alternatively, you can change your choice set by disallowing certain alternatives such as a purchase made by assuming debt. And if you can rid yourself of the incentive to choose the harmful course of action by changing the discount rate or removing the incentive by removing the alternative to which it is attached, it is much easier to make consistently good choices. More on these ideas can be found in the next chapter.

I cannot resist the tale of a young man who devised what he thought was the ultimate escape. I did not know him well, but well enough through my daughter's acquaintance with him. Behind him stretched a wake of trouble, including a trail of unpaid monetary debts. He moved to another state, assumed the new name of "Rain," and claimed he was not responsible for the debts because the person who incurred the debts no longer existed. Somehow, I don't think that tactic works in the long-run, but I credit his inventiveness and audacity.

Releases. When someone else takes care of the problem for you, a desire that seems more and common in modern society, I label that a *release*. "Bailout" is another word for release. Or substitute "rescue" or "cure" for "release," if you wish; I will use them interchangeably. The most direct example is abortion. Another example: Banks and other financial institutions made unnecessarily risky investments in the first decade of the 21st century and eventually began petitioning governments for help, seeking rescues in the form of taxpayer bailouts. Example: Homeowners who do not study mortgage contracts or do not undertake an honest review of their finances before signing, later asked the government or legal system to rewrite the contracts or to save them from foreclosure by the use of taxpayer money. Example: The person who invents a plaque-removal pill for arteries and gums will immediately become a zillionaire. Example: Runaway truck ramps in mountainous areas as a rescue from skimping on brake maintenance. Example: Nations such as Greece that appeal to other countries and the International Monetary Fund for help in untangling themselves from debt created through profligacy.

Imagine living 200 years ago with your family, located 30 miles from the nearest neighbor, and no government whatsoever. Decisions: Plow in the spring or lie around in bed, milk the cow or sit on the front porch, feed the chickens or let them starve. Think of the decision diagrams that would confront this pioneer. Winter will arrive in a few months—the future, that is—and the decision-maker and the family will perish unless preparations are made. One had better possess a low discount rate for the future if privation and death are to be avoided. Mother Nature provided squirrels with an instinct to gather nuts before the winter comes, imitating a low discount rate.

Now imagine there are wealthy neighbors and well-to-do people in a town nearby, along with the emergence of a benevolent, so-called "progressive" government. If you have made the decisions not to provide for yourself and government votes a policy that the better-off should be taxed, food and clothing purchased, and the goods delivered to you free of charge, the result is you have been rewarded for bad behavior and released at the same time. This is referred to as removing a "moral hazard," a reinforcement of bad behavior because risk has been eradicated and rescue emplaced, with the expected bailouts acting as incentives to continue bad behavior, just like large financial institutions.

But rescues are needed in certain cases. The elderly who worked hard but never earned a decent income throughout their lives, the truly sick and disabled, those struck by catastrophic natural disasters even though they had done everything else correctly as a self-reliant person, such as not building too near an oceanfront or on a hillside prone to collapse. It is where to draw the line that matters, though it is not as difficult as some would claim.

In other cases, people cry out for release rather than becoming more disciplined. Bariatric surgery as a rescue from obesity belongs in this category, along with problematical diets and weight-loss pills. The rule of law via the courts also is designed to rescue or release people from certain traps, such as pollution of a river by an upstream source because no other course of action exists in their frame of reference (they *could* pay the polluter to stop the discharges). Redistribution of wealth via taxes on some people and subsequent transfer payments or bailouts to others is a trap release, which is enervating to recipients, undoubtedly leading to loss of work incentives. Declaring bankruptcy is a legal release from debts, and most releases are the behavioral equivalent of declaring bankruptcy, e.g., bariatric surgery.

States and municipalities currently are entertaining the possibility of changing constitutions and laws to permit them to declare bankruptcy, primarily as a way of voiding union contracts involving excessive medical and retirement benefits.

Organizations such as Alcoholics Anonymous and other support groups are a mixture of escapes and releases. The initial desire to cease abusing alcohol is augmented by the encouragement and support of others. A sizeable quantity of self-discipline is required, however, making escape part of the scenario. All rehabilitation programs and institutions have trap-releases and aiding escapes as their aim.

I insert here a brief note in praise of vanity. Vanity carries a negative connotation, made synonymous with narcissism, conceit, egoism, and the like. But vanity, in bridled form, can be a powerful force in personal well-being. If a culture admires svelte appearance, that can be an incentive not to become slovenly in physical mien, which in turn leads to exercise and good nutrition. Charles Darwin would understand the purpose of restrained vanity. This incentive does seem to wane with age in some people and is never is present in many.

And, naturally (or unnaturally) there is "the government" as the ultimate release mechanism. The examples are legion, here are a few.

- Subsidies to all manner of parties, from farmers to favored industries to welfare for individuals.
- Protectionist trade policies among countries.
- The Superfund designed for toxic waste cleanup (we pay taxes to support this trap release and it has legislative power, therefore it is mandatory).
- Bailouts of financial institutions.
- Bailouts of U.S. auto companies.
- Forgiving tax cheats through amnesty programs.
- Forgiveness of or reorganization of student loan debts.

In a sloppy, undisciplined society, people look for releases, some outside force to get them out of traps rather than working their way out themselves, often involving governmental nanny solutions. Examples: Housing-crisis bailouts, pills for all ailments, back surgery rather than corrective exercise.

Personally, I find no joy in being a supplicant and would suffer considerable psychic cost if that were necessary, believing it is debilitating to self-respect, if not the soul, and certainly it is not congruous with being an adult, responsible citizen.

Remark. Some argue human evolution has slowed dramatically because of medical advances and social safety nets. Those who would not have survived before now make it through. If the hypothesis is true, the less self-sufficient remain in the gene pool. I am not making any judgments here, just putting forth an interesting idea.

Mends. I ginned up the concept of mends as an in-between idea. In fly fishing, when a line is not drifting properly, there is a rod technique called mending, which makes the line behave properly and enables the fly to drift in a natural way. In clothing repair, one also mends. And I have seen a lot of ranch repairs that could be described as temporary mending rather than fixing; we called it cowboying the problem when I owned my ranch in West Texas, and it resulted in a trap later on when a cowboyed water-line repair began leaking during the winter. Here is a good example: Methadone treatment for heroin addicts—neither an escape nor a release, but something better than the trap. Nicotine gum and patches also fall into this category, at least as a temporary mend on the way to escape. Two other examples are mediation and arbitration, especially mediation whether neither party gets exactly what was desired, but some of the rives have been mended.

Thus, escapes, releases, and mends are specific strategies for extrication. There might be other ways, such as incentives. I take those up in the next chapter.

Doomsday Traps
Alas, there is no escape or release from a doomsday trap. HIV contracted from unprotected sex is one example. Another is young people committing felonies that remain part of their life's record until death. An example that rings throughout human history, one I use often, is the destruction of one or more aspects of the environment such that recovery is not possible; for

instance, the clear-cutting of hillsides resulting in soil erosion to the extent nothing will grow there again or draining the Ogallala aquifer. And recall my example of an obese person awaiting amputation of a foot due to Type II diabetes. Emphysema as a result of smoking is another case, and the best that can be done here are various mends to partially relieve the symptoms, e.g., oxygen therapy. While presenting Hardin's tragedy of the commons in Chapter 5, I used the example of how Atlantic cod fisheries were decimated; if recovery of the cod population is not possible, it is a doomsday trap.

I once spent a long evening in Mexico with a fellow who lived in a remote Sierra Madre village. A light-skinned Scandinavian who had come to Mexico looking for silver, he had a scarred face without a nose—absolutely nothing, just two cavities where once a nose existed—and was missing both ears. While we sat on his porch through a soft twilight, every few minutes he cursed the sun and what it can do to you. Talk about a doomsday variety of trap that also included features of a time-delay trap! I excused his continual drinking of straight tequila shots, though probable sclerosis of the liver was down the track for him, another trap. Possible wealth derived from silver had been a powerful incentive for him, along with the disincentive of time and trouble required for sun protection, maybe coupled with ignorance. By the way, he found no silver.

Amidst the shrill cries from all sides about the existence of and extent of human-induced global warming, sorting out truth is difficult. Assume for a moment the direst of the predictions is true: This might be a doomsday trap, a massive social trap caused by the independent decisions of billions of humans. Attempts to mitigate present and future damage to the atmosphere are best described as mending, are costly and perhaps futile. The only real solution to doomsday traps is not a solution at all, but rather preventative measures designed to thwart entry into the traps. Trap avoidance is discussed in Chapter 9.

Chapter 8

GETTING OUT OF TROUBLE: INCENTIVES

Decisions and Incentives

Traps are the product of decisions. Therefore, if the objective is to look for solutions to traps or to prevent entry into traps, decision-making is the place to start. The scheme I have been using—decisions, discounting, incentives, small increments, traps, and so forth—will continue here.

In decision-making, an incentive is the expected outcome or range of possible outcomes if a particular course of action is taken, i.e., the outcomes act as incentives. Consider the obesity problem. First, there is the decision to exercise or not exercise; second is the decision to eat a healthy, nutritious diet or the converse. The question is: What causes people to make choices that lead to being overweight or obese? Or, to enter any other type of trap? Consider a single decision:

1. The individual is confronted with a set of alternatives.
2. Each alternative has one or more possible outcomes attached to it, depending on the uncertainty level present.
3. The outcomes of separate alternatives occur either at the same time or in different time periods.

4. The individual applies a discount rate to the outcomes, with the ultimate perceived value of the outcome depending on its magnitude, when it will occur, and discounting.

5. What influences the discounting? Three major factors: Time, patience, and risk. Patience is another way of talking about the personal value of something in the future. The higher the perceived risk, the higher is the discount rate attached to the future.[1]

6. Criteria may be in conflict with one another.

    a. Trade-offs between the short- and long-run.

    b. Trade-offs among the criteria even when the outcomes occur at the same time, e.g., cargo capacity of a vehicle versus its price.

So what underlies bad decisions (or good ones) in the obesity problem? Incentives, that's what, coupled with the individual's preference structure, and the discounting applied to outcomes. A second question immediately follows: What can be changed that would cause selection of better alternatives? I do not have the content knowledge and have no particular interest in spending years acquiring the necessary physiological and psychological background to become an obesity specialist, but I will have a few suggestions later on.

When people make decisions, they are responding simultaneously to the alternatives before them, to criteria, and to incentives. Once again, what are criteria? Think of them as preferences acting as yardsticks or measuring devices used to evaluate the desirability of outcomes and, in the end, the relative desirability of the alternatives.

How about incentives? As before, these can be viewed as the predicted or expected outcomes of decisions, the results shown at the end of each branch of a decision tree prior to the selection of an alternative. If fatty foods taste better to someone than low-fat foods, that predicted outcome of a given menu decision is an incentive to choose the "Don't Eat Healthy Diet" alternative, *if immediate taste indulgence is a highly ranked criterion* in selecting food.

Now let's be straight here. People don't open the fridge or go into a restaurant and say, "I'm going to choose an unhealthy meal." It is almost au-

---

[1] Treating risk as part of the discount rate is a conventional approach.

tomatically responding to a learned *preference* for pizza with four toppings and maybe a salad drenched with high-fat, high-calorie dressing on it instead of vinegar and oil or simple lemon juice. They are responding either to habit or perhaps, as some have suggested, an innate human preference for fatty foods based on sensors in the mouth or even a genetic tendency such as storing fat in the event lean times lie ahead. In either case, a preference for fatty food is present in the form of a criterion labeled "Good Tasting" and is ranked high, resulting in the selection of the unhealthy meal. As for exercise, the number of excuses not to exercise is almost unlimited. I know that from my own lurches toward indolence.

Fixing Things: Vomit Pills and Other Incentives

Sermons, advice, task forces, and regulations do not require much creativity. The use of incentives to change behavior does require creativity. In general, I am in favor of choice in all matters, within the constraints of civil behavior fostering a stable society. Unlimited freedom of choice works pretty well in a one-person, Robinson Crusoe social system. But in modern, dense societies where many behaviors negatively affect others, choices must either be constrained or incentives altered in the direction of better decisions. I prefer incentives, because I am given a choice and choice is the essence of freedom.[2] An outcome all lawmakers and regulators should be forced to observe is, "Does this action *unnecessarily* constrain the freedom of the innocent while constraining the behavior of those who sin, and if so, is there a better way to handle the sinners?"

A criterion for the use of incentives, remarkable for both its clarity and profundity, can be inferred from John C. Goodman (Goodman 2009, 20) talking about health-care system design but a criterion applicable to any use of incentives: "Right answers are ones that give people incentives to meet their own needs without imposing costs on others. Wrong answers are ones that give people perverse incentives to impose costs on others, while pursuing their own interests."

---

[2] Look around you and mark how many people who vociferously demand freedom of choice in one area are among the first to denounce it in another when their preferences are not served by such freedom.

Consider the "Cash for Clunkers" program instituted by the federal government to aid the auto industry in 2009. Depending on the type of trade-in and new vehicle purchased, a buyer could receive a discount of up to $4,500 directly from the auto dealer when a new, supposedly more fuel-efficient vehicle was purchased. Dealerships suddenly were packed with customers and some 700,000 vehicles were sold in a short time. The program was deemed to be wildly successful by dealers, customers, the United Auto Workers, and of course a federal government covetous of political accolades. Think about Goodman's criterion, however, and ask who carried the burden. Taxpayers, that's who. Buyers and dealers benefited, but I did not and neither did any other people who did not purchase a vehicle under the program, yet my tax dollars were used to subsidize the program. Therefore, cash for clunkers fails to pass Goodman's criterion. The program did illustrate one important idea: The power of price as an incentive. As predicted by many, auto sales declined for a while when the program ended, offsetting the advertised benefits of the program, another in the endless stream of unintended consequences ignited by government programs. Plus, usable assets in the form of older cars were destroyed in the process. The net benefit to the economy was calculated by independent studies to have been around *negative* $1.5 billion.

Antabuse (disulfiram) is a drug that alcoholics or those near that condition can ingest that will cause vomiting and/or headaches/ and/or anxiety, if even a small amount of alcohol is swallowed. The choice set would then be two alternatives each with an outcome: Don't drink and don't vomit, or drink and vomit. The relevant criterion might be phrased as "Minimize Physical Discomfort," a criterion found in most living creatures, either as product of rational thought or instinct. Thus, to minimize physical discomfort, choose the "Don't Drink" alternative, with "Don't Vomit" acting as the incentive.

Antabuse is an interesting idea that can be generalized. Perhaps we need an equivalent, metaphorical "vomit pill" for high-fat foods or neglecting retirement savings or excess use of credit cards or not studying hard in school. Or suppose, being wildly hypothetical, you became violently nauseous each time you turned the key in a gas-guzzling vehicle, resulting in the purchase of a fuel-efficient vehicle as a replacement. Once again, the problem always is figuring out a way to *bring an unpleasant future back to the present such that current behavior will be changed*. Or, alternatively, bringing a highly rewarding future back to the present that dominates current desires. And notice in particular the feedback loop associated with Antabuse: It is immediate.

Conceptually, *the vomit pill is a method for assigning a lower discount rate to the future* when present actions damage the future. Conversely, and better yet, perhaps the opposite of a vomit pill is a reward for good behavior, e.g., tax-deferred or tax-free investments for retirement, a fine invention already in place, though it irks some in the federal government as they constantly search for more revenue from taxpayers.

To solve most of the problems I have cited in the book, incentives must be changed, even if preferences in the form of criteria stubbornly resist change—preferences once formed can be inflexible to a high degree. But if the change in incentives is large enough, or clever enough, even longtime preferences can be overridden. Curiously, much *effort toward changing behavior tries to modify preferences without changing incentives*, ineffectively so.

Suppose you have a fondness for large, powerful automobiles. Now suppose that gasoline prices escalate to $6 per gallon or higher. I suspect your criterion of mileage-per-gallon would rise in importance relative to other criteria.

To repeat, say what you will, incentives drive our decision-making and therefore our behavior. Those who self-report higher sensibilities and more finely tuned intellects detest any implication we are like amoebae crawling around on a glass slide, looking for the nearest and/or largest pile of food, abhorring the idea we are so simple. But, to a large extent, we are. At least that's how I see it. I admit there are exceptions, great moments of soaring artistic achievement and exemplary feats of heroism that cannot easily be explained in such pedestrian terms, but for the most part I hold to my beliefs about the power of incentives. And even artistic or pure scientific achievement can be driven by the desire for recognition (a Nobel Prize) or money or fame, all of which are incentives. Chesley Sullenberger did a masterful job of landing his stricken, bird-disabled passenger jet on the Hudson River in 2009, and he had a damn strong incentive to get it right since he was riding on it (we will also assume he felt a deep responsibility for his passengers).

In general, if we are clever enough, it is possible to deal with traps by the use of something other than lectures, education, regulations, laws, and social safety nets. As I have emphasized, every law and every regulation instituted have the effect of constraining behavior, which is a polite term for loss of freedom.

Societies and individuals can do better when it comes to traps by providing correct incentives to people. That is, give people choices whose outcomes compete with those leading into traps or those outcomes assisting exit if a trap currently exists. Exercising outdoors in the Midwest is difficult for much of the year, the weather providing an excuse not to jog. When I lived in Iowa, purchasing a treadmill for my home changed the outcomes in the "Jog-Don't Jog" decision, *competing with* the "adverse weather" outcome and removing that excuse.

Illegal immigrants come into a country in search of work and generous social services. Those are the immigrants' incentives. Consider the work incentive. Suppose an employer who knowingly hires illegal workers is subject to a minimum of ten years hard labor in a federal prison and the probability of being convicted is 87 percent. What do you think would happen to the decision-making process of the employer? That solution requires a law involving prosecution and sentencing, but it leaves the decision-maker free to choose a course of action, one of which has enormous risk and a huge downside attached. One basic law to control thousands of employers is a cheap trade-off, and do not try to convince me I have subtracted from employer freedom when a crime has been committed. Laws exist that penalize businesses for hiring illegal aliens, but the penalties are not severe enough to prevent it. Such penalties are outcomes and must be severe enough to influence an employer's "Hire cheapest labor possible" criterion by changing it to "Minimize labor costs consistent with the law."

Another example is driving around with ice on your car, as a result of heavy weather. Why is this a possible societal trap? The ice may slingshot from your vehicle and injure a pedestrian or damage the windshield on another vehicle, which amounts to an externality trap. At least that is the claim. Washington, D.C.'s city council passed an ordinance encouraging police citations be issued to offending motorists, with no fine attached. More rules, more regulations, more work for police officers, and with no real punishment attached (no incentive), the likelihood of the ordinance's success is marginal. The argument underlying the ordinance is that people owe it to fellow motorists to remove the ice, which raises the question of how much ice is too much ice? Will the police carry measuring tapes or devices to quantify ice density and thickness? Sophocles: "What you cannot enforce, do not command." However, the city council certainly felt better having done something, even if it was nonsense.

Pennsylvania has a law incorporating a $1,000 fine if ice flies from your vehicle and harms another vehicle or person. The Pennsylvania law introduces risk and the possibility of considerable monetary loss into the decision, an entirely different set of incentives for the decision whether or not to clean ice from your car in the morning.

Through all of the above, and just under the surface, is the idea of *cost*. Cost in monetary terms, in time, in effort, and loss of pleasure plays an important role in traps and trap avoidance. Cleaning the ice from your vehicle on a winter morning has a cost in time and effort. Not choosing the high-fat meal and instead eating a salad has a cost in loss of pleasure for some people. Restraining oneself from putting an extra cow into a common pasture has a monetary cost. Exercise has a cost in time, effort, and health club fees or equipment, though access to a public swimming pool or a decent pair of walking shoes is all that is truly required. Putting on sunscreen and renewing the application every two hours has a time and annoyance cost. Someone perspicaciously said economics can be described in one word: Cost, or the flip side, *price*. Economics cannot be avoided, even if you circumvented it in your formal studies.

When the price of an item increases by significant amount, people buy less of it—price or cost as an incentive. If gas prices escalate enough, people switch to smaller vehicles or drive less, behavior we have seen over and over again. The cost of a commodity or service, monetary or psychic, has a powerful effect on our behavior, *but only if it is in the near-term*.

This should be clear from the many examples shown previously in this book. Telling people who are gaining large amounts of weight that they will pay high costs for their behavior in the future seems to have little effect on most, because the cost of the behavior tends to be in the hazy long-term and heavily discounted. This includes politicians and government spending.

Some people apparently have difficulty in visualizing futures. Perhaps a physician should have a notebook on the office shelf showing graphic and grisly photos of people's limbs being amputated due to diabetes caused by obesity and other photos portraying the ugly arterial-fat deposits built up from unhealthy diets. Give the patients one of the photos and ask them to post it on their refrigerator doors and as a screen saver on their computers or on their smart phones. The military and high schools used to show grainy black-and-white films of truly nasty venereal disease; however, the wide availability of antibiotics lessened the fear of that, resulting in trap releases. There is no antibiotic that will absolutely prevent the amputation of a foot due to diabetes.

Suppose physicians decided that no person with a BMI of 30 or greater would be given medical treatment by any doctor? A provisional weight-loss period of 18 months could be attached to the refusal, allowing the obese person to demonstrate progress toward a healthy weight. Government could provide the same incentive through Medicare or other health programs, which would relieve doctors from possible violations of their Hippocratic oath. Charging overweight people higher premiums for health insurance appears to be quite reasonable as an incentive to control weight; however, the practice inevitably and unjustifiably brings forth howls of protest concerning "rights."

Another example of incentives is the cap-and-trade programs advocated by many as a method of reducing noxious industrial emissions. The true costs and effectiveness of such programs are hotly debated and, as far as I can tell, are still unsettled. An explanation of cap-and-trade would require too much space in this book, but the ultimate incentives are those of cost whereby firms buy and sell permits to send emissions skyward. Similar programs are often proposed as a way of limiting the overfishing of a particular species, and sometimes are called trading quotas; I can sell my quota to you for a bargained price, with the overall catch determined by fisheries biologists. While having the advantage of self-regulation through markets, all programs such as cash for clunkers and fishing quotas have numerous costs attached to them: Government workers (tax dollars) to process the paperwork, economists and biologists to set quotas or the size of rebates, and, guess what, more workers to monitor and police the programs. Moreover, who polices the monitors and enforcers? Such programs always are ripe for kickbacks and other bribes, but then so are strict laws and regulations. Bring in freedom and the balance tips toward choice.

Many of our national and state parks are overcrowded, destroying the quiet and solitude of nature such places were meant to provide. So are floating parties down certain rivers, particularly the Colorado. What to do? Rationing is the first thought and is no more creative than sermons, i.e., limits on the number of people in a park or on a river at any one time, imposing a cost on those not able to participate. What about price? People object to high prices for visiting natural wonders their tax dollars already support (assuming they pay income taxes), so partial rationing may be unavoidable, but it could be augmented by price incentives. Rationing via lotteries (e.g., float trips on crowded rivers) works better because everyone feels they had an equal chance of being selected.

Consider this mildly radical use of incentives. If you pay federal income taxes, the IRS sends out a card certifying you have done so. The card gives you preferential access to float trips on the Colorado. If you pay no taxes to support such recreational opportunities, there is no reason you should have the same access as those who support the resource. The card could be used for many other similar privileges, such as access to emergency medical care or discounts at national parks. Those who pay no taxes could obtain the card by paying a flat fee to the IRS. Take it further: The more taxes you pay, the higher the privileges noted on your card. The higher the flat fee paid by non-taxpayers, the higher their privileges. This strategy would drive home the notion to free-riders that, indeed, they are riding free on the backs of others.

As I said earlier, if something desirable is free or vastly under-priced—air, water, national parks—it will be exploited until nothing is left. This includes taxpayer dollars spent by politicians who are spending other people's money and view it personally as a free good since their own checking accounts are not perceptibly damaged by the expenditure. It also includes medical care, with the federal government seeking to remove all incentives by instituting government control; if people pay only 10 percent or less of their medical costs, they will use more medical services and the medical "commons" dissipates.

Private ownership handles many such problems. The incentive structure is obvious: If you own something, there is a strong likelihood you will take care of it because the cost of neglect can be high, as with grazing pastures or vehicles or farm lands or money or . . . your body.

Underdeveloped countries are breeding grounds for terrorism. Millions of unemployed, alienated young people see no way out of a loathsome existence and are easy prey for terrorist recruiters. I long have advocated the following: Instead of expenditures on repressive military strategies to combat terrorism and social unrest, use government money to underwrite privately owned manufacturing facilities that provide decent jobs (government underwriting is necessary at the beginning because the risks of doing business discourage private investment, though customized insurance could accomplish this, as well). A person with a mortgage, family, and a job is far less likely to become a terrorist or support terrorism because such temptations are easily overridden by the prospect of losing something, rather than having nothing to lose. Some notable terrorists, however, come from middle-class or higher origins, and the use of incentives in those cases is less clear because of religious motivation and/or ideology, as they interpret their religion. But all high-level terrorists require the support of foot soldiers, so the underwritten manufacturing scheme does apply to those of lower economic standing. Plus, those who now have jobs would condemn attacks on countries that are financing the jobs. Economics knows no bounds.

Contracts and Incentives
I like simple things that work, such as Frisbees, jar openers, and pieces of sticky kitchen-shelf liner for getting a firm grip on fly rod sections that

refuse to come apart (my innovation). The use of contracts as trap-escape devices holds considerable promise for meeting the criteria of simple and effective. Incentives are a key part of the contract approach. The precondition: Trappees want to escape.

Economist Richard McKenzie (2008) signed a contract with a friend, specifying he would pay the friend $500 if he (McKenzie) did not lose a specified amount of weight by a certain date. The contract was drawn up in a semi-formal document, including a witness, and the friend was required to certify she would accept the $500 if McKenzie failed to meet the weight goal, preventing her from refunding the money out of pity if the goal was not met, and also firmly stating she had to spend the money on herself. See the referenced article for a full description of McKenzie's struggles to achieve his weight objective with a few pounds to spare.

The contract device is powerful and carries within it many of the concepts already covered in this book. I will use McKenzie's story as an example.

- McKenzie was trapped.
- Traps generally are the product of a long sequence of decisions and small increments, as are escapes. After he signed the contract, each meal required McKenzie to make a decision, choosing between a nutritious offering and his typical unhealthy choices (apparently he was obese at one time), more small increments.
- McKenzie's decisions involve short-term gain versus long-term loss. The gain is in the pleasure of eating, the potential loss is $500. There is another loss involving health in the long-term, of course, but as I have emphasized, such vague and uncertain outcomes as future health tend to be heavily discounted. The $500 acted as a *tangible proxy* for health cost—note that idea of creating tangible proxies for relatively amorphous future outcomes.
- McKenzie had incentives, with the potential payment of $500 causing the future to speak with a louder voice.
- The $500, as he reports, was seen as an addition to the price of unhealthy meals, while healthy meals were psychologically priced less because they were viewed as saving him money in the long-run.

- With money ranked high as a decision criterion, it influenced his selections of beneficial alternatives, e.g., he substituted oatmeal for a bagel at breakfast. And, though McKenzie does not discuss it, there was another criterion present: Loss of face and standing in the eyes of a close friend and her husband who served as a witness to the contract, a psychological cost. Plus, lurking in the criteria set at some place surely was the desire for a healthier body.
- Thus: Decisions, incentives, criteria, discounting, small increments, and escape from the trap. Lovely.

Here come the yah-buts who are always ready to denounce good ideas. Yah, but he had $500 and most people can't afford to risk losing that much money. Answer: The only requirement is that it be of a sufficient amount to act as a brightly flashing sign in the future. For others, $50 or $100 might do the job. The key is that the potential loss must be high enough to hurt. If having established the dollar amount a person still refuses the contract, that only implies the individual is assigning a low probability to their self-control estimate and an unwillingness to address the future.

The contract idea has been used in other settings, such as promising a young person a substantial sum if they reach 21 without using drugs or smoking. Various schemes have been devised to pay college expenses for young people who achieve in high school. These two examples are trap-avoidance programs rather than escapes from traps already forming (trap-avoidance is discussed in the following chapter).

In the McKenzie case, I mentioned the psychological cost of disappointing friends or even losing face with the general public. This can be a powerful criterion both for escapes from traps and avoidance of them altogether. Two Yale economists have (inevitably) figured out a way to organize a business while helping others to escape from traps or prevent entry into them or, more generally, to simply achieve goals such as starting their own businesses. See www.stickk.com. Here is the welcoming statement on that website: "Ready to finally stickK to your commitments? Then stand up, and put your reputation, or even your money, where your mouth is, and change your life. Reap the rewards of your hard work." You just have to love capitalism. StickK embodies the best of Adam Smith: Make a profit while others benefit in spite of how you might feel about others benefiting—that is true of all informed and voluntary exchange.

In 2008, my wife continued to smoke, declaring aggressively she intended never to quit and railing against anti-smoking campaigns. I remained silent, having followed the same path for years. That March, she was taken low with a harsh case of the flu. Two days into the ordeal while she lay in bed, she informed me she had not had a cigarette in 48 hours because she would cough to the point of nausea (a vomit pill of sorts). I casually mentioned that if she could abstain for another 24 hours, the worst of smoking cessation would be past (I only lied a little). My counsel had minor effect, I am sure, but her condition did prevent her from smoking for another day.

I then offered her a contract (this was before I read about McKenzie's contract): Don't smoke for 30 days and I will reward you with a substantial amount of money at the end of the thirtieth day, the money taken from a personal investment account I had opened long before we met. Furthermore, if she abstained for six months, I would provide another payment equal to the first. I further stated that if anytime in those six months she smoked, she would be required to return the first payment and both payments if she later resumed smoking.

The reward offered was apparently the correct amount to flash brightly in her mind, bringing the future back to the present. I also had privately hypothesized that if she did not smoke for six months, she might never again be tempted. She upheld the bargain and no longer smokes, recently telling me that I had guessed correctly on both the elapsed time and the monetary amount. Admitting she had been tempted to smoke, she said thoughts of returning the 30-day and six-month money would overcome the desire. She no longer smokes and has zero interest in again taking up the habit.

My wife and I have a wonderful relationship, two independent people who are dependent on one another while retaining our independence. Linda handles all the family accounting, consisting of 17 separate ledgers, and manages the farm, work for which she draws a monthly stipend. I do other things as my share of toting the family load. In short, I was not bribing a deprived person with a sum of money; her life would have been pleasant enough without it. But all the things discussed in this book were operating at full strength:

The Blueprint

Decisions, incentives, criteria, discounting, small increments, the lure of the short-run, and escape from a trap. The future was brought back to the present using money as a proxy, just as with McKenzie's weight-loss contract. Smoking cessation is one of the ultimate examples of the VSI, making decisions moment by moment, hour by hour, day after day, exerting self-control until the habit has vanished. Oh, yes, I had my own incentives for offering her the contract; see if you can determine what they might have been. Was my offer a matter of deep-seated affection or of my personal incentives? Hmmm.

— *Vignettes, Personal and Otherwise* —

Here are two perfect examples of the future brought back to the present. Yes, perfect, and few aspects of our wretched existences can claim perfection. One is concrete and involves discretionary decision-making, the other is discretionary only to a limited extent. Both involve skin cancer (another gladsome topic I burden you with). If you are outdoors, put on your sunscreen and keep reading.

It is a given that continued exposure to strong sunlight carries with it a high probability of skin cancer, especially the most virulent type called melanoma. Sunscreens help to some extent, especially those containing the dioxides such as zinc and titanium, but clothing that covers up exposed areas and does not allow sunlight to reach the skin is the best protection, the sole countermeasure that works with absolute certainty.[3] *The mental decision diagram is clear: Protect skin and reduce the risk of cancer to an almost nonexistent level; don't protect the skin and risk contracting skin cancer.*

People who spend a lot of time fishing or pursuing other activities around water are especially susceptible to skin cancer, because doses of sunlight are received both directly from the sun and from reflection off the water, a double-whammy. Consider fishing guides who

---

[3] The only sunscreen that offers absolute protection is one that is completely opaque, i.e., impenetrable by light. People find these cosmetically unacceptable and tend not to use them except on the nose, which inexplicably is culturally acceptable. Not all clothing adequately protects the skin, incidentally.

spend day after day on or near the water, often at high altitudes where sunlight is most fierce. Some guides are working more than 200 days a year in such conditions. Caribbean and Gulf Coast guides, a few of them, have started wearing long-sleeved shirts, long pants, and masks covering their faces except for sun-glassed eyes. Most freshwater guides do not use protective clothing, especially for the face. Some fisherpeople have started wearing fingerless gloves to protect the backs of the hands, one area where skin cancer often forms.

A fishing guide of my acquaintance contracted a nasty respiratory infection in early spring and began taking antibiotics, while still working as a guide. Antibiotics can cause severe sensitivity to sunlight, and the backs of his hands developed ugly sores causing considerable discomfort. When I fly-fished with him that spring, I loaned him a pair of my fingerless gloves, at his request. These are gloves made especially for those who fish and are designed protect the wrists and hands without compromising the ability to carry out delicate knot-tying and the like.

His sores were the future brought back to the present—a vomit pill—accidental though it may have been, and in a less dangerous and less permanent form than skin cancer. Nonetheless, the guide experienced in the present what the future possibly can hold. Will he continue to wear the gloves once he stops taking the antibiotics? I don't know, but he might, for he now has experienced a bit of what the future might be like. His experience is the equivalent of the vomit pill I spoke of earlier. Skin cancer due to overexposure to sunlight is a trap, like not visiting the dentist or not exercising, as you should be able to see by now, a trap whereby small increments add up to disaster in the longer term.

Part Two. I was born with a hereditary disease having the unwieldy name of Erythropoietic protoporphyria (EPP). All you need to know about EPP is it causes extreme sensitivity to sunlight. And, testifying here as one who has the disease, the sensitivity can be very high with a resulting pain that is indescribable to someone who has never experienced it; multiply the pain of a blistered sunburn by a factor of three, extend the pain duration over 48 hours or more, and that will give you some idea.

My father was a fisherman, and as a boy I liked to fish. I had to avoid sunlight and knew all the shady spots along the rivers of my growing. Those locations also had to protect me from reflected light, as well. I knew every such location for every time of day along several miles of river. But I was so limited as to where I could fish, I stopped fishing in my early teens and did not consider it again until I was 64 and had a little more time in my life for such ultimately non-productive activities (unless one is fishing for table fare or if you count pleasure as a revenue).

I wear long-sleeved shirts and long pants, but my face and hands are a problem. Fly fishing requires considerable dexterity in the use of fingers, so appropriate gloves were the answer there. Next, the face. I invented a particular type of headgear using an off-the-shelf, long-billed cap and a piece of Supplex cloth with a high sun-protection factor. The cloth fastens to the cap with Velcro, wraps around my face, and fastens to more Velcro on the other side of the cap.[4] *I can do the fastening with one hand. For my nose, which is not EPP-sensitive, but does sunburn like any other person's nose, I use a totally opaque sunscreen.*

How does EPP relate to bringing the future back to the present? It should be obvious. In my case, after experiencing long, brutally painful days and nights as a child—my blessed mother would sit up with me and apply ice to my burning skin—I stayed out of the sun. So I escaped the harmful rays causing skin cancer by making an easy decision: Stay out of the sun or experience pain in the right-now. I was born with a built-in vomit pill that influenced my discount rate (think about how it exerted that influence). An unintended benefit, one for which I can take no credit for being disciplined, is that I am thought to be quite a lot younger than my true age, having carefully protected my skin from sun exposure over the years. Given my love of deserts, jungles, and adventure, things might have turned out vastly different except for the EPP vomit pill.

Why doesn't everyone protect themselves thusly from the sun? We

---

[4] Some firms have begun offering caps with protective face covering attached. If you are interested, check out www.coolibar.com for an example.

are back to the never-ending story of decisions, discounting, incentives, small increments, and traps. Aside from the time required to apply sun screen and dealing with sticky skin (disincentives), men suffer a peculiar malady of American culture that often defines masculinity as behaving in self-destructive ways. If you are going to sweat and grunt around rivers and boats while trying to bring home the grub or in pursuit of simple entertainment, sun gloves and face masks do not seem to be part of the acceptable sartorial accoutrements, not even regular doses of sun screen every two hours. Evidently it is far manlier to develop ugly lesions and skin cancer. Men wear breathing masks to work in dusty conditions because they will immediately begin coughing if they do not, but the effects of sunlight are down the years, the future is not present in the present. In the case of dust, the future is immediate and uncomfortable; with sunlight, the future is distant and not immediately uncomfortable. Unfortunately, some workers do not wear masks when handling chemicals that give off damaging fumes, painters being a good example. So, OSHA stepped in with laws and regulations to force the wearing of protective masks and clothing. Incentives are constantly at work in our daily lives, their magnitude influenced by discounting, their impact influencing our behavior.

— End of Vignettes, Personal and Otherwise —

I could write a thousand pages on the power of incentives as devices affecting human behavior, but I trust you have the central idea in mind by now. Incentives also impact greatly on the decisions of voters and politicians, as we'll see in Chapter 11.

Chapter 9

AVOIDING PROBLEMS

It should be clear from previous chapters that getting into traps is much easier than the sticky task of getting out. One reason for becoming ensnared in a trap relates to the temporal length of feedback loops linking behavior to the final result of that behavior, such as not taking care of your teeth but paying a high price for that inattention further along in time or piling up government debt that traps subsequent generations. In this chapter I deal with methods of avoiding traps, relieving us of the struggle to extricate ourselves or becoming petitioners in search of release and cure. Think of trap avoidance as involving various types of vaccination.

Trap Avoidance: Awareness and Understanding
The first step in avoiding traps is being aware they exist. *But*, "From a psychological point of view, intellectual information is largely incidental to behavior determination; if we wish to make use of the potential of education for encouraging trap-avoiding behavior, we must recognize that rewards and punishments have to be made concrete. Mere descriptions of the elements of a trap cannot contribute much toward its avoidance. Facts,

by themselves, do not reinforce anything (Cross and Guyer 1980, 60)." And, "If ignorance were the sole cause of error, sufficiently large doses of information would be a cognitive panacea. You could fix *any* misconception with enough facts (Caplan 2007, 101)."

My skepticism concerning education as a complete strategy for avoiding or getting out of traps is readily seen in Chapter 7 and agrees with that of Cross and Guyer, along with Caplan. Still, education has a role, and that role can be captured in the word *awareness*, perhaps the most important early-warning signal in trap-avoidance, though inadequate on its own.[1] Awareness flows from understanding, and understanding follows from education. Understanding the nature of decision-making, incentives, criteria, discounting, feedback, and how those everyday aspects of life lead us into traps, provides a foundation for trap avoidance. I trust, if nothing else, this book accomplishes such understanding and awareness at a basic level.

A crude example of awareness and trap avoidance is the design and use of snooze buttons in alarm clocks. The button's origin is a simple recognition of human frailty, an awareness and acceptance of weakness, and is a method for overcoming a temporarily increased discounting of the long-term. Operationally, the button is a harmless compromise between the lure of the short-run and the future, with the future weighted heavily.

Age brings experience, and experience presumably entrains learning and awareness. Experience provides the opportunity to encounter decision situations a number of times and gain practice in making these decisions. That is one reason why auto insurance rates are lower for adults than for teenagers. A word of caution: Some of the nastiest traps occur where the opportunities for learning and practice have been few or nonexistent, such as buying a home or experimenting with an addictive drug.

Trap Avoidance: Visions of the Future

The ability to visualize futures and act on those visions is a key component in discounting and self-control. Concrete visions of the future influence the

---

[1] Education also helps in another way, if the right type of education has been experienced: Efficiency in problem analysis and decision-making. Skills in probability, analyzing multiple criteria and their relationship to one another, discounting, and estimating outcomes can be honed through education, whether formal or informal.

degree of patience and help prevent bias toward the short-run. If the ability to envisage futures is limited, incentives can be thought of as a proxy device substituting for visualizing the future and working toward it. So are religion and laws, which constrain choice sets and therefore what incentives will be operative. Fundamentally, religion and laws are ways of doing away with earthly time preference because they disallow certain alternatives featuring short-run rewards or at minimum prevent them from having any function in decision-making.

Baumeister and Vohs (2003, 210) present a concise set of criteria required for people to pursue distant goals.

1. The person must be able to hold a cognitive representation of the goal, i.e., what I have been calling visualization.
2. There must be a reasonable level of belief that the goal can be achieved. This is not inconsequential; experience with the power of VSI engenders belief in the process.
3. Sufficient personal skills must be present allowing organization of behavior directed toward achievement of the goal. My notion of VSI is highly relevant here, also, as is education incorporating rigorous thinking skills.
4. There must be present a capacity for denial of short-run temptation, i.e., self-control, discipline.

"We are able to form goals, our visions of the future, then we act according to our goals. But, in order to guide our behavior in a sustained fashion, these mental images of the future must become the content of our memory; thus, the 'memories of the future' are formed (Barrs and Gage 2007, 350)." I love that phrase, "memories of the future." If you have formed visions and *remember* those images each time temptation occurs, self-control can be brought to bear. A photo of an amputated limb on your refrigerator door is a memory of the future.

All well and good—memories of the future—a taut summation of human conceptual ability in an idealized sense. But it is not enough because the lure of the short-run can easily benumb us and cause behavior to deviate from good intentions, no matter how lofty our long-term goals and how well those goals are envisioned, and that is where traps originate and prosper.

Note: As a matter of future reference, the nanny state takes over all four of the Baumeister-Vohs four-step requirement for thinking about the future. This parental function is the goal of those I will label Statists in later chapters and relieves people of personal responsibility for dealing with the future.

Trap Avoidance: Commitment

A well-tested method for staying out of traps is commitment. Think of it this way: Commitment by an individual is a self-imposed reduction of a personal choice set, i.e., limiting the range of alternatives to be considered along with solidified rankings of criteria and a grasp of how short-run incentives can lead us astray. Humans use commitment as a self-control device. Societies do it through laws and regulation. The Ten Commandments and religions in general attempt to do this, though the rules are consistently bent by some adherents to a religion, in spite of feigned displays of virtue; the lure of the short-run can easily override the Ten Commandments, which act as a series of "Do Nots." The rewards of heaven and the punishments of hell are put forth as outcomes, sermons are used to influence criteria rankings, and dogma acts as a constraint on individual choice sets. For those having trouble visualizing futures, dramatic paintings and murals vividly portray both the joys of heaven and the agonies of hell. Eternity is a long time, so religions strive to attach a low discount rate to it, and the blindfold effect is not allowed or a doctrinal blindfold is substituted.

Because it is so apt, the story of Odysseus and the Sirens is a favorite illustration of commitment, though I remain certain Homer was not formally aware of discount rates and related topics. However, he understood temptation. Odysseus, aware of the Sirens' seductiveness and the danger of crashing his ship onto the rocks around their island, ordered his crew to stop their ears with beeswax, to rope him to a mast and not untie him no matter how much he cried for release. Odysseus well-understood the lure of the short-run and the traps that follow. He also understood commitment and its use in trap avoidance.

The sirens of bewitchment are all about us, constantly. And commitment has a long history of use, because it can be effective. An alarm clock is a form of commitment. If you commit to saving and investing a portion of your income, a comfortable retirement will follow. The catch is staying with the commitment in spite of short-run inducements. Mandatory retirement programs in universities are a form of forced commitment. Designers of such programs are cognizant of life's enticements and thus remove the opportunity for them by disallowing early withdrawals.

On a shorter time scale, when I was a new and lowly assistant professor, summer teaching positions were at a premium. So my wife and I adopted squirrel-like behavior, saving throughout the year and laying up food stocks in the spring to get us through the dry months. Eventually, the university offered the option of receiving my nine-month salary in 12 equal increments because too many professors did not imitate squirrels and the credit unions were busy in mid-summer; so much for education alone as a trap-avoidance strategy. But in a year I spent working outside the university, there was no retirement program and the nature of the organization's charter was such that no Social Security deduction from my monthly salary was required. Did I invest the equivalent of Social Security in stocks or bonds? No, the family spent it. Commitment can be difficult. As you mature and truly grasp the idea of short- and long-run tradeoffs, it becomes easier; at least it did for me.[2]

I have reflected on the power of habit and how habit redefines choice sets along with reducing the cognitive load imposed by making decisions. For me, not eating certain foods damaging to my health has become a habit to the point I do not consume them for months at a time. Exercising daily has become a personal habit. No decision is required each day involving whether or not to exercise; I simply do it because it has become habitual, and no conscious decision-making is required, relieving me of cognitive effort and guilt if I fail to exercise. Daily exercise is now a default option. Self-control, while trying at the outset of a program, disappears as a chal-

---

[2] The human brain does not mature until about the age of 25. Hence, higher automobile insurance rates for teenagers, among other symptoms of reckless behavior that cause parents and larger society to become semi-crazed and lachrymose.

lenge when habits form; my desire for ice cream has long abated, as it did 30 years ago for chunks of red meat and rich sauces. Habit can be mistaken for virtue, but may be virtuous in the end.

More examples of commitment:

- Policies allowing those addicted to gambling to bar themselves from casinos by formally notifying the casinos ahead of time of the desire not to be admitted and if by chance they are admitted, any winnings go to charity.
- Don't grocery shop when you are hungry.
- Make certain cigarettes are not easily obtained.
- Designated drivers.
- Christmas clubs, popular at one time and showing signs of resurgence, are used to store money for gifts ahead of the holidays, a type of squirrel-like behavior. How the Baby Jesus would view Christmas clubs, I am not sure.
- Overestimating the amount of federal income taxes that will be due, with the incentive of receiving a nice refund, e.g., understating the number of dependents one has when setting up payroll deductions. This is truly dumb, because the government has the use of your money when you could have earned interest on it *if* you had not succumbed to the lure of the short-run—the government as a self-selected nanny.
- Requiring school attendance until a child reaches a defined age.
- Mandatory immunizations.
- Add your own examples here.

As I write, the Obama administration has proposed a program for encouraging people to save. The president said: "...Making sure that folks have the opportunity and incentive to save—for a home or college, for retirement or a rainy day—is essential to that effort. If you work hard and meet your responsibilities, this country is going to honor our collective responsibility to you: To ensure that you can save and secure your retirement." There are various aspects to the plan making it easier for employers and workers to set up automatic savings plans for the workers, but also includes opt-out provisions. Behavioral economics has influenced Obama policymakers, at least to a minimal degree. The basic idea, of course, is removing the lure of the short-run (saving rather than spending), implicitly causing people to adopt new discounting rates. Because it involves making saving easier without making it mandatory, I applaud the effort, though I do not like the phrase "collective responsibility," language that reeks of much that I detest, language prominent in liberal-progressive circles.

In the previous chapter, I described the contract method for escaping traps, as modeled by an economist named McKenzie, and noted it can also be used as a way of avoiding traps. Contracts are a type of commitment. Legal contracts as a trap-avoidance device have existed for a long time and work best when as there is third-party enforcement, a legitimate and proper function of government. Homeowner associations in certain neighborhoods are a method of preventing general neighborhood decline due to the actions of one or a few careless homeowners, where the latter might affect the appearance and property values of the larger group, creating a social trap; when the agreement has been signed, commitment has occurred. Think about contracts of various types as reducing uncertainty and their impact on discount rates.

Trap Avoidance: Awareness of Current Emotional State
If rules must be followed, here is a good one: Never make important decisions when you are emotionally distraught. Before I achieved a certain level of maturity, I sometimes made choices that were lacking, shall we kindly say, in beneficial outcomes, usually when I was in a divergent emotional state. Self-awareness enters here, along with a grasp of how discount rates can momentarily shift due to emotional distress or temporary impairment, particularly the kind of risk-taking behavior associated with alcohol. The other side is a period of unusual personal buoyancy, whereby marriage is proposed, expensive cars are purchased, and risky investments are made.

Psychologists speak of hot and cold mental states. If you are of a certain advanced age, liked me, you might remember a song by Bill Haley & the Comets, which contained the lyrics, "It's Saturday night and I just got paid/fool about my money, don't try to save ... my heart says go, go, have a time... " and so forth. That's a hot state, characteristic of food, drink, and sex. A cold state can be represented by depression or extreme sadness or "the blues," and cold emotional states have their own liabilities when it comes to decision-making. Thus, know thyself and be aware of your mental state when it comes decision time. I keep the criterion "Preservation of Existing Assets" on paper and in my mind (a memory of the future) to help me make good investment decisions when emotional states might cause me to behave otherwise.

Professional gamblers understand the mental flaw of "playing with the house's money," a matter of unwarranted buoyancy. Amateurs do not. If you are having a good run at the blackjack table and piling up winnings, this is not house money, it is yours, and there should be no incentive to take on more risk, thinking it is some form of free money. In my gambling days, I always kept in mind (when not drinking alcohol) the notion of opportunity cost: What would those winnings buy? A new camera or a hundred rolls of film or two months mortgage payments, a nice dinner with sweetie in her black evening gown? Considering the opportunity cost of subsequently losing the original winnings makes the extra chips on the table take on a less abstract quality and cools the hot state. Aside from other conveniences, casinos like chips because pushing out a $100 chip is one step removed psychologically from laying down a $100 bill.

The stock market has qualities similar to the gambling table. Capital gains are not "house money." Unable to resist the temptation for a play on words, I suggest that a dramatic increase in your home's value is not house money. Put your winnings in your pocket regardless of the venue.

Trap Avoidance: The Status Quo and Default Options
Please recall what I named "the Classic Decision Problem" in Chapter 2. Choosing the do-nothing alternative often has severe consequences. Psychologists have studied adherence to a current state of affairs in some detail, and it boils down to this: Changing the status quo has costs attached to it that prevent selection of a different alternative. What kind of costs? The fear of doing something different due to uncertain outcomes, including the fear of loss. Also, what are called transaction costs, meaning the costs of hard cognitive effort, information gathering,

possible need for legal advice, and all those other details required for careful alternative selection.

At one time, internet providers made changing to another provider very difficult, at least that was my experience. Of course, the tactic was designed to cause sighs of "too much work, not worth it" (the disincentives of transaction costs, loss of email history) and maintenance of the status quo. Also, inattention results in implicit selection of the status quo. Book and CD clubs count on inattention, using automatic renewals in the background via credit card to keep you attached. So do movie rental operations such as Netflix and some magazines. Changing the Social Security and Medicare-Medicaid systems has substantial political costs, so an unsustainable status quo is maintained, at least for a while.

An interesting and accessible book by Thaler and Sunstein (2008) details the hazards of the status quo, along with many other topics related to this chapter. One of their examples concerning bondage to the status quo involves payments to employees of a corporation in the form of company stock or the opportunity to purchase company stock at a discount as a fringe benefit. The result is far too much investment money in a single company, but once underway with such programs, people seem loath to sell some of the stock and diversify their portfolios, possibly due to inattention or outright ignorance or undue faith in their company's profitability; see the famed Enron mess as a perfect example.

Thaler and Sunstein also cite simple inattention to ongoing initiatives. I have been guilty of this in my financial life, preferring to work on things that truly interested me or to pull on my waders and go fly fishing rather than pay attention to, say, reallocation of my investment assets when it was called for. The incentives here are obvious. It is more fun in the late afternoon to tromp down to my backyard pond for an hour of fly fishing than to study spreadsheets of my investments and track daily market behavior. Or changing an investment company when it is not performing to expectations. The transaction costs of changing companies are high in terms of research and paperwork, though good companies make the process nearly painless, but even then it requires some cost to do the research on a new company and make the initial inquiries, plus making new investment choices and the ever-present paperwork. Another cost that results in clinging to the status quo is fear of insulting a current investment or insurance company. Never mind, it is your money, not theirs, and companies are used to changes. A cliché but one worth adopting as a canon for your financial affairs is this: If you do not take care of your money, nobody else will. Believe me, nobody else will.

Incredible amounts of money—trillions—have been lost over the decades in the stock market because people hang on to a stock or portfolio when it is declining, hoping for a rebound that will recover their money. We hate losses and will sustain additional losses in the process of attempting to recoup losses already suffered. Stroll around Las Vegas casinos at 4 a.m. and watch things get out of hand as desperate gamblers try to recover from a long night of bad decisions. I once saw a bleary gambler yank off his suit jacket and begin flogging a blackjack table; the table did not respond, casino security did. Long ago, when teaching economics, I named this the *sunk-cost drag* or it could be called the *sunk-cost bias*. A famous example of this became known as the Concorde Fallacy, whereby England and France continued to pour money into the Concorde supersonic airplane even when it became obvious it would never make a profit.

Though I am in favor of expanded choice sets, an excessive number of options also can cause adherence to the status quo; if there are 8,000 mutual funds available for a retirement program, it is far easier to select and remain with a fund suggested by an employer as a default choice. This is particularly true if financial illiteracy is part of the baggage. Another simple, but annoying, example of a default option gaining its power through inattention is websites asking if you would like to receive emails from the company, pre-selecting the "yes" answer for you rather than allowing you to make a choice or designating "no" as the default option.

A helpful default option seeking to overcome momentary inattention is my computer asking me if I would like to save changes to a file before closing it; those of you who have been using computers as long as I have recall disasters when this option was not available. Automatic backups, if you activate them, serve the same purpose. In general, view defaults and the status quo in any situation with a hard eye—visualizing the simple classic decision tree from Chapter 2 is helpful. It might be said you should pay attention to inattention.

Trap Avoidance: Anticipatory Guilt

I have not seen what I call anticipatory guilt cited in the literature, but it can be a powerful weapon; certainly it is for me. Having a love for ice cream with my evening berries, I consistently yielded to the temptation, though with diabetes and high blood pressure heavy in my genetic background, I have to limit my intake of certain foods. I disappointed myself each time I succumbed to the lure of ice cream. I am stronger than that, I would tell myself. This reached a point where the anticipated ex post facto guilt outweighed the pleasure of consuming the ice cream and was transferred to the decision-making itself (guilt as an expected outcome competing with the anticipated pleasure of eating ice cream), which resulted in berries without the cold chocolate swirl beneath them. Eventually berries alone became a habit. Often do I remind myself that I may be subject to the forces of evolution, but I also have a reflective side, at bottom am master of myself, and needn't bend always to those forces. Overall, I am not inclined to lug around a knapsack full of guilt, but a portion of it can be useful at times. Let's call it "managed guilt"—there, that makes it sound better.

A variation of anticipatory guilt ties in with commitment. Instead of a physician pronouncing weight control is necessary and immediately so, a better way might be to distribute very basic lists of what constitutes good nutrition. Keep it simple, just two or three columns of "okay to eat this, okay to eat that on rare occasions, never eat this." Then provide the patient with a form containing blanks or a check list to fill in for each meal (including snacks) over the next three weeks, a one-sentence statement of how they intend to carry out the new diet, and make an appointment on the spot for another consultation and cholesterol test at the end of three weeks and at regular intervals after that. Keep the approach easy and non-threatening, relying on the patients own chagrin if the guidelines are not followed when they report back.

Good intentions can be a powerful incentive to overcome short-run temptations if those intentions are communicated to one or more other persons whereby guilt is suffered if a relapse occurs; remember McKenzie's contract and the stickK.com Website from Chapter 8? Exactly the same tactic can be used for exercise—typically people who are in woeful physical condition do not have the slightest idea about how to begin an exercise program. And why limit subtle pressures toward nutrition and exercise to people already in a trap? Why not extend this to reasonably healthy people, including school children, instead of grand pronouncements of new programs and periodic sermonettes? We do it with school reading programs where students receive a small award for reading a certain number of books in a time span.

A contract could be issued by a physician, similar to that employed by McKenzie the economist. Money can be a powerful proxy device for future health. Offer the patient a contract whereby a check is written to a specific charity and is held by the physician in the patient's file. If a weight target is not achieved or maintained by some reasonable date, the money is donated to the charity. Better yet, take it out of the physician's hands and send it to the charity with the check post-dated. If the goal is achieved, the charity can return the check. See if you can think of other potential trap situations where communicating intent and being provided with simple guidelines or contracts might work.

Trap Avoidance and the Government
Preventing entrance into traps is preferred to escapes, releases, and mends. Societies long have recognized this without using the label of traps. But, as I have stressed, government laws and regulations travel with oppressive amounts of baggage, are inefficient economically, and are best avoided if at all possible. If the president's suggestions mentioned earlier in terms of savings are adopted and contain the opt-out clause, that is a different matter. The role of government should be to make people's lives safer and easier, not to bludgeon them into certain courses of action and demand marching in close-order drill. As Tocqueville eloquently put it, a person should ask no more of government than "not to be disturbed in his toil."

Just about every law or regulation is nothing more than a trap-avoidance

device or a tactic for release from traps. Here are a few simple examples, and I agree with some of them:
- Required automobile liability insurance.
- Stiff penalties for driving while intoxicated.
- Mandatory deductions for Social Security.
- Mandatory paycheck deductions for taxes or required estimated quarterly payments. This is more than trap avoidance, since the government wants your money as soon as possible.
- Laws requiring the purchase of health insurance (Massachusetts already requires this).
- Enforcement of legal contracts, a reasonable and necessary government activity.
- Environmental Protection Agency regulations concerning pollution (externality traps).
- Cigarette taxes.
- Mandatory fuel efficiency for vehicles, which can be considered both a trap-avoidance scheme and an escape/release.
- Banning trans-fat in all foods (California already has a ban).
- Banning or seeking to ban fast-food in certain poor areas because of high obesity rates in those areas.
- Banning use of cell phones while driving.
- State-required annual car inspections.
- Speed limits and speed bumps.
- Requiring the use of helmets for motorcycle riders.
- Annual required physical examinations for certain professions, e.g., commercial airplane pilots.
- Required vaccinations are trap-avoidance devices, though not all diseases are due to bad decision-making.
- The multitude of safety rules from the Occupational Safety & Health Administration (OSHA).
- Highway speed limits.
- Legal age requirements to purchase tobacco products or alcohol.

The Blueprint

- Vehicle seat-belt laws.
- Limits on the number of a particular fish that may be caught and kept.
- No-smoking ordinances.
- Limitations on lawn watering or restricting landscaping to low-water-consumption designs.
- Prohibitions on the use of certain drugs.
- Zoning ordinances.

Notice how easy it is to make long lists of government trap releases and trap-avoidance measures. Does this imply something about declining self-reliance and civic responsibility by those who inhabit Western Civilization, a languid, spiritless citizenry? Or is it prima facie evidence of a drift toward a parental, statist society due to ideology on the part of a few? I will return to these troubling questions in Chapters 11 and 12.

Trap Avoidance: Nudges

The Thaler and Sunstein book, *Nudge*, was referenced earlier in this chapter. Nudges are nothing more than what we have been calling incentives, the difference being (in the main) that nudges are small changes in the incentive structure, as the word "nudge" implies. *Nudge* contains a large number of ideas relevant to trap avoidance. I cite two of them here.

A good example that ties together our previous study of decisions, incentives, and feedback is having a home thermostat that instantaneously flashes increases or decreases in utility costs as the thermostat is adjusted. The trap is an unexpectedly high utility bill at month's end. With utilities, the reward in the form of more comfort is immediate but the cost is delayed, typical of the many situations already detailed in this book. The eventual savings, however, are a longer-term reward in the form of lower utility bills. In other words, the thermostat becomes an instantaneous feedback device indicating future costs or savings occurring now rather than receiving the news in some complicated utility bill later on; think of this in terms of discounting and feedback where the loop is shortened.

Like my vomit pill in Chapter 8, the smart thermostat can function as an archetype for bringing the future back to the present and is a prime example to keep in mind when thinking about, for instance, retirement savings or obesity. If you spend $300 on a non-durable consumer good, imagine a "retirement fund thermostat" that would flash in your mind indicating the effect on your long-term happiness. Lacking such a thermostat plus the ever-powerful temptations of the short-run, Thaler and Sunstein suggest an innovative trap-avoidance program called "Save More Tomorrow" and claim success with it.

The authors also promote cooling-off periods as a contrivance for trap avoidance. Examples: Texas has a 60-day window before a divorce can be made final, plus waiting periods between issuance of a marriage license and when the marriage can occur. Certain states have laws regarding a consumer's right to abrogate a contract within a specified period of time. When purchasing a home, I pay the seller a small fee to allow cancellation of the offer contract within a specified period of time, and I have used this flexibility twice to exit an agreement after pondering my decision or a professional engineering assessment of the property. Cooling-off periods are simple, powerful trap-avoidance devices serving to overcome the blindfold effect due to emotion. When writing an unpleasant letter to someone or transmitting anything incendiary, I suggest putting it aside for 48 hours before sending it.

Trap Avoidance: Competing Alternatives

The use of competing alternatives is a method not only for avoiding traps but also for escapes and releases. Given our lengthy considerations of incentives, this approach should be obvious. The idea is to be more creative and expand choice sets to provide alternatives having better outcomes that compete with an alternative having an undesirable outcome. I can illustrate this with a personal vignette.

— Personal Vignette —

> For reasons not discernible, my daughter refused to learn the multiplication tables when she was in elementary school. Naturally, she was falling behind her classmates and entering a trap from which recovery would be onerous. At the same time, she craved a stereo system for

her room. I bought the stereo system but left the components in their sealed boxes where she could see them each day, while guaranteeing the system would become operative when she learned the tables and could recite them from flashcards in a time limit I specified. Until then, it would remain in the boxes.

There was whining, there were tears, her mother accused me of being cruel. In one week the tables had been mastered, the stereo made operative, my alleged cruelty forgotten. All that I had done was set up a decision simple enough for a child to grasp: Learn multiplication tables (alternative) and receive stereo (the incentive), don't learn tables and suffer the outcome of no stereo. That was far easier than lectures in the form of verbal horse whipping (the moral exhortation approach). See also my earlier description of providing incentives for my wife to quite smoking.

— End of Personal Vignette —

Renting is an alternative to owning a home. Ideologues of one or more stripes decided 30 years ago everyone should own a home, characterizing it as a "right." The Community Reinvestment Act was jammed through congress in 1977 and along with its later addendums contributed greatly to the issuing of sub-prime loans to people with poor or questionable credit histories. Of course, a high proportion of those loans went into default and was an integral part of the housing meltdown from 2007 forward. Homeowners were trapped until they walked away from their obligations (an escape), due to home loans being non-recourse debts, unlike credit cards, and little or nothing in the way of down payments that would have made the borrowers stakeholders. Lenders found themselves trapped and so did society as a whole when economic conditions deteriorated.

Renting is a much better choice for many people (White 2010). If rents increase beyond affordability, the flexibility exists to find a different place when the lease expires. More important, it is easy to be "house poor," as many people have discovered over many decades. Home ownership results in a concentration of assets rather than diversification. Plus, along with mortgage payments, there are bills for maintenance, property taxes, and insurance. These expenditures detract from saving for other purposes such as retirement, college, emergency medical expenses, and a rainy-day fund in case of unemployment. For trap avoidance, renting should be advanced as a competing alternative to owning for those with limited financial resources. Those who constantly push for home ownership by people with limited resources are, perversely, harming the very people they seek to help, a common result of statist policies, including minimum-wage laws.

Trap Avoidance: Abstention
Abstention is the sacred formula used by those of sermonical bent, e.g., "Just say no." Abstention is effective, if practiced appropriately, that appropriateness being somewhere short of a pinched and overly constrained existence. *If practiced*! We have studied enough lure-of-the-short-run examples in this book to be skeptical of abstention as an effective device. Uganda once claimed success with abstention in avoiding the HIV plague besetting Africa, but the development of antiretroviral drugs has lessened fear of the disease, resulting in discount rate shifts, changes in incentives, and the old, old lure of the short-run has appeared once again.

In 1836, economist N. W. Senior advocated abstinence as a trap avoidance device, but admitted, "To abstain from the enjoyment which is in our power, or to seek distant rather than immediate results, are among the most painful exertions of the human will." Bravo to brother Senior for such a succinctly powerful encapsulation of the difficulties surrounding abstinence and patience. When abstinence is practiced, it works well, such as saving for retirement (abstaining from current consumption), but unfortunately it has failings as we have seen in the obesity problem.

Another economist, John Rae, writing in 1834, stated that deferral or abstinence is difficult in the "actual presence of the immediate object of desire." In my less exalted language, the summer nights never end. Rae examined the idea of saving from the standpoint of leaving a legacy and also on its larger economic impact.

Abstaining from criminal behavior is a form of trap avoidance. And the debate lingers: Is punishment a deterrent? The only true deterrent against criminal behavior is the hypothetical and unachievable world where *certain* punishment is present at the moment of alternative selection. There are criminals for whom I wish only the worst and their deaths bother me not. But in the case of death penalties assessed, the costly appeals process can absorb 20 years between sentencing and the outcome of the sentence, so it is difficult to see how this is an effective deterrent, given what we know about discounting along with the apparent inability to think rationally during or even before the commission of homicide, along with limited intellectual capacity causing an inability to conceptualize futures.

Criminality is evidence of aberrant criteria rankings and incentives, resulting in the choice of alternatives promising gain without lawful effort, alternatives that dominate lawful alternatives. Risk of apprehension does play a role, no doubt, but people are not good at estimating probabilities and the lure of gain in the short-run can easily bias probability assignments in the direction of low perceived risk. The certainty of punishment by death may be 1.0 for a terrorist suicide bomber, but this is dominated by the incentive of promised heavenly delights to follow immediately, where the punishment and rewards both occur at the same time.

If we knew much of anything about preventing people from committing crimes or launching suicide bombings, our prisons would not be bursting and airport security would be lessened. My thoughts on all this should be viewed as speculative, since I know nothing about the formal aspects of criminology.

Trap Avoidance: Cost/Price
Of the many problems we confront, the one receiving the least attention, relatively speaking, is the dwindling supply of fresh water. Living in rural areas, as I have for the last 17 years makes you acutely aware of water. One of the high-desert ranches where I lived depended on wells that were 1,500 feet deep, the water brought up by pumpjacks like those you see nodding away as you pass oil fields, where a new well could cost upwards of $40,000. My dogs and I checked the pumps and storage tanks every afternoon to certify they were still functioning properly. People who live

in urban areas turn on faucets and blithely assume water will spill forth from somewhere, but farmers in the San Joaquin valley are far less certain water for crops will be available.

The economics of water requires a long book to adequately explore. But the core of the problem is simple: Price, or cost on the flip side. As I said before, if a good is underpriced, such as clean air or fresh water, people will use more of it (one of the problems with socialized medical care or blue-ribbon medical insurance). Price can be a powerful incentive not just to change behavior but to prevent certain behaviors from being contemplated in the first place. Think back to the discussions of discounting earlier in this book where cost and price were front and center as incentives. Do you shave in the shower with the water running? Would you shave in the shower if you knew it cost you $50 a month? Would you let the water run while you brush your teeth if it cost $30 a week? Living the country life provides an incentive to be parsimonious with water use, and I never shave in the shower. We need a device on our faucets similar to the thermostat mentioned earlier along with the pricing of water high enough to act as an incentive for conservation.

Free or extremely cheap goods always are over-exploited. See Garret Hardin's tragedy of the commons, explained in Chapter 5. If ground water was accurately priced, I doubt there would be massive cotton farming in the high desert of west Texas or huge farms in other parts of the arid American West. "It will put us out of business" is a common refrain when higher water rates are proposed. Maybe, maybe not, depending on what consumers are willing to pay for fruits, vegetables, and clothing, and overdriving aquifers will result in business extinction anyway, but of course that is viewed as a long-term problem. I admit the pricing of water and air is subtle and tricky business, but it can be done and it works. The alternative is rationing, which is subject to anguished cries of "Me first" and political influence.

American hospitals have been trapped because existing law demands emergency-room care for those supposedly unable to pay for services. Consequently, emergency rooms are flooded with a surfeit of people who are suffering no real emergencies but rather are there for complimentary medical care of a routine kind, free-riders who are transferring costs to those who do have insurance. Hospitals make up the free-rider losses by charging higher fees to those with insurance, resulting in higher insurance premiums for policyholders, especially under Obamacare, or reimbursements to doctors and hospitals by federal, state, and local governments, which is cost-shifting via the tax system. One solution is to impose a non-monetary cost or price on those claiming insufficient funds for treatment by demanding payment in the form of labor, e.g., janitorial work or lawn mowing. Therefore, a price for services is levied and I suspect the pressure on emergency rooms would be lessened. See Staib (2009) for an extensive discussion of market-oriented solutions to emergency-room overload.

Remark. Suppose all those without sufficient medical insurance were refused care. That would be a powerful incentive. After about a dozen people died on hospital lawns, there would be a rush to purchase insurance. Cruel? Inhumane? I suppose that's a reasonable conclusion, but is it more inhumane than asking others to pay for your care? Is it more distasteful than the federal government passing a law forcing everyone to buy insurance?

Other examples of price as an instrument for trap avoidance are peak-load pricing by utilities, varying road tolls by the time of day, and higher prices by airlines during favored arrival and departure times, which all are variations on the same idea. I belabor the point. This entire book has dealt with such matters, either implicitly or explicitly. The conclusion: Price is a powerful incentive if left to do its job. There is little more to say about its role in trap avoidance.

Trap Avoidance: Other Preventative Measures
Condoms are useful in the avoidance of STD, HIV, and pregnancy. The birth control pill was designed specifically to avoid unwanted pregnancies. If you are seriously overweight or concerned about weight, try not to associate and, especially, dine with other overweight people; there are various social pressures at work in being one of the crowd and other overweight people reinforce the idea that it is just fine to join them. Think about conformity and social pressure in parenting pre-teens and teenagers. One of

the reasons I favor school choice and charter schools is the opportunity for poverty-stricken young people to experience cultures that value intellectual effort and achievement as a way of avoiding a trapped adulthood due to injurious cultural influences promoting the delights of the short-run.

I want to reinforce the point just made in the previous sentence and implied earlier. As I am writing this in winter 2010-2011, the United States unemployment rate is about 10 percent, officially, but is much higher when those who have stopped seeking work are included. There is wringing of hands, the usual non-productive chatter of the political class, and a general sense of frustration. Yet, there are good jobs available, many of them paying $70,000 and up. It is a trap; people did not invest in the kind of training that would prepare them for such conditions. If you counted on a lifetime, well-paying but routine assembly-line job in manufacturing or construction, things are tough.

Yet jobs go begging in fields requiring some expertise, such as pharmacists, medical technicians (e.g., MRI operators), engineering, and accounting. Preparation for a good job requires an investment in time and money, and such an investment involves a tradeoff between the present and the future. One is tempted to condemn failures in the labor market or the common villain of "outsourcing" when the underlying cause is a failure of will and planning. Becoming an engineer is difficult, but other available employment only requires basic technical training. A trap escape: Instead of complaining, go back to school, or better yet, acquire training before a trap arises and avoid the trap entirely.

The housing trap and credit card debt have been mentioned. Transparency and clear, easy-to-understand information is critical in all financial transactions. *Caveat emptor,* meaning "let the buyer beware," is something we all learned in grade school or through rough experiences. Still, transparency cannot compensate entirely for financial illiteracy and, for that matter, a low level of general literacy. Responsible lenders will seek to disclose information and educate credit applicants, especially in home purchases, but there are plenty of subprime lenders who engage in chicanery. The following simple question can go a long way to avoid the housing trap: "If the interest rate rises to x percent or you are unemployed for six months, here are the results.

Can you still make the monthly payments?" A trustworthy lender will help make that determination based on not only income, but also stability of job prospects and other factors. Worst-case scenarios should be examined, just as a benchmark, but excessively dire worst-case forecasts would result in few loans ever being made.

Technology is being developed to prevent people with elevated blood alcohol levels from driving. One proposal is sensors in the vehicle's steering wheel that can measure such levels and cause the vehicle to stall or fail to start. That would entail a nice short feedback loop independent of human decision-making.

Summary

From the beginning of the book to this point, I have presented what I believe is a unified view of problems and how to conceptualize them, along with avenues leading to solutions and prevention. As you have sensed, this chapter on trap avoidance and the previous chapter concerning escapes, releases, and mends have overlapped. That is, some escape strategies can be used as preventative measures and vice versa. Following a short case study in Chapter 10, I turn to a two-chapter essay on democracy and its prospects, the discussion making use of the concepts covered thus far. But first, a lesson in trap avoidance or "A big whirring saw as one reason why you should get an education rather than dropping out of school."

— Personal Vignette —

My father believed his son should always get up early, work hard, and save money. Approaching the summer of my eighteenth year, he informed me the local lumber yard needed an extra hand for the busy summer season. I acquired the necessary special license permitting me to drive the big delivery truck and reported to work on a Monday morning in May.

And then I saw the SAW. A big saw, a really large, pernicious saw with an exposed blade whirring at 7 zillion revolutions per second (there was no OSHA in those days). I also noticed the grizzled regular workers all had at least one finger missing. But that first morning, some sort of complicated board-feet calculation came up that was puzzling the workers. They scribbled on boards with their carpenter pencils, adding and subtracting and multiplying and maybe even dividing. I could see they probably would arrive at an answer sometime in the next hour, but it was clear to me the calculation essentially boiled down to a rather simple algebra problem with a single unknown. I used one of their pencils, laid out the equation on a #2 pine 1 x 12, solved for the unknown, and presented them with the answer. They were awed. In less than 60 seconds, the kid had solved the sort of problem they confronted several times every day. An agreement was struck: They would operate the saw if I would do the calculations. My father's words about the value of an education hummed in my ears. As it turned out, he was right about most things, and, out of his bib overalls and into a jacket and tie, he uncharacteristically wept when I received my doctorate, with a university teaching job already secured and all five fingers intact on both hands.

— End of Personal Vignette —

Chapter 10

A TSUNAMI TRAP: THE CASE OF PUBLIC PENSION FUNDS

Seldom is one example sufficient to illustrate almost every concept discussed thus far in the book, but the public pension funds tsunami is a perfect summary case. It also mirrors the well-publicized problems of Greece and other countries in dealing with massive public debt. Every concept we have discussed will be found here: Decision-making, discounting, incentives, small increments, the lure of the short-run, feedback, and traps. Warnings about problems with public pension funds now appear as daily news items; however, when I originally wrote this chapter, few were aware of the problem. Nonetheless, the problem still is worth exploring because it illustrates so perfectly what has been covered previously in the book.

Public pension funds—sounds boring doesn't it? Trust me, it is not, if you are fond of your own money and object to governments flushing it down the public commode. Read on and be dazzled by prevarication and a trap about to be sprung involving the decline of your checking account (you just have to love all the cheery, uplifting examples in this book).

The Tsunami

In mid-ocean, tsunami waves are barely noticeable, a slight roll on the surface, nothing more, unremarkable. As they approach shore where the water shallows, the wave height grows, sometimes to mammoth proportions and terrible destruction occurs. Tsunamis are thus an apt metaphor for time-delay traps, almost unnoticed until the trap closes, the waves ascending toward dwellers on the shore.

Public pension funds are a tsunami as they presently exist. Some people have been aware of the coming disaster, most have not been until recently when reports have begun appearing in the popular press. Even so, a substantial percentage of the electorate does not grasp the immensity of the problem. The result will be destructive, another "crisis" will suddenly be upon us, and for an America already struggling with massive debt, panic and recriminations will ensue.

I will use small numbers to reduce computational effort and then expand to real-world numbers as we progress. Furthermore, this subject is an accounting and actuarial specialty with many subtleties, and I will omit certain details without being deceitful and corrupting the analysis. Incidentally, the nomenclature involving retirement plans can be confusing, since "retirement plans" is used to talk about private-sector plans and "pensions" is commonly used in the context of public-sector employment. I will bypass convention and use the terms interchangeably. The type of thinking relevant here was briefly explained in Chapter 1 in the context of discounting. I will keep it simple and non-technical for this book.

Gloria's Retirement

Gloria is a public-sector employee. She contributes to her retirement plan and so does the governmental entity she works for. The money in Gloria's account is invested by the government so it can grow over time, typically in a combination of stocks, bonds, real estate, and sometimes hedge funds. Gloria plans to retire in 20 years and the financial reports sent to her show she has $100,000 in her retirement account. Using an interest rate of 8.5 percent, the government estimates the future value of her retirement account when she retires in 20 years will be $511,000 without further additions.[1] Gloria is happy, but principled accountants and financial people are not, because 8.5 percent is an unrealistic return on her invested capital. More lugubrious, Gloria may not even have $100,000 in her account, but the government entity for which she works assures her that she does.

Private-sector retirement-fund managers are required to use low rates of interest in computing future value as a way of accounting for risk (see Chapter 1 and the appendix at book's end). Not so with governments. Taking risk into account, suppose 3.5 percent is the appropriate interest rate, a reasonable figure. Gloria's $100,000 would grow to only $199,000. But Gloria has been guaranteed she will have $511,000 at retirement. Thirty-two states, either constitutionally or by law, guarantee retirement benefits and for all practical purposes retirement funds in the remaining states are impossible to cut. At her retirement Gloria will receive benefits as if she had $511,000 in the account; she is guaranteed that principal amount. And there are lots of Glorias.

But there is another problem, a nasty one. Gloria really does not have $100,000 in her account because the investments are not being valued at *market value*. Recent stock market declines have lowered the real value of her retirement account to $57,000. In financial language, her assets are not "marked to market." Now, $57,000 compounded at 3.5 percent over 20 years amounts to only $113,000. Subtract $113,000 from the $511,000 she is guaranteed and the difference is $398,000. Gloria's pension is *underfunded* by $398,000. If the true valuation is $57,000, Gloria's government employer would have to earn 11.6 percent per year on average over the next 20 years to reach $511,000—not likely.

Is Gloria in trouble, is she being deceived? No and partially are the answers. It is taxpayers who are in trouble and being deceived. Even before the stock market collapse in 2008-2009, public pensions were estimated to be underfunded by one to $2 trillion. That's *trillion*.

Andrew Biggs (2010) says it is worse than that: "Pension plans for state government employees today report they are underfunded by $450 bil-

---

[1] Of course there will be additions to Gloria's account, but those additions can be omitted for this example. If $5,000 were added to Gloria's account each year, the total would be $774,000 at 8.5 percent based on the starting value of $100,000.

lion, according to a recent report from the Pew Charitable Trusts. But this vastly underestimates the true shortfall, because public pension accounting wrongly assumes that plans can earn high investment returns without risk. My research indicates that overall underfunding tops $3 trillion."

What is occurring is the worst sort of government chicanery—no, the proper word is dishonesty at a level dwarfing Enron, WorldCom, and all the rest of the inexcusable private-sector scandals that so rightly enrage politicians and the citizenry. It is called "cooking the books" in the private sector, and federal or state agents flashing badges will appear at your door when the corruption is suspected, possibly followed by a perp walk with television cameras tracking your journey from office to courtroom. As mentioned, in handling retirement programs private firms are required to use conservative interest rates as a way to account for risk in projecting retirement benefits. Not so for the government, and the reality is that the government cannot earn the necessary 11.6 percent to fund Gloria's pension, but Gloria is nonetheless guaranteed her $511,000 as a result of shifting risk from her to taxpayers.

There is one single reason why the dishonesty exists: To deceive taxpayers by concealing over-generous public employee retirement benefits and pushing the managerial responsibility and electoral consequences for the deficiencies further into the future. In a 2008 letter to his shareholders, investor Warren Buffet bluntly stated (Evans 2009): "Public pension promises are huge and, in many cases, funding is woefully inadequate. Because the fuse on this time bomb is long, politicians flinch from inflicting tax pain, given that the problems will only become apparent long after these officials have departed." Now where have you seen that kind of trap before? Throughout much of this book. Notice also the length and velocity of the feedback loop at work where punishment is pushed far enough in the future such that it does not influence present voting decisions by the electorate.

To cover the *unfunded pension liabilities*, there are three possibilities. First, cut non-pension government spending and use that money to make the pension funds whole. A second one is to immediately raise taxes, which would disclose the tsunami of unfunded liabilities that is rolling toward us and is just over the horizon of the citizenry (tsunami is exactly the correct word).

The third is what are called "pension obligation bonds," issued by governmental units to make up for the unfunded liabilities, though I suggest "pension bombs" might be a better term. These bonds are not exempt from federal taxes, as are standard municipal bonds, so higher interest rates of, for example, 6.5 percent must be paid to the bondholders. To reduce the unfunded pension liabilities, the government must earn more on the money received from the bond sales than is paid out in interest, requiring investment returns beyond what most investors earn on investments. This does not occur, quite the opposite: Government investments have returned less than the bond interest rate, which exacerbates the problem because not only are the pension liabilities underfunded but also a deficit is being incurred on the bonds intended to reduce the liabilities. It may amount to job-keeping and electoral rationality for bureaucrats and politicians, as reckonings are pushed into the future, but it is lunacy to the rest of us.

Here are two examples from Evans (2009). First, the Chicago Transit Authority (CTA) borrowed $1.8 billion to cover pension shortfalls, the bonds paying 6.8 percent; the proceeds from the sale were then held in a money market account earning 2 percent for the CTA. Even those possessing a low level of financial literacy can understand that doesn't work. A sixth-grader could understand it. Second, the seventh-largest public pension fund in the United States is the Teacher Retirement System of Texas. The fund routinely reports 8 percent expected rates of return, while actual results over the last ten years have averaged 2.6 percent.

Let's reflect a moment. *Decisions* were and are being made to pay generous benefits to public workers as part of union contract negotiations. Examples: Detroit is teetering on the edge of bankruptcy; union fringe benefits of the public employees are 68 percent of their base salaries. Average fringe benefits for federal employees are $41,000 per year and average annual salaries are slightly over $71,000, meaning fringe benefits are 58 percent of salaries.

Alternatives and Outcomes: Taxes will have to be increased to pay for the excessive benefits as pension payments come due to employees or other government expenses will have to be severely curtailed. *Dominant Criterion for politicians*: Electability in the short-term. *Possible additional alternative*: Increase the retirement age for employees and/or pass revised laws reducing new benefits and already promised benefits, which will anger the public employees and their unions contributing large sums of campaign money, along with votes in the next election against anyone who tries to make corrections.

Implement new alternative: Issue pension obligation bonds and use accounting trickery to hide the forthcoming debacle by not marking current assets at market value and inflating expected rates of return on the assets. *Additional Consideration*: Underfunding pension liabilities in the present allows more money for new or current government programs, increasing reelection chances for politicians and job security for bureaucrats. *Choice*: Use the last alternative of bonds plus bogus accounting because it will help in the next election. *Ultimate outcome*: A gigantic trap that will be sprung and ensnare future taxpayers. This is a sliding-reinforcer, time-delay trap where the further you get into the trap the more costly it is to get out.

A final alternative is for a governmental entity to declare bankruptcy, which will nullify contracts with unions and place the solution in the hands of a bankruptcy judge. This latter tactic is not available to the federal government due to its impact on the national economy, not to mention international humiliation, and is unnecessary because of its ability to "create" money. States also are not permitted to declare bankruptcy, though municipalities can (the process is arduous). True to the nature of many such traps, it is far better to avoid them than try to extricate yourself once you are trapped, but the lure of the short-run persists, the summer nights never end until they do. As ever and always: Decisions, incentives, criteria, discounting, the lure of the short-run, and traps, illustrated here by another touching story from the statist's world.

Chapter 11

**DEMOCRACY AND ITS SABOTEURS
(INTENTIONAL AND OTHERWISE)**

"Experience should teach us to be most on our guard to protect liberty when the government's purposes are beneficial. Men born to freedom are naturally alert to repel invasion of their liberty by evil-minded rulers. The greater dangers to liberty lurk in insidious encroachment by men of zeal, well-meaning but without understanding."

-Justice Louis Brandeis

"In the end, more than they wanted freedom, they wanted security. When the Athenians finally wanted not to give to society but for society to give to them, when the freedom they wished for was freedom from responsibility, then Athens ceased to be free."

-Edward Gibbon

At the outset I promised to provide a useful conceptual framework for quickly grasping the central features of problems, whether personal or societal. In this chapter you will discover all our old friends present and accounted for as I sift through political complexity and the implications it has for freedom, for liberty, for democracy: Decisions, incentives, discounting, criteria, VSIs, the lure of the short-run, feedback, and traps.

Though I am normally of a sunny disposition, this chapter is mildly elegiac in tone, the set of ideas having the color of middle gray fading to darker shades where dots of red ire can be seen. When it comes to liberty, to freedom, I admit to a disquietude bordering on sadness, with a not-so-vague sense of an ominous presence hovering over me. The unease I feel is due partly to the ascendancy of ignorance to positions of power—almost a studied ignorance by ideologues—and partly a matter of self-interest among voters and politicians that is translated into public policy. Recent events have provided some muted cheer, as citizens have sought to rein in governments, but the central problems remain and cast doubt on democracy as a sustainable form of political organization.

Understand, I am entering here a world in which I am a nonprofessional, an alert, educated citizen of the United States but no more than a decently informed amateur in this realm. It is a world of Rousseau, Jefferson, Paine, Locke, Hobbes, the Greeks, Frederic Bastiat, Montesquieu, de Tocqueville, Edmund Burke, Rousseau, Adam Smith, John Rawls, Milton Friedman, Robert Nozick, Amartya Sen, and hundreds of other penetrating minds who spent and are spending their lives contemplating notions of liberty, rights, and political organization. For me to attempt an emulation of those minds would be epigonic at best, a conceptual shambles at worst.

That said, I have a way of thinking about such matters that serves me well, and that framework is anchored in the preceding chapters of this book. The framework provides a perspective I find useful in voting, discussions with others, and making rapid sense of political events as they unfold. If I cannot resist a strong opinion here and there, you need not forgive me, for I neither seek nor require absolution. And keep in mind, I examine trends but am no better than the next person at forecasting the long-term future; I remain humble in confrontations with complexity, avoiding the conceit that afflicts many politicians and some economists (though not many economists).

I do not want to fuss overlong about the exact definition of democracy. And I am most interested here in what passes for democracy in America, which can be characterized (ideally) as a representative democracy. That is, we do not vote directly for various policies and governmental actions but rather elect representatives we believe speak for our interests and concerns; we are a republic, strictly speaking. Direct democracy would be a case where no representatives are inserted between the electorate and governmental action; California's public referendums do allow people to vote directly on certain matters such as property taxes, though constitutionally the state is a representative democracy, albeit a highly flawed one.

As you will see, I fear we in America are rapidly moving toward—perhaps already have reached—what I call *nominal democracy*, a Potemkin village having the exterior trappings but none of the essence characterizing anything approaching true representative democracy. Rahe (2009) calls it "Soft Despotism," Levin (2009) uses the label of "Soft Tyranny." Regardless of the name, it has dire portents for my dominant political criterion of freedom.

A proviso here at the beginning: I will come down hard on voters, politicians, and other entities. I realize there are millions of serious, thoughtful members of the electorate, but they presently are in the minority or at minimum are bludgeoned incessantly and severely by the rancorous voices of ignorance and the votes commensurate with that ignorance. I recognize there are dozens of serious, thoughtful politicians, but they are presently in the minority. Astute voters and politicians are to be roundly applauded, even if my applause for the intelligent and thoughtful may appear far too muted in what follows. Naturally, all readers of this book are excluded from the more venomous criticism, except when you are not, and it is up to you to determine the latter.

Voters and Their Criteria

See two looks away,
That is the image of your life
Down the years
And you thought it was only
... a meaningless vote.
(The Author)

In any decision, people choose among alternatives. The choice is based on expected outcomes, which serve as incentives. Those outcomes occurring in the future are *discounted* and were illuminated in the chapters on traps. Alternatives are judged by a set of criteria and a selection of one alternative is made from among those available. The larger the number of feasible alternatives available, *the larger the choice set and therefore the greater the freedom.*

What criteria do voters bring to bear? Here are the most prominent: Self-interest (including security and loss avoidance), compassion, national well-being (for the thoughtful), and a desire for a reasonable amount of temporal certainty—call the latter societal stability, if you like. Two less obvious criteria are social pressure or conformity and "expressiveness" in voting. Notice I have omitted my dominant criterion—*freedom*—since freedom seems to be misconstrued as a given by many voters, even as it drifts away in small increments and occasionally large ones, like the depletion of a scarce resource.

The first four criteria listed above need no explanation. As for conformity, people want to be able to say or imply they voted in a fashion preventing them from being viewed as outcasts in whatever social structure they inhabit. Think of a university social science department or a circle of friends on the Upper West Side of Manhattan, both bastions of modern liberal progressivism. The slightest hint of nonconformity would result in a shunning of sorts, and future invitations to dinner parties would not be forthcoming, let alone promotion or the granting of tenure. Of course, electoral voting is by secret ballot, but voting one way and pretending to have voted in the opposite direction would cause great cognitive dissonance and the charade would soon be discovered by an offhand remark while the entrée is being served—dinner invitations and the like are incentives for many.

Expressive voting, suggested by Brennan and Lomasky (1993), is something different and interesting, though empirically debatable. As summarized by Caplan (2007, 137), "...citizens might vote not to help policies win, but to express their patriotism, their compassion, or their devotion to the environment." Economist Caplan makes an excellent point when he states (18), "In real-world political settings, the price of ideological loyalty is close to zero. So we should expect people to 'satiate' their demand for political delusion, to believe whatever makes them feel best. After all, it's free." He means the individual cost of a particular policy may appear tiny relative to "doing the right thing" and thereby obtaining cozy feelings about your behavior, though to me it seems directly related to ideological loyalty.

I call expressive voting comfort food for the conscience. For example, I suspect a vote for Barack Obama made some people feel racially tolerant. I interpret compassion in the context of expressive voting as a generalized sense of wishing better things for those viewed as less fortunate. The way I interpret its use in the initial list of four is as a specific criterion applied to a particular policy such as approval of minimum-wage laws, a misguided attempt at fostering national well-being, which perversely damages the most vulnerable people in society while putatively attempting to help them.

It is more than reasonable to inquire where concepts such as fairness, justice, and equity enter into voters' criteria. The literature on these subjects is broad, deep, and historical. As yet, no general theory of justice has emerged. These topics might best be placed under the broad heading of compassion, though the fit is not perfect. Konow (2003) states that fairness does seem to influence the thinking of many people; however, I remain skeptical of that contention when self-interest is put to the test. It is one thing to advocate fairness on a survey or in a behavioral laboratory when participating in an experiment and quite another when your personal well-being is at stake.

Caplan (2007) devotes an entire book (*The Myth of the Rational Voter*) to the theme of voter irrationality. He argues, with varying degrees of persuasiveness, that other criteria such as expressiveness and enthusiasm override self-interest. The result is voting skewed toward irrational policies, which are easily observable in democracies. Caplan (2007, 2) bluntly states, "... voters are worse than ignorant, they are ... irrational and vote accordingly."

If you doubt enthusiasm plays an important role in voting decisions, consider the mindless chant of "Yes, we can!" during Barack Obama's presidential campaign in 2008. "Can" what? Didn't matter, it was enough to believe or feel that something can be done about an unarticulated something, followed with the equally ambiguous "Change You Can Believe In." What change? How much change? At what rate will the change occur? Who will the change affect? As Blinder (1987, 197) points out, "...in politics it is more important to sound right than to be right."

Performance art has come to dominate substance and rationality, and it can achieve the quality of being downright grotesque. Recall Obama's acceptance speech when he received the Democratic nomination in Denver. He was backed by faux-Roman columns, apparently to represent the wisdom of the ages now personified by a candidate for public office. The columns made me squirm in embarrassment for those who designed and approved the backdrop, plus those who stood in front of them. President George W. Bush's landing on the USS Lincoln with a "Mission Accomplished" sign in the background falls in the same category.

Caplan's arguments concerning voter irrationality are good ones, but I have trouble with his dismissal of self-interest. I resolve the difference between Caplan's and my view as follows: For large, complex issues such as minimum-wage laws or tariffs, I can agree with him that some sense of, say, compassion may influence voting. For more specific policies where direct and substantial financial impact on the voter is salient, I favor the self-interest criterion, as would be true of matters such as gun control or required military service for everyone or a substantial tax on household consumption of energy or—see the brouhahas in various states in 2011—asking public workers to pay a larger share of their wage and pension benefits in the interest of making the states financially solvent. Anthropologist Robert Edgerton (1992) would agree with my distinction between personal and more general issues: "The bulk of available evidence suggests that people in all societies tend to be relatively rational when it comes to the beliefs and practices that directly involve their subsistence... The more remote these beliefs and practices are from subsistence activities, the more likely they are to involve nonrational characteristics."

For my purposes here, I will define irrationality as the casting aside of reasoning or simply a lack of sound judgment. More precisely, in the framework of this book it would mean one or all of the following:

- An incomplete list of feasible alternatives, due to ignorance, lack of information gathering, ideological bias, unnecessary haste, or sheer laziness (remember, cognitive effort has a cost).

- Misestimating the outcomes of alternatives due to ignorance, lack of information gathering, faulty calculations, biasing estimates in favor of ideology, haste, or misrepresentations by political elites. Errors in estimating outcomes due to uncertainty or rationality bounded by the limits of available knowledge are a completely different matter and cannot be classified as irrational, though the results may appear to be the product of irrationality.
- Failure to carefully think about criteria sets and the importance of the criteria relative to one another.
- Failure to observe how the various outcomes are operating as incentives and how outcomes possibly are being manipulated or misrepresented by those presenting them.
- Failure to understand discounting and the impact it has on decisions.
- Failure to understand the cumulative power of small increments. As Caplan (121) observes, "In economics terms, the private costs of an action can be negligible though the social cost is high," a form of social trap where each individual suffers little but the cumulative costs of many individual actions are high.
- Failure to understand how present decisions can lead to traps in the future.

An example of irrationality is voting for protectionist measures favoring a particular industry, i.e., a tariff. Many Americans who are not economists would agree with the desirability of tariffs, an *expression* of the "Buy American" ethos. But tariffs on basic commodities raise consumer prices over a wide range of goods and services, so overall national well-being is severely damaged. When I built a steel building on my farm in 2004, the price of steel had risen dramatically, partly due to strong demand by the Chinese and partly due to tariffs on steel instituted by the Bush administration in 2002 for political reasons. Multiply my experience by millions of steel purchasers in the United States and you have a large decline in national benefit measured against the benefit for a relatively small segment of the American economy. This is an unintended consequence of protectionist measures, though the consequence is predictable. Tariffs depend on irrational voting, in Caplan's terms. Notice that steel tariffs benefited a particular voting block (steel workers) while having an almost indiscernible effect on most members of the electorate, so the cost to an individual seemed low in comparison to protecting the steel industry from foreign competitors, even though the overall cost to society was high.

Suppose, however, you work in the steel industry and, because of lower labor costs or more efficient production methods, foreign suppliers are selling steel below what can be charged by domestic producers. Before congress is a bill to institute high tariffs on imported steel, thereby providing additional protection to your wage level or perhaps even your job. Do you favor the bill? I am certain you do favor it, illustrating the criterion of self-interest and apparent rationality. Yet, if tariffs are imposed on widely used products, the overall level of economic activity will be affected to the detriment of all, including steel workers. Evidence exists to indict the infamous Smoot-Hawley Tariff Act of 1930 for deepening and prolonging the Great Depression. Economists have long agreed on the damaging effects of economic protectionism and stand firmly against such misguided and irrational measures.

Or consider price controls: They result in shortages. Socialist Hugo Chavez, President of Venezuela, imposed price controls on coffee in 2003, destroying incentives for Venezuelan coffee producers. So the producers exported their coffee to Columbia where prices were higher, with a resulting coffee shortage in Venezuela, which now is forced to import coffee. Price controls are inefficient and distort markets—see rent controls in New York City as a prominent example.

Nearly all major issues of the day—any day—have economics at their core, and the average level of economic and financial literacy among the American people is abysmally low. Ignorance coupled with other criteria leads to irrational voting, and irrational voting leads to failures of democratic societies.

Prejudice (raw bias) as a criterion is easy to understand. President John F. Kennedy was viewed as suspect because of his Catholicism. Mitt Romney, a Mormon who sought the Republican nomination for president in 2008, was likewise denigrated for his religious faith, even though he appeared eminently qualified in other respects. Before Barack Obama was elected, enough racial prejudice had existed to immediately disqualify people of color from seeking the American presidency.

At its core, voting exemplifies multiple-criteria decision-making similar to a vehicle purchase decision. People make silly mistakes in buying homes or vehicles, and there is no reason to believe they are more rational in "purchasing" political issues and candidates. On the contrary, there is good reason to believe they behave even more irrationally in the voting booth. Caplan (2007, 140) states, "Shoppers have an incentive to be rational, voters do not." As before, he means an individual vote counts for little in the typical national or state election; therefore, one can behave irrationally in the voting booth with zero or a very small perceived personal cost because even large governmental initiatives appear to have little cost to the individual.

But ... the VSI appears. As mentioned before, the total of millions of irrational or simply ignorant votes sums to failed policies and societal problems that remain unsolved or worsen. And democracy falters, democracy fails, not in theory but in application.

People tend to be risk averse. Not entrepreneurs, not the risk-takers who invent, innovate, and build enterprises that employ people. But for ordinary folks, security plays a large role in their decision-making, including political decision-making. That troubles me, for I worry we will trade freedom for the security of a parental state, an irrational, hubristic, federal government promising cradle-to-grave care if the electorate will only vote for certain types of ideologues. I use the adjective "irrational" in the previous sentence to emphasize all attempts at such a utopia have failed throughout history. Rahe (2009, xi) offers a poignant observation about the end of the Cold War and what ensued: "...the old communists with a name change and face lift were soon returned to power by a newly liberated electorate nostalgic for a past offering in predictability what it had denied in the way of opportunity." A recent Pew poll would show agreement with Rahe among older citizens of those countries but not entirely with younger, better-educated people.

Now toss in doctrinaire-based efforts to "get out the vote," which traditionally involve chicanery of all types. Estimates of illiteracy in the United States vary, sometimes as high as 40 percent, and the standard is low in terms of what constitutes literacy, i.e., basic reading skills. Now add the number of voters who have limited or no comprehension of the English language and/or lack the education or intellectual ability needed to conceptually grasp the economics and future implications of complex issues. Finally, account for people leading busy lives with little time for serious study, even if they were so inclined, and stir that into the unholy stew called "election results." The end product: An absolute mess called democracy, at least from the voting angle.

Frederic Bastiat, the nineteenth-century French political economist stated, "The right to suffrage rests on the presumption of capacity." Alas, a large portion of the American electorate sorely lacks capacity and is constantly misled by those who feign understanding of the issues. Elitist? No, a fact, and I doubt if things are much better in other democracies. Fortunately, there are portions of the American electorate who intuitively grasp certain fundamental ideas, such as the importance of freedom and the virtue of not bequeathing to future generations the results of a selfish present one.

Politicians and Their Criteria

Politicians are easy targets: The approval rating of congress presently is 13 percent based on a recent Gallup poll, and carping about politicians has a history as long as people have elected representatives. Some politicians are honorable and dedicated to public service, many deserve the worst opprobrium that can be offered. Here, I briefly examine the politician's world using the framework in this book.

· Politicians have decision criteria. The dominant criterion, in virtually all cases, is "Electability." For those in safe districts where re-election is not a factor, the highest ranked criterion becomes "Maximize Personal Ideological Agenda," though such personal agendas usually and necessarily match closely the thinking of the home folks. "National Well-being" is somewhere in the criteria set and for an honorable, thoughtful few will be ranked ahead of personal agendas or even the electorates they represent, though the ranking usually is dependent on whom the politician is addressing and the issue at hand.

Study the politician's incentives to understand why alternatives maximizing electability are chosen. Having power certainly is an incentive. In spite of polls showing disapproval of congressional behavior, the prestige associated with higher office brings self-satisfaction and an unwarranted sense of privilege.[1] Salaries are more than decent at the federal level, especially in terms of opportunity cost, i.e., best alternative employment. Comfortable fringe benefits are another incentive, including premium quality health care and retirement plans more generous than those in the private sector for jobs with comparable salaries.

More important than salaries and fringe benefits, however, is the opportunity for what amounts to legal insider trading of the sort that would send a private-sector insider to prison. If you sit on a committee that makes decisions about an industry or a company, you have access to information the rest of us do not have. A call to a broker or personally handling a transaction regarding forthcoming (but not yet public) negative or positive impacts on company x or industry y results in a tidy profit, a very tidy profit. It is unconscionable, but it is legal. This is a powerful incentive, indeed powerful, satisfying the criterion of personal well-being, which can be viewed as a subset of the electability criterion. Arrive in Washington with modest means, depart a multi-millionaire while proclaiming the sacrifices you have made in the interest of public service. Life is good when it is impossible to lose.

Plus, sizeable and subservient staffs, the size depending on the rank and duties of the congressperson. Plus, prime, free parking space at local airports.

Add opportunities for travel to exotic or highly desirable locales under the guise of "fact finding" or "learning first-hand about the views and concerns of other countries regarding X," at taxpayer expense. The politicians often fly on military jets accompanied by military baggage handlers and military chauffeurs. Spouses and significant others accompany them. The hotels are first-rate, the dinners at fine restaurants are elaborate, hospitality rooms well-stocked, and generous time is allowed for sightseeing. When

---

[1] Constituents typically give much higher approval ratings to their own representatives than to congress as a whole.

I watch Air Force One or several lesser jets carrying politicians take off for dubious journeys, I am forced to concede, as my teeth grind and blood pressure mounts, that all the tax dollars I will pay in my lifetime will be consumed by one or two of those trips. I regard such behavior as decadent and childishly egocentric, along with being evidence of complete insensitivity to taxpayers struggling to earn a living—behavior that is the result of an unwarranted sense of privilege.

Also, lots and lots of time off bundled under various categories such as recesses and district work days. And there is the glitzy social life of some capitals, especially Washington, replete with black-tie dinners while unemployment soars.[2] Plus, a measure of respect derived from political power, accompanied by toadying on the part of both the electorate and those seeking favors. There are more incentives, the ego-gratification of handing out plum jobs to friends and supporters, for example. Too cynical? Okay, some aspire to public office for the idealistic reason of public service, work very hard, return unspent office funds to the Treasury, and are to be commended.

Prima facie evidence of the incentives present, particularly for those at the federal level, is the enormous effort and money put into campaigns and the constant worry about re-election once in office. Washington has a strong pull and few want to return to the farm or small-town law practice having experienced the delights of our nation's capital. It is interesting that 45 percent of our congressional people have a net worth of $1 million or more, which casts doubt on their ability to empathize with the average American, regardless of bathetic proclamations otherwise, e.g., "I feel your pain."

If electability is so highly ranked in the politician's criteria set, what does this say about policymaking? If it can be assumed that a large portion of voters are ignorant and/or irrational and the politician seeks office or a return to it, then there is a strong incentive to satisfy the electorate regardless of how misguided voters may be. As Blinder (1987, 196) observes, "The successful politician instinctively feels what the voters feel, regardless of what

---

[2] Instead of Washington, D.C. I will only "Washington."

facts and logic say. His guiding principle is neither efficiency nor equity but electability—about which he knows a great deal." Sensing voter opinion, by the way, is not the same as heartfelt empathy.

Thus, if you wonder why democracy fails, and fails more severely as America ages, you have a few answers. Almost the entire political strategy of acquiring votes for passage of a national health-care package involved two criteria: How will my vote play with the home folks and will my vote satisfy special interests, including the leaders of my party? Concerning the latter power brokers, committee chairmanships or largesse for the politician's home state act as incentives. Criteria sometimes come into serious conflict: The electorate strongly desires A, the Speaker of the House demands a vote for B and controls both incentives and disincentives.

Seldom is there concern for the rightness of the garbled, complex legislation in terms of the national weal—the jabber is almost entirely about re-election prospects and, more subtly, trying not to incur the displeasure of trial lawyers, unions, large corporations, and other favored constituencies. John Fund (2009) details how Democratic senators had great misgivings about the massive health-care bill they passed, knowing it would not do what they promised it would accomplish, and in fact would raise health-care costs and insurance premiums, but were intent on passing it solely to mollify their liberal-progressive constituents as well as their party leaders—a clear case of form dominating function. Fund quotes Democratic pollster Doug Schoen, "They believe the liberal base expects them to deliver and will punish them if they don't." Just why the liberal base so fervently approved of a health-care bill—any health-care bill regardless of its content—can only be answered as follows: Because it had something to do with increasing government intrusion into our lives and what is viewed as compassion. Rationality, knowledge, and national well-being are submerged relative to the dominant incentives before the politician. And democracy continues to stagger like a drunken fraternity boy after a hazing ritual.

Our study of discounting and traps earlier in the book emphasized why short-run thinking is so powerful. If the electorate thinks short-run, as do special interests, then the politician concerned about electability will submit to the lure of the short-run. As the wind changes direction or

The Blueprint

strengthens or abates, so politicians change the configuration of their sails and tactics, but mostly without guidance as to goal and direction, except as electability dictates—new alternatives are devised, outcomes are tweaked, announced positions on various issues are modified. And the long-term is heavily discounted, or ignored, which amount to the same thing when outcomes are considered. My poem that began with "See two looks away" befits this contention: Politicians, most of them, see one look away—the next election—and therein can be found one of the major sources of unintended consequences.

To the extent a correct course of action coincides with the politician's re-election criterion, good will be done, but that happy occurrence is a matter of coincidence, not of rationality. Thomas Hobbes speaking of representatives in general: ". . . and for the most part, if the public interest chance to cross the private, he prefers the private: For the passions of men are commonly more potent than their reason. From whence it follows that where the public and private interest are most closely united, there is the public most advanced."

The result is the various traps in which we find ourselves as a nation. If a politician lost 1 percent of her electorate's vote for each month nothing was done to repair the finances of Social Security, something would get done because there would be an incentive to do something, with the feedback loop between consequence and decision-making a short one. But there is no vomit pill (Chapter 8) available for such decisions, or so it seems.

Two segments of the population are most likely to vote, the better educated and the elderly. The latter wish no trifling with their Social Security checks and undoubtedly would like them increased, even though the Social Security program faces bankruptcy. Little electoral punishment occurs in the short-run for leaving Social Security alone; on the contrary, much damage to electability likely would be done by tackling the problem. In discounting terms, the electability cost of fixing the program is high in the short-run and the long-term costs of not doing so are assigned a heavy personal discount rate by politicians. The same is true of the huge expenditures inherent in Medicare and Medicaid. Similarly, those representing districts with a large number of

Hispanic voters—and, in fact, most politicians—flee from rational policies and legislation concerning illegal immigration.

Remark. As I write, there is much discussion in Washington about taking on the Social Security problem because of its contribution to a soaring national debt. The dire consequences of an unsustainable system have finally arrived; the future or near-future has become the present and the necessary incentives are in place, the vomit pill has been swallowed. However, electoral politics have engendered a two-actor game: Whoever goes first in reforming Social Security or Medicare will be bludgeoned by the opposing party as being insensitive to the needs of the elderly; the criterion of electability dominates. If both parties would put aside electability and concentrate on national well-being, simultaneously announcing an agreed-upon plan, reform could commence.

Now think about the national debt (or don't, if you want to have a buoyant day). In 2000, there was $5.6 trillion of federal debt outstanding. In October 2011, this had increased to $14.9 trillion, rising currently by $4 billion per day, and headed toward some higher trillions with new proposals forthcoming, probably about $20 trillion by 2020. Interest must be paid on this debt. To service the debt, taxes must be raised or existing government programs need to be slashed; consider the unpleasant electoral consequences of those alternatives if voter self-interest is important, which it is. Of course, more debt can be issued to help pay for the existing debt (adding to debt service costs), but supply and demand problems exist, since higher interest rates will be needed to attract new lenders from home and abroad. Higher interest rates drive up the price of business borrowing, consumer borrowing, and home mortgage loans, which affects economic growth, employment, consumption, and the housing industry.

Thus, a gigantic intergenerational trap forms: It will be left to younger people and future generations to pay off most of the debt incurred by present-day discounters in the legislative and executive branches of what passes for our democracy, helped along by voter discounting and demands on politicians.[3] Talk about the lure of the short-run! The intergenerational government debt is a trap like polluted oceans, declining fish stocks, denuded hillsides, and (yes) the costs of obesity where younger people will bear part of the medical costs for the all-around gluttony of their elders. Obese governments know they should go on stringent diets, but the pasta with cream sauce is just too tempting.

In the summer of 2009, unemployment was around 10 percent, and the 2010 elections already were flashing in politicians' minds. There was palpable desperation in Democratic ranks concerning the unemployment problem. Pseudo-rosy forecasts based on fudged or insufficient data, along with various "stimulus" and other giveaway programs were forthcoming in an effort to correct the problem or at least present the illusion that something was being done. The result? A higher federal debt level with all the ramifications mentioned above. The utter nonsense never ends and seems to worsen over time. Why? If you have absorbed the way of thinking I have outlined in the book, the answer should be clear.[4]

---

[3] As noted, the per capital share of U.S. federal debt is over $40,000 per person. If current trends continue under the Obama administration, it will be nearly $70,000 per U.S. citizen by 2016. Hello out there to all you young people and you who are yet unborn.

[4] Democrats presently are in the office, as I write, so perhaps I am coming down too hard on them. Republicans in the George W. Bush administration (2000-2008) were also spendthrifts.

PART II: MATTERS PERSONAL AND GENERAL

Chapter 12

VIEWS OF HUMANS

Over time, I have come to agree with the view of humans as expressed by the great political thinker, Edmund Burke: "We cannot change the Nature of things and of men—but must act upon them the best we can." The smart money understands human nature cannot be changed, but behavior can be changed. Along the same line, economist Thomas Sowell (1997, 12) provides an astute interpretation of Adam Smith in Smith's *Theory of Moral Sentiments*: "The moral limitations of man in general, and his egocentricity in particular, were neither lamented by Smith nor regarded as things to be changed. They were treated as inherent facts of life, the basic constraint in his vision. The fundamental moral and social challenge was to make the best of the possibilities which existed within the constraint, rather than dissipate energies in an attempt to change human nature—an attempt that Smith treated as both vain and pointless."

In the interest of that scarce commodity called transparency, my personal stance cooks down to Burke and the ideas in this book as they are applied to politics. Russell Kirk (1997, 230) captures it well by summarizing the philosophy of Burke: "On the model of Burke, a conservative statesman is one who combines a disposition to preserve coupled with the ability to reform." Focus on the words *preserve* and *reform*. Over thousands of years, through trial and error—by torturous trial and error, by calibration—humans have developed methods of government that work reasonably well when reasonably practiced, and those things should be preserved. *Reform* is different from *change*. Change discards those practices that have worked pretty well in place of an entirely new system, while reform seeks to improve them in *small increments*. Burke (quoted in Levin, 2009, 13) elaborates: "There is...a marked distinction between change and reformation. The former alters the substance of the objects themselves, and gets rid of all their essential good as well as all the accidental evil annexed to them."

And why small increments? Because errors can be corrected without huge dislocations to society; massive change is difficult to undo and frequently leads to doomsday kinds of traps. Burke emphasizes the classical liberal point of view, "a state without the means of some change is without the means of its conservation," but his use of "change" is modified by "some," meaning reform. Burke had witnessed the sickening, dreadful path of the French Revolution. So it seems the failure of prudence is the birth of profligacy.

The previous paragraph captures well the course I follow. And only one more piece of my personal outlook needs to be noted. Many so-called conservatives do not conserve in the old Latin sense of preservation, whether that conserving is in matters fiscal or in environmental concerns. Instead, these fractional conservatives focus on social issues of the sort that never will be completely resolved and should be treated as matters for continuing debate while the financial and natural systems of that sustain us, physically and aesthetically, must be tended to and preserved.

Beginning here, a little nomenclature will be useful. I define my terms as follows:

- *Classical liberals* have a strong commitment to personal freedom, a political system answerable to the people, free markets, and small government, particularly as the latter applies to government monopolies. The root of "liberal" is the French liber, meaning *free*.
- *Mid-20th century American liberals* believed education of the people would produce enlightenment and in an active central government harmo-

nizing the economy through various fiscal measures (Keynesian economics), along with a large array of social-welfare programs. These are *not* classical liberals, the word having been perverted in 20th century America.

- Contemporary *Statists* are the product of 20th century liberal evolution, have no illusions about mass enlightenment and simply want ever-increasing government control of almost everything, a cradle-to-grave set of policies designed to govern the masses, with themselves as the sole arbiters determining the wisdom and application of said policies. They prefer the term *progressive*, which I find disingenuous and misleading, unless you consider loss of freedom as progressive. Their ranks include high-level government officials of the leftist stripe, union leaders, political activists who advocate large and meddlesome governments, business people who know how to game the governmental systems and have the resources to do so, certain public intellectuals, and most academics. In short, Statists are those who have large, loud, and influential voices and who lead the charge for government control in all areas of life. I will use Statists with an upper-case "S" to refer to this segment of the political spectrum.
- I will use statists, with a lower-case "s" in reference to those members of the general electorate who support and vote for Statists.
- I will capitalize "State" when referring to the federal government or to governments in general.

A classical liberal of the nineteenth century variety sees humans along the following *continuums*: Happy to sad, productive to idle, joyfully creative to dull, intelligent to something less, achieving to sluggish, builders and innovators to the sedentary, good to evil.

Until I was about 30, I could have been classified as something approximating the early- to mid-20th century version of an American liberal. That is, I naively believed enough education for the masses coupled with Keynesian economics could produce an enlightened, prosperous society and all would be well. Statists see humans quite differently. True ideological Statists have a long history, believing with radical fervor in socialism, communism, fascism, or an entrenched social-welfare state as the path to utopia, a utopia as they define it.

For a long time, I struggled with why liberals and conservatives (*conservatives*, not necessarily members of the Republican Party), living in the same social and economic milieu, seemed so far apart in their ideologies. I fumbled around, eventually understanding it had something to do with how humans are viewed at their core, different takes on the essence of human nature. I was already starting to get a pretty clear sense of it when some years ago I came upon a book by Thomas Sowell (2007, originally published in 1987). Sowell, mentioned earlier, is a man of wisdom, a man who sees the world clearly and unhesitatingly shares his thoughts in a most direct way, providing instructive language and concepts when he wrote about "a conflict of visions."

A little parsing of said language is required here. When I use the word "vision," I am talking about a rather concrete view of the future and how that future might be attained. Sowell, on the other hand, is using the word vision as a synonym for "view," as in views of human nature. Keep those differences in mind for now, as I yield to Sowell's usage for a short time.

Sowell speaks of two disparate views of human nature: The constrained vision and the unconstrained vision. Like all dichotomies in the socio-economic world, there are muddy in-betweens that do not fit perfectly into either category. But as statistician George E. P. Box once said, "Essentially, all models are wrong, but some are useful." Sowell's is useful, with qualifications I will note below.

In line with Burke, the constrained vision takes humans as they are, as flawed and imperfect organisms, more or less unchangeable at their cores. The constrained vision is therefore a hard-nosed, no-nonsense view of humans, e.g., "there always will be poor people," with the problem being how to make the poor better off without trashing an entire socio-economic system. The unconstrained vision, at the other extreme, sees humans as perfectible, as malleable creatures that always can be improved, largely through higher forms of learning, sees them as capable of acquiring advanced wisdom and using such knowledge to create ideal societies, e.g., "No child left behind." Yet, and curiously, in spite of a purportedly genial outlook on humans, people of the unconstrained vision are the first to revert to government fiat as a way of solving problems, as the vision warped into Statism and statism.

In the interest of full disclosure, as I intimated above, I subscribe to the constrained vision. Until my early thirties, however, the unconstrained view gave me a nice place to hang my idealistic hat and flail about with comforting thoughts of nirvana out ahead and being on the side of God while moving in that direction, but years of experience and study caused a shift in my thinking. I suppose a subscription to the constrained vision places me around the politically conservative campfire, though I prefer to think of myself as a classical liberal, since "conservative" in many people's way of thinking would link me immediately to certain dogmatic minds I would rather not be linked to.

How does all this relate to incentives? As I judge it, the constrained vision would subscribe to the power of incentives in solving problems and doing the best we can, given the human raw material we have to work with, always recognizing the best is the enemy of the good. The pure, unconstrained vision, in Sowell's usage, would find the conscious use of incentives as odious—as something of an insult to the envisioned potential and (assumed) essential goodness of humans—preferring education as the path to human enlightenment and improved behavior. The world has been waiting a long time for the rise of general enlightenment and apparently will have to wait a good deal longer, while problems fester and grow worse.

And be careful; there is a difference between descriptive and normative treatments of problem situations in economics and other fields. Descriptive is just what it sounds like—objectively describing the elements and relationships of a problem. Normative usually means prescriptive, recommendations about how to fix a problem, and inevitably such prescriptions have the prescriber's personal values embedded in them or the values of a group the prescriber represents. Keep that up front when possible solutions to complex problems are forthcoming in this book and elsewhere. I suggest striving for an objective, hard-headed view of a problem, and only then bring forth your values at the solutions stage, if you must.

In the last 20 years, my overall view of modern liberalism-progressivism has shifted from Sowell's characterization of the 20th century liberal's unconstrained vision to something else, something approximating a truly repellent conclusion when it comes to those who operate under those monikers—Statism. Modern liberals-progressives cum Statists implicitly view humans (except for themselves) as puerile creatures for whom enlightenment is not possible. That is, the Statist vision is that humans are mostly out of control and must be harnessed, though all of this is hidden behind the masks of "compassion" and "fairness."

Therefore, the only approach is to treat humans as needing a devoted parent, that parent being the State—a large, custodial government in full flower, looking after the welfare of all, since none of us is deemed competent to fend for ourselves. In Chapter 9, I listed the Baumeister-Vohs requirements for thinking about and moving toward futures. The nanny state preferred by Statists (and statists) seeks to assume all such toil, providing a superficially comfortable life for those who evade thinking and responsibility.

Rossiter (2006, 29) ticks off but a few of the custodial functions commandeered by the government: Early infant care, preschool and public school education, sex education, employment regulations of all types, occupational safety, product quality and liability, money and banking regulation, food and drug regulation, health care, disability compensation, retirement security, and so forth. Great Britain with its long tradition of socialistic leanings even has established government policy to intrude into private homes to search for indications of inadequate protection against childhood accidents, including the installation of various safety devices, appropriate stair gates, restrictors that govern hot water temperature, oven guards, and acceptable door and window locks. I find the British policy indicative of a fearsome trend, with the U. S. not far behind the Brits.[1] The Brits recently proposed competence tests for dog ownership as a good thing, along with required microchip implantation in the animals and third-party insurance in case the dog misbehaves. The nanny State hovers in the friendliest of manners and behind the counterfeit smile dwells a sneer at the very idea of freedom.

---

[1] The state of Pennsylvania has banned the serving of homemade pies at events such as church suppers, deeming Mrs. Everyday Smith's blueberry pies a potential health hazard, since her kitchen was not a state-inspected facility. The California Energy Commission has proposed direct controls on home thermostats that could be adjusted by utilities as they choose. Massachusetts law demands that children in day-care centers for at least four hours and have been served a meal must have their teeth brushed.

Personal note. I once worked for a so-called progressive, a former federal bureaucrat who had been in charge of doling out welfare money to an underdeveloped area of America. He consistently referred to citizens of that region as "my people." I still cringe when I recall him saying those words in a lofty, paternalistic fashion. He was, I might add, the most dictatorial administrator I ever worked for, one who expressed humanity for people in general but not in the specific cases when he was brought into close juxtaposition with us, an example of Edna St. Vincent Millay's famous quote, "I love humanity but I hate people." Furthermore, he knew absolutely nothing about economics or mathematics or the sciences and regarded people such as me as "technicians" and not well-educated. And, lastly, he was totally disorganized, chaotic in fact, in his managerial function. I lasted one year in his "care."

At least the liberalism I embraced as a young man was hopeful in terms of human development, though quixotic it may have been. The Statist version views people as a mass of unfortunates to be managed by grand words and political performance while herding them into enclosures fit only for cattle when it comes to the human spirit. Perfectibility is passé, cradle-to-grave care and feeding is now the goal, based on the revised view of humans. In fairness, there are segments of the right-wing of American politics who share the view of humans as children or perhaps sheep requiring management from above, e.g., pastors who speak of "my flock." And, it must be admitted, when shoppers are observed trampling one another at shopping malls on the day after Thanksgiving, I sometimes wonder if those of a custodial bent are correct, after all. Then I remember the shoppers are there to buy a flat-screen television in honor of the Baby Jesus.

If not true compassion, then what motivates Statists, what are their incentives? That is clear: Power and the accoutrements of power, such as the social life of capitals, world travel, high and rapidly increasing salaries and benefits, appearances on television, loving audiences, a sense of control and superiority. It is a fine life for those who anoint themselves.

Chapter 13

POLITICAL ECONOMY

"The American people will never knowingly adopt socialism, but under the name of liberalism they will adopt every fragment of the socialist program until one day America will be a socialist nation without ever knowing how it happened."

-Norman Thomas

A market economy requires a tolerance for oscillation and uncertainty, coupled with rewards from skill, hard work, and intelligence. A Statist economy requires a tolerance for complete and utter failure.

-Present Author

Economic Organization

Here is a malicious little sport to play with your Statist/statist acquaintances, and the use of it will turn big-government advocates into melted pools of exposed ignorance. Oh, oh, you are a proponent of big government? Too bad; you need the tutorial here as much as your statist friends.

Ask: What are the essential economic problems all societies must confront? You will gaze on a befuddled countenance that speaks without talking, the silence indicating, "Never thought about it." They are:

- *What* should be produced?
- *What price* should be charged for the goods and services produced?
- *How* should the goods and services be produced, i.e., the technologies?
- *How much* of each good or service should be produced?
- *When* should the good or service be produced?
- *Where* should the goods and services be produced?
- *Who* should get the output and revenues from the output?

Each of these problems, in fact, is a *decision*. More, within each of the categories are a multitude of smaller decisions serving as subcomponents of the central decision problem. The number of decisions and their interrelatedness with decisions from other categories defeats central planning, utterly and invariably this is so. In confrontations between complexity and humans, complexity wins every time.

When I need a certain bolt and a nut to fit the bolt, I head for my local hardware store on the east edge of a nearby town. With a very high probability, the correct bolt and nut will be available in their respective bins or neatly packaged and hanging on a hook with the price attached. How did the pieces get there? If I lived in a true Statist economy, the probability of the exact nut and bolt being there would be infinitely close to zero.

Imagine a government Czar of Hardware Supplies, call him Inchargeikoff, with a spreadsheet before him and mumbling, "Let's see, comrade Boltsandnutsikoff who runs the Revered Dear Leader Hardware Emporium in rural Texas might need a supply of 2-inch bolts and nuts to fit them. That means I have to figure out a bunch of stuff before I dine tonight at the Czars-Only Restaurant: Where can they be produced, who should produce them, how will I specify they be produced right down to the metallic composition, how many should I order for all the comrades, when should I order them, what factory can I requisition them from, and what price should be charged to the comrades who want to buy them. And, sigh, screwdrivers or Allen wrenches of some kind probably will be needed, as well, causing me to make more decisions. And Boltsandnutsikoff said something in a recent letter to the Czar of Invention Control about a power screwdriver, but I think that's silly because all the murals of the worker comrades show they have strong arms. Furthermore, power supplies to most areas are limited since the Central Committee ordered rationing of coal because our coal-train locomotives need new bolts but the bolt factory is running behind because it presently is producing parts for Czar Cars."

So how do the bolts and nuts we need come to be at my local hardware store? Elementary: *Prices*. It should be writ large: *PRICES*. People think of prices solely in terms of dollars or rupees or yen, but beyond that, and fundamentally, prices are signaling devices; they are information transmitters. And this brings us to markets. Prices are set in markets by the interaction of buyers and sellers. Demand too low at a given price? Lower the price or stock less or stock none at all. Demand exceeding supply? Raise the price or order more stock. That is about as elementary as economics can be made, and it has been going on since Ugg traded two arrows and a bow to Zugg for a stone hatchet, with three crystals for Zugg's woman included in the bargain—the price of the stone hatchet was two arrows, a bow, and three crystals, all of which could be converted to a single price when money was invented. Ace Hardware has what I need because there is enough demand at a reasonable price to pay for the manufacture, shipping, store overhead, and cost of stocking the items, with sufficient revenue left over in the form of profit to provide the *incentive* to deal with the headaches of operating the store and as a reward to the owner for taking risks, not to mention the critical role of profit in supplying working capital for purchasing more stock or hiring additional employees.[1]

If the fatuous example just presented comes off as patronizing, I am not contrite, because the level of economic ignorance afoot is staggering and it is necessary to start at the bottom. People who propose ever more

---

[1] See Leonard Read's "I, Pencil" for a charming essay on free markets (Read 1958). Read traces the complex workings of Adam Smith's invisible hand in the production of a common lead pencil, a production operation a government bureaucrat could never accomplish.

government intervention simply do not understand the power of prices and markets as *information devices*. Statists are largely the product of social science and humanities programs, along with law schools, and the idea of markets does not enter their thinking. How does a government official decide on the price of any product produced or controlled by central authorities? How does a *Pay Czar* (Obama has one) decide on executive compensation? Why is it okay for a famous baseball player to earn $30 million per year while the Pay Czar sets arbitrary pay levels for business people, large and small (taxation on small businesses comes directly from the profit of the owner and therefore indirectly sets pay)?

Another magical aspect of markets is they work in spite of ignorance. I am largely ignorant about the internal workings of internal combustion engines but I make reasonably intelligent choices in my car buying. I have no idea of exactly how my cell phone works, but I can purchase one at a decent price and use it. All of the complex economic transactions involved in making a simple pencil are unknown to me, but I can write with one. I am ignorant of the person or machines who harvested the cotton for my shirt, the transportation that delivered workers to the cotton gin, the shipper that delivered the cotton to a mill, the machine that wove it, the entrepreneur who raised capital to provide the box it was shipped in, and those people are ignorant of me, but because of prices set by markets we came together to provide the shirt and to produce more of them. Thousands of airline workers I will never meet coordinated via prices to fly me from Texas to Rome on a recent journey. The toleration for ignorance is a beautiful aspect of markets that goes completely unappreciated by most. A central planner would be mired in the details of shirt-making and store shelves would have too many or too few shirts, while markets coordinate the process with aplomb. Outfits such as Overstock.com and Sierra Trading Post handle excess supply.

For a colorful and accurate description of private enterprise versus government in producing goods and services, see Patrick O'Brian's novel *The Letter of Marque* (1992). O'Brian describes how a nineteenth-century sea captain in the British navy, having been discharged under false pretenses, assumes the life of a privateer. Dealing subsequently with private merchants for his stores, he is amazed at the speed and efficiency with which his privately owned ship is refitted, manned, and prepared for sea. His previous experience had all been with the government supply yards where workers and their bureaucratic superiors worked slowly, where sailors were pressed into service against their wills, where supplies were problematical, and where corruption in the form of theft and bribery was rampant. It reminds me of tales from Soviet Russia when communism ruled. It reminds me of Medicaid.

But what if there is no identifiable demand by individuals or firms for a particular good or service, but that good or service is judged a good thing by society as a whole? I take that up next.

The Proper Functions of a Central Government

> *"I have never known much good done by those who affected to trade for the public good."*
>
> *- Adam Smith*

Let us inquire as to the proper functions of government. There are three.
- National security/defense against the encroachment of other nations.
- Internal security to protect citizens from one another, i.e., law enforcement and the courts (including contract law). I include the protection of private property rights here, though newly broad interpretations of the Fifth Amendment are weakening those protections as described below.
- Provision of only *the most necessary* public goods.[2] Governments operate by passing laws and laws are enforced by police power, making government the lone entity in American life possessing the legitimacy of force (other than self-defense). Paraphrasing Charles Murray (1997, 10), anything permitting a drastic intrusion on the life of a peaceful, self-supporting citizen, through the use of governmental police power, had better be an authentic public good. As Murray (84) incisively states, "...the government can back up its tastes and beliefs

---

[2] In this context, "good" is used in the sense of "goods and services," not in a normative sense meaning "positive."

with the police power. That is why it cannot be permitted tastes and beliefs. Most emphatically, it cannot be permitted to define one group of people as being privileged over another group of people. It was wrong in the days of Jim Crow laws; it's wrong in the days of affirmative action."

When it comes to the first two functions, disagreements arise concerning the wisdom of foreign intervention, size of the military, appropriate use of police power, and judicial renderings. Provision of public goods is where most of our day-to-day controversies involving economics appear, and the question of what constitutes or should constitute public goods strikes at the very center of freedom and its continuing disappearance. Various definitions—entire books, at times—attempt to deal with what are or are not legitimate public goods. I will keep it simple. Murray (1997, 11-17) treats the definition succinctly and well, and I am relying on his treatment here, though almost any thoughtful and objective source will follow a similar path.

1. A public good is a good or service that cannot be provided *selectively*. National defense is not only a central function of government, it also is a public good. No one citizen or group of citizens has exclusive rights to national defense. Therefore, non-exclusivity is one criterion for determining what qualifies as a public good.

2. The consumption of a public good by me does not diminish the availability of it to you or others. Examples: Breathing air, street lighting, feeling secure because of our national defense systems. This criterion breaks down at times, such as rush-hour traffic reducing the availability of speedy transit to everyone traveling public roads, a trap.

Those two criteria do a good job of generally defining what constitutes a public good. Murray adds five additional criteria, which operate as tests for refining the two basic criteria above. These are direct quotes.

A. Is the good something that cannot be provided by individuals on their own?

B. Am I asking my neighbor to pay for a government service that he doesn't want?

C. Am I asking my neighbor to pay for a government service that benefits me, or people whom I favor, more than it benefits him.

D. The public good in question must enjoy popular support, as determined through the democratic process. Just because something meets the technical criteria for a public good doesn't mean the government has to do it.

E. Private property shall not be taken for public use without just compensation. That one comes straight from the Fifth Amendment of the Bill of Rights.

Government abuse of E above has increased, as evidenced by the classic case of *Kelo v. the City New London* and similar takings for economic development purposes. It is worthwhile to read about the Kelo case if you are not familiar with it, for it stands as an incomprehensible and brutal application of government police power; not only the supreme court decision but also the aftermath of the taking will make you weep and mourn. Coincidentally, five days after the Kelo decision was announced on June 23, 2005, my novel *High Plains Tango* was published, the central theme of which is the combined force of government and business interests to confiscate via eminent domain a home lovingly built by a South Dakota carpenter.

I would add one more criterion to Murray's list: If you were asked to invest a substantial portion of your own money in Program X, would you do it? People are far more profligate with the wealth of others than with their own. When I taught in executive development programs and M.B.A. classes, I would present hypothetical problems to the students, designed to probe their risk tolerance. The results were always the same: Executives were willing to incur far more risk with the firm's money than with their own. For voters and politicians, the impact of large programs usually is distant from their personal checking accounts, or politicians buffer themselves and favored constituencies from the impact (for numerous examples, see the health care reform law of 2010 and waivers from its requirements).

Murray's handling of a complex subject is beautifully done in its clarity and simplicity. Nevertheless, public goods still comprise something of a set with fuzzy boundaries and reasonable disagreements can occur. But applying Murray's criteria and auxiliary tests provides a good place to start and rapidly whittles down the possibilities.

First, why the need for public goods at all? Markets are magical in many respects, but there is continuing prospect of *market failure*, about which economists have been writing for decades. Clean air always has been viewed as a *free good*. In the U. S., fresh water nearly so. Both pure air and fresh water tend to be overused because of a zero or low price. Markets have trouble providing for national defense since a price mechanism is absent; how much is a country's security worth? Who will make it and buy it? Each person or county cannot have missiles because there is no effective demand at that level and hence no supply and hence no market where prices can be set, along with the fact Floyd County, Iowa might be upset with Cerro Gordo County next door and decide to launch (let us not even think about neighborhood squabbles). It is painful to imagine ICBM silos sprinkled around individual counties and operated by private firms.

The same is true for interstate highways, though experiments with privately owned toll roads are ongoing and are promising. Street lighting is another example, as is maintenance of county roads (privatization is always a possibility), along with public school systems and law enforcement. These are public goods, though I expect the slow privatization of schooling over time, in spite of objections by the teachers unions. Is medical care a public good? Is child care a public good? Is housing a public good? The arts? Scientific research? How about power scooters/chairs for people who have trouble getting around (see Medicare)? Should taxpayers foot the bill for trap releases such as careless hikers stranded on mountains or abortions using federal tax dollars?

Should taxpayers in Minnesota be responsible for helping pay New Orleans' costs of Hurricane Katrina? If the creek 70 yards from where I am sitting flooded and caused damage to my house, would I, having no flood insurance, expect the government to declare my property a disaster area and pay for repair of the destruction, affording me other living quarters while the work is being done? When a wind gust blew away part of the roof on one of my outbuildings, no government official appeared to provide fix-it money. Why then New Orleans, when it was obvious to all that one day a hurricane such as Katrina would arrive and will arrive again in the future? Not only was government assistance expected in New Orleans, much criticism was directed at the timing and effectiveness of the help.

Should people in South Dakota help provide disaster relief to people who build along seacoasts or on unstable hillsides in California, knowing those who enjoy the sea and distant views are taking a risk in doing so? Try this one: As I write, a Florida court will pony up $150 per day for a makeup artist to cover the tattoos of a neo-Nazi, fearing the violent nature of the tattoos could bias a jury; now there's a public good worth hanging a sign on that reads, "Public Bad."

As always, small increments are at work. Almost daily another service or commodity is added to the list of public goods. The sum of these small increments mounts to billions and trillions of dollars, which must flow from somewhere. Similar to Ralphie's meal choices in Chapter 1, the thinking seems to be, "It won't cost much to add just one more item to the public-goods list; besides, such a small increment will hardly be noticeable and the cost to me is less than a penny per year." How about you? Do you feel compassion for a neo-Nazi who requires makeup to cover obscene body art? I do not.

Food stamps are a public good. Philosophy professors are a public good because it is doubtful the individual demand for philosophy professors is high enough to establish a market for them (I am not denigrating the teaching of philosophy). So are public-school athletic programs at all levels, except for the very few showing a net profit.[3] I once proposed a market solution to replace taxpayer subsidies for university athletic teams but it has not yet caught on, and, jiminy, I received substantial abuse for even raising the issue (Waller 1990). Should I be forced to pay, via property taxes, for a high school football team if I fail to see the long-term value of high school football, even if my neighbor enjoys such activities and attends all the games?

Allow me to partition the world into ten fuzzy and incomplete sets, incomplete in that the list could be a very long one if broken down into more exact

---

[3] Even those athletic programs claiming to make a profit usually are not paying all their costs, such as liability insurance provided by a state, building maintenance, parking lots, and so forth.

categories. My purpose in formulating this list is not to be exhaustive but rather to provide examples of where public assistance might be needed and justified, or not needed. As you read the list, apply Murray's criteria and ask the following questions of each category: "Worthy of public support?" and "Worthy of public support through governmental transfers of wealth?" Think about both general government revenues and your wealth when answering the latter question. Answering the questions with unfettered honesty will locate you on the continuum from classical liberal to statist.

- Children born into unstable homes and/or socially chaotic circumstances.
- Those who, through no fault of their own, are truly disadvantaged, e.g., the mentally and/or severely physically handicapped, including military veterans disabled in the service of their country. For reasons of genetics or unavoidable chance, they have been grasped by the talons of the world and it appears to be a matter of common decency to provide them with support and comfort.
- Those who have worked hard at low-paying jobs, making it difficult to save for retirement.
- Those who are "disadvantaged" because of their own behavior, but otherwise would be fully functioning, productive adults, e.g., the obese, drug addicts, profligate spenders, school dropouts, the slothful, criminals.
- Those engaging in foreseeable risk against which insurance can be purchased or can be underwritten in some fashion, e.g., hikers who may need rescue, people who build or purchase homes in potentially dangerous locations such as cliffside dwellings or low-lying areas subject to hurricane or flood damage, New Orleans residents and business people.
- Those who have advantages in mental and/or physical realms, including good families in many cases, and are successful, productive citizens.
- Business firms—non-human, but organized and operated by humans.
- Domesticated Animals. Yes, animals. The quality and compassion of a civilization can be measured by how it treats its animals (I am not certain whether this is someone else's idea or mine).
- The natural environment, needed to sustain life, the place where we live, work, play, and wonder. This includes wildlife.

- Foreign aid of all types, which includes several of the preceding categories.

Something to notice: We spend much of our societal time and resources on children, the truly disabled, the elderly, those who take uninsured risks, and the fourth category, those who find themselves in difficulty because of their own failings.[4] In fact, we continually are merging the latter two groups with those who truly are disadvantaged.

Now apply Murray's criteria and auxiliary tests to a few public goods. Start anywhere amidst the multitude of government goods and services. Say, food stamps, which fail immediately on Murray's first criterion. Food stamps seem to pass the second criterion if both you and I receive them, since your stamps do not deduct from my stamps. But stop here for a moment to examine how I think about public goods; you may find it helpful. Grocers accept food stamps because reimbursement will be forthcoming from the government. They will receive money when the stamps are redeemed. What is the ultimate source of this money? One way or another, it is private citizens and businesses that pay taxes or support government debt. Therefore, converting food stamps to the common denominator of dollars makes it clear that they *do not* pass the second criterion, since the use of your dollars or my dollars to finance the food stamp program diminishes the availability of dollars to us. Converting high-sounding government programs to money, especially your own money, clears away all the misty-eyed language typically attached to numerous public goods currently provided.

How about national defense? It easily passes all criteria. High school football fails miserably on all counts. Philosophy professors? Here it gets sticky, one of those boundary problems I mentioned. The good and kindly professors apparently pass the second criterion but things become less clear on the first, since you cannot have a right to the professors' teaching unless you attend college. The professors do not pass sub-criterion "A" since one can visit a library or purchase books and do independent reading, which many have done to their credit. The teaching of philosophy fails completely

---

[4] Take note of how often "the children" are cynically used as a straw man for questionable government enterprises.

on sub-criteria "B" and "C". In terms of market demand, compare philosophy professors to, say, engineering or accounting professors.

Hikers stranded on mountainsides are an easy call: They fail. Make those who take risks post a bond or buy insurance before setting out and convert the public good to a private good, guaranteeing that those who take risks pay for taking chances that result in taxpayer-funded rescues. Spending thousands of dollars in search-party costs and helicopter flights is an externality created by the hikers. If the hikers have a good time and do not require assistance, they do not compensate the taxpayers who did not participate in the psychological revenues of the hikers.

Alternatively, simply announce in the clearest possible language that no rescue attempts will be allowed, period, and hold to the pledge. This will have two effects. First, people will be more careful. Two, fewer people will even attempt hiking in risky conditions. Thus, in traps language, we are demanding escapes rather than releases, along with trap avoidance. My solution to risk-taking hikers is the classical liberal point of view. Proponents of the nanny State, never considering costs and benefits, and ignoring scarcity, would proclaim, "Every life is precious, no matter the cost." The differences are stark. Nobody rescues the owner of your local cafe when it fails, so why hikers? Similarly, a new cancer drug called Provenge extends the life of those with prostate cancer for four months, on average—at a cost of $93,000 per year, should Medicare and any supplemental insurance (i.e., taxpayers and the premium-paying public at large) pay for the drug?

Try this one. Spending billions of dollars, the United States provides nearly one-half of the world's foreign aid for HIV antiretroviral drugs, which allow people with the disease to lead normal lives. Currently, 4 million people are receiving the drugs, but under World Health Organization guidelines, 14 million are eligible to receive treatment, with the number growing by 2.7 million per year. It has been hypothesized, quite plausibly, that the availability of the drugs lessens the fear of contracting the disease and encourages unsafe sexual behavior (an incentive). Should the United States continue the funding? Think about the question using Murray's criteria and the 10 categories listed above. Include HIV patients in the United States after thinking about foreign aid. HIV is a trap that is mostly preventable, except for fetuses and babies snared in the misbehavior of adults (a social trap). Then contemplate what incentives and disincentives the United States has in making decisions about such foreign and domestic aid—obtaining votes from various groups to satisfy the electability criterion and providing a veneer of compassion.

Think for a moment about time preferences, discount rates, and social safety nets of all kinds. Clearly, the presence of guaranteed or implied bailouts affects the discounting of possible outcomes (contracting HIV and antiretroviral drugs, failing financial institutions), therefore affecting incentives, and therefore affecting decisions. Bailout protection and the availability of releases increase the discount rate for potential future costs and thereby extinguish careful evaluation of all costs and revenues in decisions. Moral hazards disappear, just as they do for hikers, just as they did for Fannie Mae and Freddie Mac and their prominent roles in exacerbating the 2007-2011 housing crash, just as they did for General Motors, just as they did for certain large banks.

Consider entitlement programs. Examples: Medicare, Medicaid, Social Security, school lunches, Head-Start, low-income energy assistance, maternal and child care, Job Corps, summer youth employment, foster care, Indian Health Care, and a long, long list of other such programs. Entitlements consume about two-thirds of the federal budget, with the remainder composed of defense and other discretionary spending.

Entitlements have the following characteristics, based on Murray's criteria: They are selective and the use of them diminishes the welfare of nonrecipients; therefore, they fail both of Murray's two criteria. That does not mean all of them should be eliminated if honest compassion is introduced, but all projections show that the growth of entitlements at present rates eventually will consume the entire federal budget. Once an entitlement is put in place, the incentives for politicians to eliminate it are all negative. Scarcity, understand, is like the "Whack-a-Mole" carnival game: When scarcity raises its head, it is ignored by whacking it back down as too constraining and unpleasant to think about. But scarcity is implacable and cannot be interred forever, continuously popping back up.

Lastly, here is a conspicuous example of entitlements and incentives. Texas has a "Robin Hood" law whereby communities with high property values, and hence substantial property tax income, must share school financing with poorer communities. A bustling, industrious community is therefore penalized for its achievements while less wealthy school districts receive a redistribution of income and have no incentive to improve. More bluntly, there is an incentive for the recipient community not to spend money on improvements because it might lose the nice transfers from its better-off neighbor, enabling it to keep its property taxes low. Indeed, the label of Robin Hood is appropriate. After all, Robin Hood, for all his alleged romantic daring, was a socialist.

I leave you to apply the criteria to any public good you can think of. When you do, the result will be very small governments carrying out only the basic functions for which governments were intended. A final note here: Does this mean I think food stamps should be discontinued or university philosophy departments phased out? No, but stringent limits must be set on who benefits from them and exactly how they benefit and how long the benefits last. This should be the case for all public goods that lie uneasily on the fuzzy boundaries, such as unemployment benefits providing disincentives to seek work. Personally, I strongly favor the care and treatment of animals as well as the preservation of wild spaces, but those need to undergo the same scrutiny as other categories. Question: Should terminally ill people without any hope of recovery be kept on expensive life support? My physician's directives and powers of attorney clearly specify that I should not.

Remark. Beware of those who want to add the following to the public goods criteria list and to rank it higher than all others: "Benefits society as a whole." Almost any government program can be construed to pass under that standard, and that is exactly the criterion that has been used for decades by those who favor government control of nearly everything. Murray once again (102), "To think it is right to use force to override another person's preference 'for his own good' is the essence of the totalitarian personality. If you have the right to do that to someone else, then someone else has the right to do it to you. That way lies the rationalization for every conceivable kind of coercion." See the insurance requirements of the 2010 health-reform law for examples.

Thus, markets work much of the time but not always. Markets involve people making their own decisions to sell or buy, without coercion and ordinarily under more or less competitive conditions where an array of variations on a good or service are presented. Governments inherently are monopolists with all the abuses ascribed to monopoly power plus some powers a private monopolist does not enjoy, the use of force being the most prominent—government robber barons wearing T-shirts inscribed "For Your Own Good."

And, so very critical, all government intervention into markets reduces freedom, one way or another, including the freedom to spend your money as you choose. Market systems embody free exchange between individuals, including businesses, where each party believes benefit is to be had by the exchange. With governments, the exchange is not free, legally or monetarily. The IRS says PAY!, and you pay or face severe consequences, and if you resist, the IRS will use your own tax dollars to fight you. Because of all I have discussed before, you have little discretion over how your money is spent, so any personal benefits are either dispersed beyond recognition or may support policies you detest (e.g., government funding of abortions).

Government monopoly power is similar to the power exerted a hundred years ago by monopolists who controlled company towns or factories. The owners hired thugs to prevent the unionization of workers. Likewise, citizens always face the coercive power of the State. As things turn and go, unions now partner with governments to impose monopoly power on the rest of us (see the activities of the Service Employees International Union).

Because markets are imperfect or may not exist at all in some cases, *none of us pay the true cost of our existence, including business firms*. Think of clean air. Each of us contributes a small amount of pollution to the atmosphere when we drive. But a charge does not appear against our checking account or on a Visa statement. Earlier in the book such costs were called externalities. Likewise, a coal-fired generator plant is not required (as yet) to show a pollution expense deducted from revenues in the process of calculating profit. Cases of market failure due to externalities do allow a role for government, though it seldom is played with a light hand when controls on externalities are imposed through excessive regulation.

In general, I have no problem with taxes on polluters, though Republicans rail against such levies, contending the taxes will be passed on to consumers in the form of higher prices. They are correct. We final consumers of, for example, electricity or automobiles would then paying part of the true cost of our existences, assuming clean air is valued. If the taxes raise prices, less damage to our air will be forthcoming, substitutes for current activities will be used, and markets will adjust. As with all of economics, it comes down to tradeoffs, to scarcity.

Where I *do* have a problem with such taxes is this: What happens to the taxes paid? If they are used for political favors or simply the expansion of government, I dig in my heels. When money flows to governments, it seems to disappear in congressional expense accounts or subsidies for blocks of voters who are supportive of whomever is handing out the money via that maw called the U. S. Treasury. Regulations cause all sorts of problems and interfere with the orderly operations of markets. So in the case of externalities I instead favor incentives such as taxes, as long as those taxes are used to reduce government deficits or to pay down the national debt or are allocated with close scrutiny to helping fix the problem for which they were levied in the first place, e.g., research into making nuclear power plants as safe as possible, or rigorous and unbiased studies to determine if global warming (if it exists) is caused by humans. Consumption-based taxes give us the freedom to make choices.

I temper my enthusiasm for free markets with the recognition that some regulation is necessary. Markets themselves are amoral, but people are not, and immoderate human desire for wealth or status or power can result in damage to others, creating externalities that must be held in check by regulation, but regulation that operates with a light hand and stops short of throttling economic efficiency. Furthermore, complexity and human inventiveness always outrun control systems, so small changes continually must be made as long as the changes are not cumulative small increments that multiply to choking constraints.

Am I my brother's keeper? Yes, but to a limited extent and according to strict criteria, e.g., children incontestably in need and truly disadvantaged adults. There also is the segment of people who have worked hard and honestly all their lives but whose incomes were never high enough to permit saving for even a subsistence-level retirement; they have faced what I call an "imposed high-discount rate" where all of their current incomes must be spent on barely getting by. The central problem now, however, is we have an increasing number of would-be brothers who want to be kept and who rely on a relatively few keepers supplying government with the keeping resources. Morality has its limitations when "fairness" is thrust constantly forward as a rationale for the "keeping." And, as we know, each new government initiative seems to require a new government bureaucracy, where salaries, fringe benefits, and operating expenses absorb part of the resources destined for those genuinely in need of assistance.

Remark. Discuss this while drinking coffee with a friend. Virtually all government policies impact the future. If the frontal lobe of the brain does not fully develop until age 25 or thereabouts, and the frontal lobe deals with the "executive" cognitive functions such as decision-making, planning, and goal-seeking, why do we allow those younger than 25 to vote? Should we rephrase an old 1960s screech to read "Never trust anyone under 25!"? I am not suggesting we bar young folks from voting, since it will never happen, but it does drive home the notion of how the future is discounted.

Something else to consider: If you are in the 50 percent of Americans who pay little or no federal income taxes and you would receive increased government benefits resulting from higher taxes on those who do pay taxes, should you be allowed to vote on any matter that raises my taxes? I am doubtful you should. Why? You are not a *stakeholder* on the input (revenue) side of the distribution system, even though you are on the receiving end of the wealth transfer. You are not allowed to enter my home illegally and steal money or goods, to commit theft, so why should you be allowed to vote on policies that will take my money and give it to you? Put another way, by not paying federal income taxes, you have not "purchased" the protection offered by the State, although you have basic claims arising from your payment of other taxes such as for gasoline or payments into the Social Security system.

Freedom and the State

> *"Life limits options. Governments limit freedom."*
>
> *- Charles Murray (1997, 30)*

Discussing views of humans in Chapter 12, I concluded that modern liberal-progressives, called Statists, believe humans cannot manage themselves and need custodial care from cradle to grave,[5] partly to protect them from becoming "victims" of shadowy, inexplicit, and pernicious social forces under the rubric of "culture" or "society," partly to protect individuals from harming themselves or to provide succor when they do. My position, as should be clear at this point, is that if freedom is to be preserved, people must be held responsible for their own lives, the truly disadvantaged excluded.

Refer to the Brandeis quote at the beginning of Chapter 11 and notice the phrase "well-meaning." That has become an obbligato, a frequent conciliation found in critiques of the Statist mind—well-meaning people who simply are misguided. If the phrase were "well-meaning, but ignorant" I would have an easier time accepting the qualification. In general, however, I am more skeptical and attribute Statist behavior to a combination of well-meaning (though ignorant) behavior and self-interest. Both Statists and statists have substantial self-interest mixed in with what they see as a compassionate society. To a large extent, the mixture is such that self-interest dominates all other criteria. Though the usual conciliation is present ("no doubt sincerely"), Milton and Rose Friedman (1979, 97-98) capture it well: "Believers in aristocracy and socialism share a faith in centralized rule, in rule by command rather than by voluntary cooperation. They differ in who should rule: Whether an elite determined by birth or experts supposedly chosen on merit. Both proclaim, no doubt sincerely, that they wish to promote the well-being of the "general public," that they know what is in the "public interest" and how to obtain it better than the ordinary person. Both, therefore, profess a paternalistic philosophy."

---

[5] Again, certain elements of the right want to manage what people read, watch, and do.

See Figure 13.1. If you are a government employee, a larger state augurs well for a more secure and better paying job. Therefore, the more people who work for governments, the more votes there are from this group for increases in both the size and funding of governments. The average salary of a federal worker is twice the average salary of a private-sector worker, and the federal employee receives four times the amount of benefits.

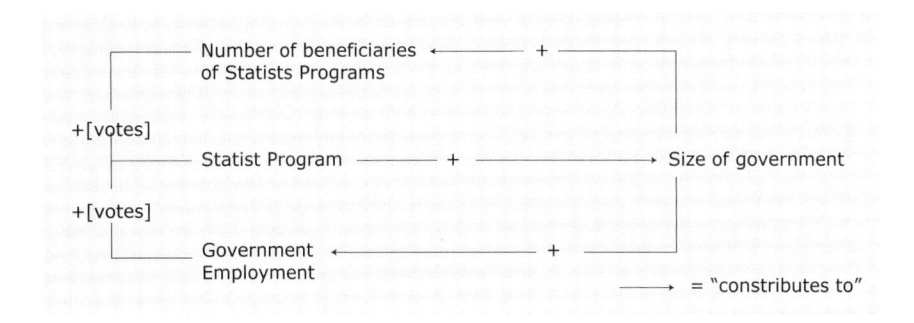

```
                    Number of beneficiaries  ←——— +  ———
                    of Statists Programs
   +[votes]
                    Statist Program  ———— + ————→ Size of government
   +[votes]
                    Government  ←——————— + ———
                    Employment
                                                 ——→ = "constributes to"
```

Figure 13.1 The Growth of the State

Question: Should those who work for governments be allowed to vote on any issues involving tax increases or reduction of government expenditures? For statists, the larger the government the greater is the likelihood of largess in the form of government-ordained transfers from others, and therefore it is propitious to vote for a larger state.[6] This is the self-interest criterion in naked form.

The goal of Statists is to condition people to always look toward government as a place of succor, security, and solutions to problems. Levin (2009, 111) argues, "It is the Statist's purpose to make as many individuals as possible dependent on the government" and that (171), "The poor and uneducated enhance the Statist's electoral and welfare-state constituency." In other words, gather the lumpen proletariat and prom-

---

[6] According to recent data, 383,000 federal workers have six-figure salaries, with 22,000 having salaries above $170,000. Average annual fringe benefits for federal workers are $41,000. Much of the growth in federal salaries has occurred during the worst recession in decades. Source: USA Today, December 11, 2009, page 1A.

ise them stuff in exchange for votes. According to the Tax Foundation (Hodge 2009), and this is astounding, 60 percent of Americans receive more from government than they pay in taxes. When self-interest dominates so thoroughly, thinking about constraints on choice and the loss of freedom wane in comparison.

For political activists, including non-profits and foundations, larger governments provide the opportunity for more funds and organizational expansion. For academics employed by state institutions, the more government revenue the higher is the probability of increases in salary and fringe benefits, providing a solid platform from which to proselytize for even larger government. And large academic research institutions, both public and private, benefit greatly from government grants. Students benefit from lower tuition costs.

If you manufacture wind turbines, you are in favor of ever more extensive alternative energy programs subsidized by governments; you "market the government" directly for goods and services and indirectly for subsidized sales of generators to private parties. If you are a farmer, you learn to "farm the government," reaping gains from the many and ever changing farming and ranching programs, of which there currently are 198 consuming $991 for each American household. Some of the agricultural programs were established during the Great Depression and, characteristic of government programs, have a half-life equivalent to infinity. Real estate agents approve of government rebates to home buyers, most car dealers like cash for clunkers programs. If you are in the housing industry, you benefit from the huge taxpayer subsidies provided to the Federal National Mortgage Association (Fannie Mae) and the Federal Home Loan Mortgage Corporation (Freddie Mac), subsidies that distort the housing market and contribute to dubious lending practices. As the State increases in size, the more money there is to be had, and the greater are the incentives for business people to engage in and support the growth of the State.

Jonah Goldberg (2009) writes, ". . . businessmen are opportunistic and their money follows political power." Not surprising, then, that General Electric favors government-subsidized wind energy programs, since the firm produces wind turbines and supports any political party favoring such efforts. Particularly as governments have grown to Leviathan proportions, business has turned toward Statism every bit as much as activist organizations such as ACORN that have functioned as professional mourners. The media, as well, seems to have followed suit, though the motivations in that realm are more ideologically driven and cloudy in origin, possibly a result of university educations.

The upshot is that government becomes larger and more intrusive because it becomes larger and more intrusive. In 2009 while the U. S. unemployment rate exceeded 10 percent, the federal government added 25,000 new jobs, meaning more voters for larger government, meaning . . . well, you get the point. Plainly, a positive feedback cycles are at work (see Figure 13.1 and the discussion of feedback cycles in Chapter 6), having a toxic lethality when it comes to freedom. As with public goods, it often happens in small increments, hardly noticeable: A law here, a regulation there, a new staff person, an additional one-cent tax on gasoline, a 5 percent surtax on high-income earners, a new program or continuation of an old one buried in some inordinately complex funding bill. From Chapter 5, once again Whitehead's observation about the essence of tragedy is pertinent: "The essence of (tragedy) . . . resides in the solemnity of the remorseless working of things." I see liberty as a commons that can be despoiled in small increments, just as Garrett Hardin's commons suffered ruination (Chapter 5). Thus, the source of my disquietude, as democracy and freedom drift away, replaced by a trap in the form of a hovering and obdurate state.[7] Of course, the Statists do not sense any loss of freedom because they are the ones determining what the rest of us must endure and have their own privileged ways of circumventing their policies, such as politicians sending their children to elite private schools in Washington while denying black parents funding for charter schools.

Tax dollars also have a direct correspondence to the grass in Hardin's commons. Once the money flows into federal and state government

---

[7] If you doubt the implacability of the State, you have never had to confront it head-on. I have. The State uses your tax dollars to fight the very complaint you have against that State and serves up a faceless creature called "the government" to confront you. The State is never wrong or if it is, pretends it is not. The State admits to no wrongdoing even when it is wrong.

treasuries, nobody seems to own it. Elected representatives spend freely because it brings them votes and private pleasures (the revenue from extra cows in Hardin's terms) because nobody "owns" the tax dollars. See the discussion in Chapter 11 on congressional perks. Speaker of the House Nancy Pelosi spent $101,000 on food and liquor in two years while flying here and there on Air Force jets, part of the $2.1 million travel costs spent on the trips (Unruh 2010). Moreover, politicians attempt to expand the commons—the pasture—by issuing debt or raising taxes.

Question. Congress loves show-trial hearings where members of the business community or athletic community or whomever are paraded before television cameras and grilled about their behavior. Why don't we have the same type of hearings—serious ones, this time, run by knowledgeable private citizens—where members of congress are subpoenaed and put under oath, required thenceforth to testify and justify their various activities?

If a small proportion of federal income taxpayers are subsidizing everyone else, which they do, and you pay little or no taxes, a vote for higher taxes will have minimal or zero effect on you. Thus, why not vote for higher taxes? There is no reason not to and plenty of reasons to do so. And your vote will bring smiles of parental approval from the mandarins of policy and manipulation, the tutelaries of your fate who will escort you toward a false utopia. You may even be invited to spend a token night in the Lincoln bedroom at the White House.

Figure 13.2 summarizes the basic problem, where the dashed lines indicate the wealth transfer is indirect via government. Let A represent an individual or group of individuals, a business firm or industry desirous of government subvention, a foundation or non-governmental organization looking for research funds, or some mixture of all these. Now add to that the intrinsic government demand for funding that stems from government employees in search of higher salaries and benefits, pressures from public-sector unions on behalf of the employees, and the straight-ahead demand by advocates of big government for ever-increasing government size, the latter due to ideology and personal incentives. To fund A, B is taxed. Government siphons off its cut and passes the residual on to A. Thus, B's income and wealth is redistributed to both government and A.

Even if there is no demand from A (unlikely), there will be enough ideologically based demand to cause some redistribution. Even if debt financing is used, the debt must be serviced and B will be called upon to supply that funding. Thus, demand and supply, with B as the supplier but only due to coercion by the one entity in all this with police power: Government. Unlike private markets, supply emanates from the threat of force or the use of it, not free choice.[8]

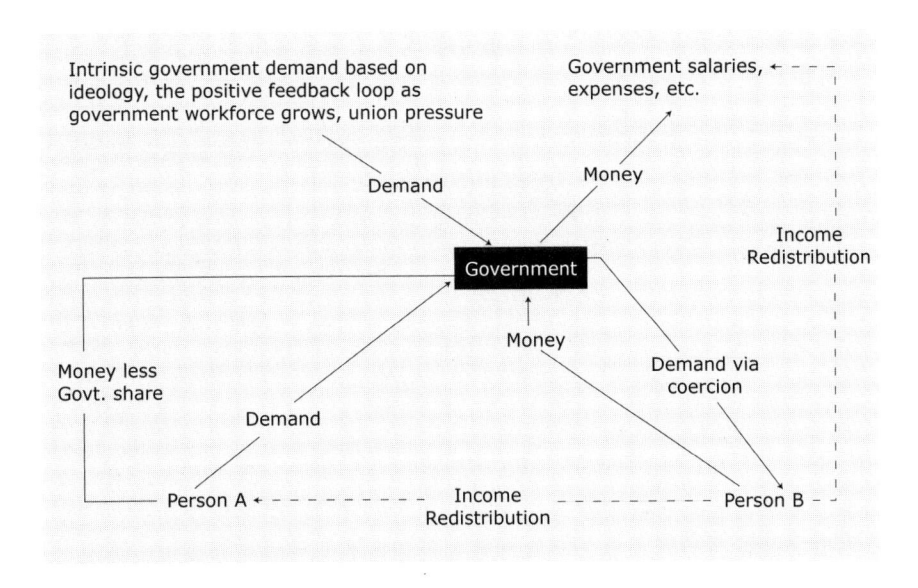

Figure 13.2 Demand and Supply via Government Coercion

Let us all then scramble from the curbsides as goodies are thrown from Statist floats moving by in an endless parade of benefits paid for by others. One float displays a banner called "Cash for Clunkers." And here comes the "Farm Subsidies" float and the "Energy Subsidies" float is rumbling along just behind it with a smaller banner underneath reading "Ethanol Subsidies." The tractor-trailer truck with a "New Rules and Regulations" sign flapping in the wind is not so much fun but, what the heck, you got $4,000 off your car purchase from the clunkers giveaway, as well as a rent subsidy or an $8,000

---

[8] I am indebted to Rothbard (2006) for the idea of demand and supply as used in this context.

government kickback from purchasing a home. The Buy Your Vote Parade stretches far back, further than you know, but there is no "Freedom" entry because that has been deemed obsolete, a quaint idea from the past that is no longer relevant; it would require a 1920 Model-T Ford draped with wet crepe paper to characterize that anachronism. So most everyone is happy and most receive prizes courtesy of the real stakeholders, those who pay the bills now and those doomed to pay future bills. It is enough to make a reasonable person writhe in agonized disbelief.

Freedom is an abstraction for most people, and those who try to place it in a dominant position in our national criteria sets are but faint and distant voices in a heavily discounted future. They are shouted down by an ever-growing chorus: "We are not talking about freedom here—sure, we want freedom, we absolutely demand freedom—but we are talking about subsidies to get us through the next year and to help us overcome the harmful decisions we have made! We'll worry about freedom later on." (See the Gibbon quote at the beginning of Chapter 11.) And Keynes was more right than he knew when he said, "In the long run, we are all dead," though he meant it in a different context.

Young people and those yet unborn will shake their heads in wonder and disgust at the labyrinth of regulations they must navigate while reading disingenuous history books claiming freedom was always an illusion marketed by the wealthy. And they will bend and chafe under the weight of the financial burdens thrust forward by their ignorant and foolish ancestors as the intergenerational traps weigh full upon them. Since fairness is a constant mantra of progressives, is their support of large, current government expenditures that will beggar future generations "fair?" I could modify my earlier poem as follows:

See two looks away
and listen.
That is the wail of your children
down the bloodlines
and you thought . . .
. . . it was only the wind.

Remark. If debt and a staggering economy are passed to future generations in the name of present-day rights, then what about the rights of those yet to come? Ignoring those future rights leads me to one conclusion: Self-interest dominates, base electability rules, and arguments justifying a huge welfare state on the basis of present-day rights are not only morally wrong, but downright tawdry. Compassion and justice are the reasons offered, but behind that rhetorical curtain lurk reasons far less benevolent.

Even if we assume purity of heart and mind as characteristic of Statists and statists, well-meaning and with the best of intentions, complexity defeats central planners. Statist promises to "eradicate hunger," "eliminate poverty," and conduct a "war on drugs" probably make the speakers and some listeners feel better about themselves, but the difficulty of gritty and grinding details in strategy or on-the-ground tactics are horrendous, impossible for central planners to execute, while markets do it effortlessly—remember Comrade Inchargeikoff? And why is there so much fraud in the Medicare program? Because it is too complex, making it impossible to administer.

In my consulting work, I confronted many similar problems at the corporate or national level, and "grinding" is the proper word. In my managerial life as a university dean, grinding change was the rule in establishing new programs, updating old ones, or doing away completely with outdated ones. It is far more satisfying to speak of "change" in general terms with a jejune, doting audience wildly applauding at a campaign rally. In the face of difficult problems, hubris is our enemy, humility our prudent and helpful friend. Not humility in the sense of head-bowed, foot-shuffling pietism but rather a deep respect for the challenges of complex problems when dealing with those problems. And Statists are anything but humble and prudent. The adjective "comprehensive" applied to government proposals makes me shudder, for complexity will always outwit the planners' desire for comprehensiveness that is workable. When I hear the word comprehensive from governments, my first instinct is to secure my pocketbook and curl into the fetal position with my freedoms clutched to my chest.

True conservatives or classical liberals who speak of freedom have little chance against the immediate blessings held in the outstretched hands of those who control government funding, siphoning off their own bureaucratic cut while dispersing the remainder to those who demand ever more. It is called decision-making, incentives, criteria, discounting, the lure of the short-run, and traps.

William McGurn nicely summarizes what I have said thus far: "Of course, the kind of people who are apt to push for government-imposed solutions are those who also are apt to believe they will be the ones imposing decisions, not the ones who have to live with decisions imposed by others. Sometimes that's because they enjoy the wealth that gives them escape hatches unavailable to the less affluent, such as their ability to ensure that their own children never have to set foot in a public school. Mostly, however, their trust in government reflects their confidence that they have all the answers and that it's government's job to enforce them."

Cycles and Implosions

The sources of funding for generous governments that create no wealth and have no earned income or profits are two: Taxes on those who *do* earn income (businesses and individuals) and government debt. Oh, yes, the Federal Reserve System can, speaking loosely, print money simply by making entries in their accounts and using those funds to purchase assets such as bonds or mortgages from other institutions, along with other transactions such as loosening reserve requirements for banks. If these funds are then loaned to business and consumers, more money enters the economy. Since there are limits to what I can discuss here without writing an entire economics book, I will focus on taxes and debt.

So how about taxes? Got a problem with funding national health care or any other government enterprise? Tax something or somebody.[9] But what or whom? The first thought, always: How about incomes of "the rich," that apparently undeserving group of people earning money by (mostly) productive effort? How about oil companies and private health insurers; they surely must be gouging the public somehow, aren't they? Doctors—we will lower doctors' Medicare and Medicaid fees because everyone knows they make

---

[9] Insatiable governments often tax items under the guise of health when it is nothing more than a way to raise more tax revenues, e.g., taxes on soft drinks and liquor.

too much money (lowering fees by government fiat is a form of tax). Ronald Reagan spoke truth when he said, with dark humor, "Government's view of the economy could be summed up in a few short phrases: If it moves, tax it. If it keeps moving, regulate it. And if it stops moving, subsidize it." Comes then Hillary Clinton, providing a short, paternalistic tutorial on fundraising to the government of Pakistan while lifting a bit of Reagan's outlook, "We (in the United States) tax everything that moves and doesn't move." Spoken like a true Statist, except Secretary of State Hillary Clinton was not being funny.

"The rich" are constantly redefined depending on how much money the government wants to raise. In addition, there is the implied, dimwitted view that the affluent have their money in a box under the bed, just waiting to be distributed to others.

Remark. Those in favor of high taxes on the so-call rich seem not to understand the difference between income and wealth as measured by net worth (assets minus liabilities). You can have an income of, say, $250,000 per year without having a high net worth, but progressives will place you into the "rich" category based solely on your income. The reason, I think, is that defining the rich in terms of income rather than net worth is that it captures many more people in the tax net.

Taxing the rich involves, one way or another, a real indirect tax on those who make the things the affluent buy or those whose jobs depend on investments. Thus, transfers of wealth to the less-well-off changes consumption patterns in an economy and results in job layoffs in certain industries. While publicly worrying about national levels of unemployment, politicians cast a wide tax net that captures small business people whose profits are reported as ordinary income. These businesses employ people, many people, though that basic fact seems to escape all those shouting, "Tax the rich!"[10]

---

[10] A Stanford University Poll taken in the autumn of 2009 showed 57 percent favored taxing higher-income Americans to pay for a health-care overhaul, with 36 percent opposed. Why not pilfer more from the box under the bed? Self-interest prevailed in the poll, for most objected to any increase in their own taxes or their own health expenditures.

How about the abundance of licenses and permits required to start a business? Along with basic health and safety requirements, the primary aim of such hurdles is to provide a record for tax collection (and to insulate favored constituencies from competition). Government of the Statist ilk, you see, is a carnivore that eats its own babies in an effort to grow ever larger and more omnipotent until there are no babies left, at which point the State must take over everything and fail miserably once that has been done, eventually eating itself.

Therefore the tax spiral must stop somewhere. If it continues, there will be no income left to tax. Everybody knows this, but by golly our politicians have the votes because only a tiny proportion of the electorate is taxed heavily, so we will push forward in small increments as far as possible with the support of those who pay little or no taxes and the future be damned. All the while, other taxes will be gradually increased by inconspicuous amounts on almost everything, ranging from gasoline to hotel stays.

Still not enough for the Statist programs? There is always debt. Along with taxes, governments fund themselves by borrowing money. In the United States, public borrowing breaks down into four categories: Bonds (state and local governments), and treasury bills, notes, and securities issued by the federal government (the difference among them is length to maturity). As with any borrowing, interest must be paid; in financial parlance, the debt must be "serviced" by paying interest and returning the principal, just like a home mortgage. In the case of governments, however, refinancing of the mortgage can repeat endlessly, *as long as somebody is willing to loan the money* (purchase new debt).

If tax revenues are less than government expenditures in a given fiscal year—a *deficit*—the difference is made up by debt, the same as for a household. For that year, when expenditures exceed revenues, the *national debt* increases, which must be serviced via interest payments. You are smart, you can see the cycle beginning to take shape: More spending contributes to more deficits if taxes are less than spending, contributing to more debt, contributing to more interest to pay. *Voila!* It's a Ponzi scheme and a subsequent trap. The first into a Ponzi scheme get paid back, at least for a while, e.g., current beneficiaries of government programs. With government debt, older people who die before things get out of hand profit from the scheme via Social Security and Medicare, among other programs. Those who have decades of living yet to go eventually have to help service and repay the debt, as will future generations, the equivalent of being a late-arrival into a Ponzi scheme. Think of it as consuming now instead of investing for the future. Figure 13.3 illustrates a positive feedback cycle related to the aforementioned Ponzi scheme. Even squirrels know better, and what we need, it seems, is a Department of Forever.

Statist Ideology → Excessive Government Spending — + → Government Deficits — + → Government Debt — + → Debt Sevices Charges

⟶ = "contributes to"

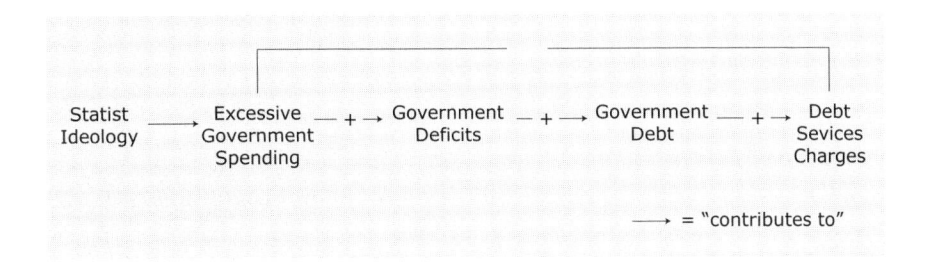

Figure 13.3 The Government Spending Cycle

And just how much government debt are we talking about? Forget the $14 trillion figure currently bandied about, even though that is a mountain, but it is a small mound compared to what is truly out there. Add in unfunded pension liabilities, state and local debt, plus forthcoming Social Security and Medicare benefits, and the total becomes something in the neighborhood of—get ready—$130 *trillion*. And that is just the United States portion; other welfare states are in similar dismal condition.

From an intergenerational perspective, later arrivals pay for the sins of their fathers and mothers as the scheme expands and eventually implodes, the bubble bursting. Crucially, financing and refinancing the national debt requires the willingness of foreign and domestic investors to lend the money. When enough such investment is lacking, and it likely will be as the debt climbs, the trap is sprung and derangement in Washington and international financial markets will follow, i.e., another "crisis." Finally, if governments must pay higher interest on debt to attract lenders, overall interest rates rise, causing severe problems for business and consumer borrowing. It is—and there is no other word for it—insanity. The thinking and behavior is so tragic it makes voodoo look like hard science, and to contemplate the amazing ability of carbon-based life forms with a prehensile thumb to destroy themselves is . . . well, amazing . . . and the essence of tragedy in undiluted form. [11]

Remark. What has been done in the past can place major constraints on what is possible now or in the future, for individuals and societies, sometimes called path dependence. Increasing government debt and taxes in the present removes alternatives for policy decisions in the future, as the commons becomes more barren.

One other matter concerning taxes: Arguments against higher taxes ordinarily center on loss of incentives for the income earners. But when money is taken from you without your consent, it is not only theft of a kind but also a *loss of freedom* to dispose of your private property as you wish. It also results in capital market distortions as investors seek to avoid taxes.

As discussed in Chapter 6, positive feedback cycles have a tendency to implode and fall to pieces; witness the housing crash for the most recent example, which was helped along by government insistence on lending to buyers with doubtful credit. And recall the tech-stock boom of the 1990s that imploded. Remember, government *transfers* wealth (while taking its own cut) but does not create it; only the private sector creates wealth. Governments act like the house in a Vegas poker game, transferring money from one person to another while removing a slice for itself.

At the very foundation of everything I am talking about is scarcity, which I have mentioned before. Someone once said the main problem with modern liberals (Statists) is they do not understand scarcity. Our parents told us, "You can't have your cake and eat it, too." However, ignorance, discounting, and incentives lead Statists and statists to exist with the rosy illusion that scarcity can be surmounted, that somehow there is more than

---

[11] I am not certain whether the phrase "carbon-based life forms with a prehensile thumb" is original or whether I read it somewhere. I cannot find a reference in my files. If not original, I apologize to the originator.

there is. As taxes flow to the federal, state, and local governments, there is less money for investment and consumer spending, leading to a decline in economic growth, leading to less employment, leading to less income to tax, leading to higher tax rates, leading to . . . can you hear my teeth gnashing all the way from rural Texas? Even those who think they are operating as free riders with their subsidies and income transfers eventually will be caught in the traps because the summer nights seem never to end until they do. As Bastiat famously said, "Everyone wants to live at the expense of the State. They forget that the State lives at the expense of everyone."

Remark. NOT EVERYTHING CAN BE DONE FOR EVERYONE, EVERYWHERE, ALL THE TIME. Scarcity rules.

Government is a voracious animal whose appetite is never sated. Aside from damage to society, it is downright unseemly watching Statists playing a tax-police version of Keystone Cops flitting from one taxing possibility to another, guttling our money and our freedoms. As my wife is wont to say about Statist politicians babbling into microphones about new Statist programs, their voices reverberating in cavernous government buildings, "Are their clown suits at the cleaners?"

There is another place in political life where feedback is germane. If you are a politician or average voter supporting a complex government initiative that ultimately leads to societal tragedy, the negative effects of the initiative may not occur for some time, i.e., the feedback loop is temporally protracted. This is entirely analogous to the time-delay traps presented in Chapters 4 and 5. Hence, the politician may be long-removed from office or the voter dead by the time the trap is sprung and the ill-effects recognized, as with public-sector pensions. Therefore, those who caused the trap are not made to suffer, but others who remain do suffer.

Remark. My friend Tom Reuschling suggested to me that the transient nature of modern society, where people move from job to job, also may contribute to short-run thinking in many sectors besides government. That is a point worth considering.

Chapter 14

MISCELLANEOUS TOPICS

"Why has government been instituted at all? Because the passions of men will not conform to the dictates of reason and justice without constraint."

- The Federalist Papers

The Case for a Parental Government
Make a list: Obesity, drug abuse, lack of retirement savings, illegal immigration, school dropouts, excessive credit card borrowing, home foreclosures, smoking, traffic jams, air and water pollution . . . make the list as long as you like. When you have finished, ask what underlies the problems? You know already: Decision-making, incentives, criteria, discounting, VSIs, the lure of the short-run, and traps.

At the heart of it all are incentives and discounting. In Chapter 7, I discussed various conventional solutions to the problems besetting humans and societies. There I dwelt at some length on government regulations and how we have increasingly and reflexively lurched toward government for problem solutions of all kinds. In fact, we seldom even consider more creative approaches.

And I fully understand such lurches because they appear straightforward—make a law, bring forth a new regulation, spend taxpayer money. Moreover, in some cases an overarching central authority or caregiver is the only approach, particularly in those situations where markets fail or in regulating natural monopolies such as urban water systems. On the other hand, there are relatively few instances where government intervention is the only solution.

If freedom is to be a dominant criterion, then freedom of choice is the key. But as we have seen over and over again, government intervention always reduces choice, the available alternatives are narrowed. Think about obesity and incentives. Instead of myriad state and national regulations regarding sugar in soft drinks or the use of trans-fats in restaurants, suppose obese people are charged significantly higher premiums for health insurance and refused medical care if they do not have insurance or are forced to pay cash for treatment. Who pays for the extra-large ambulances, winches, and other accommodations currently made for the obese? Like mountain hikers, the obese must pay for the externalities they create.

Already I can hear the Compassion Police accompanied by the Discrimination Patrol approaching my home. The alternative, the burden we now carry, is that those who observe nutritious diets and exercise routines, keeping their bodies in good condition, must subsidize directly or indirectly those who do not. Our *private property*, in the form of our personal incomes and wealth, is transferred to obese people for diabetes treatment, joint replacements, scooter chairs, special hospital beds, oversize MRI machines, and the like. Is there no compassion for those asked to pay bills on behalf of others they do not even know?

As Thomas Schelling wisely stated (1960, 2), "There is a disaffection toward those whose demands are insatiable and whose gratitude is inconspicuous." Thus, one of the many problems with government redistribution of income is the divorce between the givers and the takers. The takers have no one to thank and the givers never receive any thanks; in short, the givers receive no compensation even in the intangible form of gratitude. Statist politicians call this *sacrifice*. I, quite frankly, have no interest in sacrificing for the *avoidable* sins or indolence of anonymous others, nor should others feel obligated to pay for mine.

I prefer freedom and therefore I prefer choice. Freedom of choice, in the way I employ it, implies responsible behavior, doing no intentional harm to others as a result of my choices. What could be clearer than that? But, oh, cries the pseudo-compassionate Statist, "He just made some bad choices." Well, that's tough, and now he can make some responsible choices to extricate himself from whatever trap has sprung.

Thaler and Sunstein (2008) propose a system they label "libertarian paternalism." An oxymoron—that term—or so it seems. What they are proposing is preserving freedom of choice (libertarianism) but with the proper incentives in place to help people make better decisions about everything from obesity to retirement planning. But here is the catch: They propose using "choice architects" (the paternalism aspect) to design contexts in which people make decisions; the incentive systems, in other words. And therein rests the possible, glaring flaw of using incentives: Who chooses the incentives and where incentives should be applied. That is, who chooses the choice architects? One presumes, or hopes, they would be objective experts in the pertinent field and they would be transparent in the deliberations and construction of their choice edifices.

Libertarian paternalism comes very close to what I argued in all the discussion of incentives and their uses at many places in this book (no, I was not aware of Thaler and Sunstein's work when I wrote those chapters). Using insurance rates as an incentive for obese people to correct their deleterious behavior is an example of libertarian paternalism; it also would be an example of sensible business practice by insurance companies, and it also would be far more equitable to those forced to pay for the sins of anonymous others. Those gaining weight would have a choice: Pay higher insurance rates or switch to improved diet and exercise.

In sum, the alternatives are a heavy-handed government and huge government expenditures versus freedom of choice incorporating incentives. But there is yet another alternative, one that adheres closely to the classical liberal philosophy, a view expressed by John Stuart Mill: Allow people to make bad decisions and suffer the consequences. That is fine with me as long as innocent bystanders are not forced by government coercion to supply releases from the traps in which the bad decision-makers find themselves. The latter would be characterized by the progressive mind as inhumane and lacking in compassion, but embodies a simplicity I find attractive and perhaps greater humaneness and compassion when viewed from a more general level.

Incidentally, a true libertarian would disagree with both government regulation and the conscious use of incentives, preferring to have centralized authority of any kind removed from our lives, except perhaps for the bare necessities of national defense and contract enforcement. As Rockwell (2008, 27-28) observes, using privatization as just another tactic of the political class for a social goal is not the same as government completely disengaging itself from that area once and for all: "They don't cut the chains or throw away the yoke. They forge the steel with different materials and readjust the yoke to make it more comfortable." The economy is a huge organic system that is difficult to tinker with and not cause all sorts of unintended consequences in the process. Society in general has those characteristics, as well.

Take your ... well, take your choice.

What Would Make American Democracy Work Better?
There is nothing intellectually misguided about defining perfection and then considering how far removed present reality is from the ideal. First, a comment on our federalist system. Axiom: All government policies and programs should be designed and operated at a level as far as possible from the central government. The great strength of federalism is that if you do not like what is occurring in your state or community, you are free to migrate to a different area. When the central government is all-powerful, there is no escape, which is exactly what Statists desire. I am certain that at some point there will be a Statist movement to equalize taxes at a high level across all states, since migration from high tax states such as California and New York to states such as Texas is damned annoying to Statists. I am also certain countries will band together to enforce common taxing and regulatory powers, preventing inter-country migration for purposes of finding more sane economic policies.

At minimum, a well-functioning American democracy would require the following:
- Smart, well-informed voters who strongly prefer federalist principles but at the same time are able to account for national well-being, including sensitivity to burdens placed upon future generations, i.e., are willing to pay the full cost of their existences.
- Smart, well-informed politicians who strongly prefer federalist principles but, at the same time, are able to account for national well-being, including sensitivity to burdens placed upon future generations.
- Perfectly honest, transparent elections.
- Perfect transparency of all policy debates and procedures, save for certain military concerns.
- A completely unbiased media to purvey news and offer useful criticism.
- Civility in debate and the exchange of ideas.

We have none of these, and we are not even within range of them. More dismally, it seems America is retreating further from those ideals. That is why I am skeptical of democracy's survival in the long-term, not just in America but more generally as a form of societal organization anywhere. The skepticism stems from all I have sketched in this book. You may be weary of my list, but here it is again: Decision-making, the lure of the short-run and personal discounting, criteria, incentives, the value of the small increment, and traps. Pogo was right: We have met the enemy and he is us, one of the wisest observations ever made.

To survive, democracy requires an educated electorate, voters and politicians who understand the lure of the short-run and are willing to balance that lure with the long-term. In short, it requires a smart, serious, and thoughtful populace that refuses to attend the Buy Your Vote Parade in numbers great enough that the parade is canceled. Given the traps we have entered or are about to enter, it is hard to imagine people willingly sacrificing part or all of the goodies being currently being delivered or promised in the future. Adults seem to be relatively few in number.

To state "It has always been this way," a common red herring used to excuse bad political behavior, may be true but solves nothing. We are like the audience at a tragedy, watching what is occurring onstage, simultaneously realizing it is ourselves we are observing. Yet apparently we are helpless to prevent the plot from moving forward with its sad ending clearly in view.

Equality and Equity

The subjects of equality, equity, and justice are deep water for a short book such as this. They are deep water for a long book. The arguments are subtle, dense, and unresolved, the products of clever people dueling with one another using the weapons of language and inherent ideologies they cannot avoid though the pretense is there. For example, genetic good fortune plays a role in income inequality, i.e., smarter people tend to earn more money, which contributes to inequality. Is this sufficient reason to redistribute income? Some would say yes.

I decamp in this book from exalted philosophy and present a straightforward, more or less bare-knuckled approach to the subjects. I just wanted to let you know I am aware of the ongoing debate found in, for example, John Rawls' *A Theory of Justice*, Rawls' *Justice As Fairness*, G. A. Cohen's *Rescuing Justice and Fairness*, and Robert Nozick's *Anarchy, State, and Utopia*. Konow (2003) provides a decent survey of various philosophic attempts at theories of equality, equity, and distributive justice. Though I admire grand visions of anything, including a just world, in most of the justice literature I personally find an airy sense of academic naiveté and the unreachable dreams of societal purity as discussed over sherry in faculty clubs on Friday afternoons. It causes me to wonder if these thinkers have ever held a construction job or drank with the cowboys in a West Texas honky-tonk on Saturday nights.[1] My view of human possibilities tends to be far more restrained and earthbound than that of the philosophers.

Traditionalists argue that all are equal before God. On a more secular basis, we can accept that all are equal or should be before the law and in terms of opportunity (impossible to achieve in an exact sense). Understandably, opportunity is scoffed at by some, rightfully so, arguing that a child from a

---

[1] Rawls did serve in the Pacific campaign in World War II

poor family does not have the same opportunities as a suburban child from a financially comfortable family. What they mean is the poor child faces a *constrained choice set*. That is true. And those people born with fewer natural gifts than others confront similar circumstances, what Rawls (2001, 40) calls "life-prospects." For those with equal natural endowments (intelligence, physical skills), the same set of opportunities exists for all, in the abstract, but some are not prepared to exploit the full range of alternatives, partly by circumstances.[2]

The next question is why? Stop! Don't tell me it is lack of spending on education, for that does not account for the differences. Growing up in a small Iowa town of 900 people and attending classes in a crumbling school building, as I did 66 years ago, did not provide a wide range of opportunities, either.[3] But let us assume that certain sub-cultural differences have an important role in constraining choice sets, though the advent of computers, the internet, and television should be overcoming much of those differences. We spend billions on education, the differences among people remain, including both minorities and non-minorities.

Perhaps equality of opportunity is quite enough—to the maximum extent it can be achieved—and let the chips of genetic inheritance (natural endowments) fall where they may. When attempts are made to extend equality of opportunity to account for individual genetic differences, all sorts of problems emerge. Nonetheless, equality of opportunity as we commonly think of it is unsatisfying for some. Peter Singer (1993, 39), for example, argues ". . . equality of opportunity is not an attractive ideal. It rewards the lucky, who inherit those abilities that allow them to pursue interesting and lucrative careers. It penalizes the unlucky, whose genes make it very hard to achieve similar success." He admits, though, that under conditions of competitive private enterprise and allowing for human self-interest, it is unavoidable that inherited abilities ultimately will create inequalities. In short, Singer has no

---

[2] Check Geoffrey Canada's "Harlem Children's Zone" on the internet to see how a remarkable man is attempting to remove the constraints, but only with substantial outside funding.

[3] I send my gratitude to the dedicated teachers in Rockford, Iowa who worked with limited resources and did their best. They were competent and professional, and they were supported by parents, to a large extent.

answer beyond basic equality of opportunity as it is commonly understood and neither do other theories of justice as I interpret them.

Now a problem arises, making a grand, sweeping entrance in tasteless and mendacious clothing: *The demand for equality of results or outcomes*, accompanied by cries of "social justice" and "fairness," words that today cause me to experience tremors and, like the word "comprehensive," to tightly grasp my billfold and my freedoms.

I brazenly propose the following axiom: We may be created equally in terms of rights, but genetics vary the raw material in other ways, and all are not created equal in intellectual abilities and physical characteristics. There should be nothing audacious about such a commonsensical observation, but it has been judged unacceptable, taboo in our times, and its very utterance brings forth invective from certain coteries of ideologues and societal titans pursuing a monotonous, gray-hued equality in all things for all people. But it is self-evident, of course, even if political correctness holds it is not. The imposition of constraints on our language has caused us to stop speaking truth to one another.

No matter how you slice the data, whether anecdotal or empirical, intellectual capabilities are dispersed over a fairly wide range. Consequently, former president George W. Bush's "No Child Left Behind" mantra and subsequent law must rank as one of the ultimate and cruelest works of fiction, not because it requires regular testing but rather because the program's name is itself a lie. Some will get ahead, some will be left behind; it has been ever thus and will thus be so except under social and economic restrictions so dire as to circumscribe joy, laughter, innovation, creativity, and achievement. Likewise, some are deemed beautiful or handsome, using admittedly nebulous standards, some are not.

We are all prey to the vagaries of genetics and that is an irrefutable fact. I have Erythropoietic protoporphyria, an inherited gene making me less than equal when tolerance for sunlight is a criterion. I suppose I could file a lawsuit under the Americans with Disabilities Act if a business firm would not hire me for inside work when the firm's business involved outside work, or if it failed to provide an umbrella carrier on a construction site. I qualify for a handicap sticker for my car, though I do not need or want one. Perhaps

I am eligible for government assistance through a program of which I am unaware; I'm pretty certain there is such a program somewhere.

We have an easier time accepting inequality in physical ability than we do in intellectual ability, because the former is so much more obvious and less delicate in a hypersensitive society. Most of us are not troubled by the fact that a certain Jamaican sprinter can run faster than we can, because it is obvious and measurable. Not everyone can win, some will be left behind. If we handicap those with extraordinary speed so that all finish the race simultaneously, it will be a race that eventually will no longer be run by anybody, for there will be no point in exerting effort. From *Alice in Wonderland*, we hear the cry, "Everybody has won and all must have prizes," followed by other voices, "But who is to give the prizes?" Following such guidance, schools have outlawed dodge ball and, yes, even tag and scorekeeping in games.

Intelligence also is obvious, but the measurement processes are more subtle. For instance, awareness and understanding of the topics in this book require a certain level of conceptual ability, of reading and comprehending moderately difficult material and putting that material to work by thoroughly understanding it. Alas, as a matter of probabilities and genetics, such comprehension will always be outside the reach of a segment of any society's population, no matter how much one believes in education and equality of outcomes. Furthermore, we all have observed highly intelligent people who have contorted their lives into unqualified muddles, so sheer intellect alone does not guarantee success or trap avoidance. Rothbard (2000, 6) sums it up nicely, "There is one and only one way, then, in which any two people can really be 'equal' in the fullest sense: They must be identical in all of their attributes." And that is a ridiculous aspiration.

We come now to the inequalities of wealth. I introduce a second axiom: Freedom in a general sense and reasonably free markets are inseparable. See Friedman and Friedman (1979) for a cogent and persuasive presentation in defense of this axiom. Free markets, for all their flaws produce wealth faster and in greater quantities than any other system ever tried. Period. Don't even argue about it unless you are totally ignorant in economics and economic history, in which case find somebody else to argue with because I have better things to do.

Speaking of free markets, Blinder (1987, 27) writes, "...playing the game well takes both hard work and willingness to bear great risks. To encourage daring individuals to grab for the brass ring, the prizes must be commensurate with the risks. Therefore, the gap between the rewards of the winners and what is left to the losers must be large. *That is what incentives are all about* (my italics). That is why strong incentives go hand in hand with large inequalities." See the Classic Decision Problem in Chapter 2 for a decision tree illustrating such incentives and those who choose to take the risks.

Rossiter (2006, 378) adds, "In a *free* society with vigorously enforced property rights, inequalities of wealth are both expectable and large because citizens differ greatly in their motivation to seek wealth, their ability to produce it and their willingness to preserve it. These differences represent normal variations in human ambition and ability." Rossiter (379) goes on to argue that the politics of equality, as espoused by Statists, are such that only one conclusion can be drawn, "...the idea that inequality is somehow wrong in itself," which creates "...an evil where none existed before." He then carries forth an important insight from John Kekes, namely "...it is *insufficiency*, not inequality, that causes suffering and is therefore an evil to be remedied."

In the 1970s, while I was teaching in a university, an attorney's office was next to mine. He was fixated year after year on how much singer Wayne Newton was paid for nightly performances in Las Vegas. I would explain to him over and over that Mr. Newton monopolized what I called "Wayne Newtonness" and since Wayne Newtonness was in high demand, he could command such high fees while singing "Danke Schoen" because people wanted to see him sing and were willing to pay a high fee to be in the audience and to be lured to the slot machines and gambling tables in the attached casino. Do I think a baseball player should be paid $30 million per year? From the standpoint of some vague morality, it does not seem right, and I intuitively sense my doctors should earn far more than a baseball player. But putting on my economics cap, it does seem right, though uncomfortably so. In the interest of freedom, I think the baseball player *should* earn the high salary based on demand for his services, because if I complain about his income, somebody will complain about mine and about my doctors' yearly incomes. I feel the same about what seem to be excessive bonuses doled out to Wall Street bond traders and investment bankers.

An example to consider. Suppose you are an intelligent, hard-working person who invents a new Website that gains a huge following and generates large amounts of advertising revenue. After several years you sell the company for $500 million. Meanwhile, I, though healthy and able, have not been so ambitious or diligent in my work or so fortunate (success always has a measure of luck embedded in it). Suppose I have a net worth of minus $410,000 due to $20,000 in credit card debt and a second mortgage I took out on my home to finance the purchase of a Porsche and a second home in the Colorado mountains, the value of which has fallen by 60 percent along with a decline of 40 percent in my first home. Should I be entitled to a share of your assets or at least the earnings from those assets? Even a small portion? No one has ever presented a compelling argument that convinced me such redistribution is either necessary or deserved except for one practical reason and that reason is my own: Those instances where the stability of civil society is in danger of tipping toward instability because of wealth inequalities.

If, however, I was born with a substantial disability that prevents me from engaging in productive activity, it is in the interest of social stability for you and others each to share a very small portion of your money with me. In fact, you have an incentive to do just that, since without social stability your assets will soon disappear in the chaos of anarchy. A nicer-sounding word would be compassion, but underlying all compassion is some type of incentive. For me, however, to demand and receive income from you via the political process and against your wishes for no other reason than you have more than me, is simply and brutally a form of larceny. It can be characterized as nothing else, and cries for "distributive justice" do not obscure that fact—most who argue for distributive justice in our current national politics are not using the subtle arguments of philosophers but rather are employing some vague criterion they are unable to define, such as "fairness." Some would use the term "allocative justice" in the way I am using distributive justice, both of which are designed to have a resonance milder than theft.

See "Cash for Clunkers" in Chapter 8, a 2009 program where other citizens stole from me (and maybe you) via the federal government for the purchase of a new car. Because the government was an intermediary does not lessen the charge; no referendum was organized concerning the desirability of the clunkers program and money was taken from me by federal officials. Purchasers of vehicles under that program could have refused to participate as a matter of principle, but self-interest ruled and no thought was given to the fact they were taking the money of other citizens—the government as an intermediary disguised the taking. While I do not shy from helping a person who is truly disadvantaged, it is not my task as a citizen to help another perfectly capable citizen buy a car for his benefit, the benefit of an auto dealer, and ultimately the benefit of auto workers (the real reason behind the program was to retain union political support). All three of those parties have arrogated my rights with the prodding of a State that has the police power to implement its preferences with force.

Suppose I inherited a small amount of money and squandered it in Las Vegas, thereafter claiming my profligacy caused me to become addicted to drugs. Should you have to pay for my rehabilitation? My heating bills? My medications? Unemployment benefits? For the cases just cited, multiplied by the tens of thousands, you soon will run out of money.

— *Personal Vignettes* —

When I lived on a ranch in southwest Texas, theft by illegal immigrants was a problem; in the interest of speaking truthfully and plainly, they were illegally in the United States, not merely "undocumented." Doors or windows in my buildings would be smashed, what could be carried was taken, some of it valuable, and rain and dirt blew in the broken doors and windows. In a conversation I had with two progressives, both of them argued vehemently that the theft was justified since I had "so much more" than the illegal trespassers committing burglary possessed; a naked version of distributive justice. I was stunned, since theft is never a way to adjust inequality, assuming it needs to be adjusted at all. If it were, society would collapse. The conversation caused my brain to swim in a miasma of incredulity and I walked away. I later reflected that Statist governments do the same thing, take my assets simply because I have more, but with the implied threat of breaking doors and windows via police power.

On another occasion, still in southwest Texas, my wife spent well over $100 on a list of school supplies for her son by an earlier marriage. The school dispatched the list and parents were required to trundle the child off to the classroom with the exact quantity of items so specified. We walked up and down the aisles of a Wal-Mart in Midland, Texas where she purchased pencils, crayons, tablets, and the like.

The day after the term began, her son informed her that he would be needing pencils for his homework. It turned out the teacher had confiscated all the required items on the first day of school and rationed them to the entire class, since many parents had not purchased the supplies. That, my friends, is called theft of private property, no different than a mugging on a city street. It also is called socialism. It also is called Marxism, for Marx stipulated, "from each according to his ability, to each according to his needs." The remains of imploded communes that attempted to follow Marx's dictum smolder all over the world, including (on a larger scale) Soviet Russia and North Korea. Incidentally, a number of parents did not purchase school supplies because they knew others would and enjoyed the benefits of being free riders. It was cash for clunkers in a different costume.

— End of Personal Vignettes —

Ideologues encouraging class envy and economic warfare usually are doing so entirely for their own profit and gain. In the process, they damage society and they are to be despised without limit.

Remark. I believe there are two sure signs of maturity: The ability to laugh at yourself and to view the accomplishments of others with admiration rather than the debilitating sickness called malevolent envy. When my wife says,

"Be careful about asking Robert a question unless you have three hours to spend listening," I laugh, because like all good humor it has truth contained within it, especially my tendency to become extra-garrulous when drinking beer. Listening to the Brandenburg Concertos, I exhibit pure admiration for Johann Sebastian Bach. Studying calculus, my admiration for Sir Isaac Newton and Gottfried Leibniz goes unbounded. I also admire and envy without malevolence the British fellow I met who left school at 15 and became wealthy in the scrap metal business, the skills of my plumber, the mind of my now-deceased friend John Warfield, and NFL quarterbacks who can throw a football 40 yards into a 3-foot-square window of opportunity. Envy is normal, but attaching a vicious quality to it is debilitating to the person and to society. Statists cultivate envy, class envy, as one tactic in their drive toward social leveling.

One more interesting idea on the matter of compensation. Professional athletes are renowned for the enormous salaries they command, as are coaches at schools with highly ranked athletic programs. Why? They win or lose, and the scores are posted for all to see, along with attendance figures and organizational revenues. Poor revenues bring lower salaries. For college professors, the effects of their teaching may not be obvious for decades, such as when an alumnus donates a large amount of money to a school in gratitude for the education received, but seldom is an effort made to compensate specific professors for their past work. The feedback loops are short for coaches and athletes, long for professors. If you break your leg, you are willing to pay a doctor almost anything to repair it; the feedback loop is a short one.

I leave you with this to consider, a contention by philosopher Peter Singer (Singer 1993, 20-21): "There is no logically compelling reason for assuming that a difference in ability between two people justifies any difference in the amount of consideration we give to their interests."

Incivility, Incentives, and Choice Sets

Many have lamented the decline of civility in American life. This is true in political discussion perhaps more than elsewhere. Ad hominem attacks substitute for thought, abrasive and foul language in critiques of others' ideas appear daily on the internet. The authors often remain anonymous, their words approaching if not libel, then the appearance of uninformed illiterates. The tactics are designed to suppress the speech of those who think differently than the critic by creating venomous disincentives, i.e., "If you don't shut up or change your mind, I will hurt you." It is an attempt to constrain choice sets—the expression of certain views—by promising punishment if you do express those views.

This incivility is designed to throttle competing ideas, an end run around the First Amendment. You are free to speak or write, of course, but punishment will follow immediately if the speech does not follow a designated party line, as is true of all dictatorial societies. Thoughtful people are at a disadvantage here, because their standards do not allow name-calling and personal destruction of those who disagree.

A perfect example of such barbarous tactics occurred when the United States Chamber of Commerce (of which I am no admirer) expressed opposition to health care reform and climate change legislation, as proposed by congress and the Obama administration. A collection of liberal-progressive groups then offered a reward of $200,000 to anyone who could uncover any evidence of personal wrongdoing by the Chamber's CEO, as a way of constraining the Chamber's choice set or, in this case, attempting punishment for behavior unacceptable to the liberal-progressives. Therefore, if your opinions are threatened, you can always suppress opposing ideas by roundabout thuggery. Such gangland conduct distances us from not only the First Amendment but even further from the ideals of democracy, and from each other.

One Man's Self-Interest in a Vibrant, Civil Society

Why do I dutifully pay my taxes and obey all other laws? I have pondered this question and answer it as follows: I have self-interest, an incentive, in helping to foster a stable, civil, organized society. If anarchy ruled, I would be forced to spend nights and days with an arsenal propped around me. I would prefer, instead, to have quiet days working in my office or fly fishing or sitting on a bench outside with my cat Harper or listening to Bach or contemplating a painting or watching a football game in the evening.

Therefore, I have an incentive to be a good citizen, to do my lonesome part in promoting a civil, stable society. This includes providing help to less fortunate humans, to a pair of well-run animal shelters, to a university, to an effort to save the wild Bengal tigers, and to medical research. Some would call it altruism or generosity or the retch-inducing label of "giving something back." I prefer self-interest, but I am unwilling to accept that somehow that label diminishes my actions. On the contrary, I believe it fairly reeks of humility, of understanding that I am not a vainglorious altruist feeling all cozy and warm from being concerned with the larger world, but rather a human being doing the best he can to get along and get by while assisting his society to do the same, because that is necessary for his own happiness and productivity.

On "Giving Back"

Treat this section as a parenthetical remark. For the successful, it has become all the rage to "give something back." Such proclamations—ordinarily made in a self-serving, public relations mode so that others are aware something ostensibly beneficial is or will be forthcoming—have reached the level of charity chic, the phrase uttered with a demeanor of humility and blessedness, with the expectation of praise in return. If a person has worked hard and gained wealth in an honest fashion, why is it necessary to give something back? It has the ring of theft in the first place: "I should give it back." Give what back? To whom? If you have provided income and employment or joy and contentment to others while making your way, what more do you owe? Besides, the IRS has already forced you to give rather a lot back and will demand more when you die. If you choose to do volunteer work or give to charity for purposes of a more orderly and stable society, that is your choice and is to be commended, but there should be no compulsion to do so or to shout "Look what a good thing I am doing." "Give something back" has the ring of a Statist training manual, one of the most sloshy, meaningless, ill-considered phrases to enter the language, as if some undefined and undeserved good fortune must be expiated along with guilt at having done well.

Unless one has wealth wholly inherited or has been given money without cause, one already *has given,* not *taken,* as the phrase implies. Perhaps a person with inherited wealth or someone who has done well receiving politically motivated subsidies, needs to give back. Other than that, feel no compulsion beyond the personal satisfaction from charitable work.

President John F. Kennedy is famous for his ringing imperative, "Ask not what your country can do for you, but what you can do for your country." If you have lived an honorable, honest, productive life, there is no need to ask anything from your country except the basic functions of government cited earlier, and there is no obligation to do anything more for your country than you have already done by paying taxes and being a good citizen. In fact, Kennedy's dictum has a strong nationalistic ring to it, i.e., service to the all-encompassing Mother State.

Small Increments or a Darwinian Flush?
A score of books could be and will be written on reducing the United States deficit and debt. Here I offer a few ideas on what can be done and must be done, trusting the reader will understand these are only examples. Variations of some of these recently have been proposed, an example of the times catching up my writing of this book. For a more extreme view, see Murray (1997). What should be done? First, general ideas.

1. When it comes to solving complex socio-economic problems, recognize our imperfections as humans. Replace hubris with a modicum of humility. This will be difficult given the fraudulent self-esteem gibberish handed out in our public schools and elsewhere, as well as the tendency of humans to believe they know more than they do know and think better than they do think.

2. Rebel against politically correct speech so we can begin speaking truth to one another, with civility present, of course.

3. Use a sledgehammer approach to getting public finances under control or attempt to do it through small increments, or, better yet, use a combination of both.

4. Preach the doctrine of scarcity—drive it home in our schools and public discourse that everything cannot be done for everyone everywhere all the time. That alone will not change behavior, but it will create awareness.

5. Rigorously apply Murray's criteria for public goods, or a similar criteria set, to all government programs, existing or future.

Specifically, a small-increment (relatively speaking) program would include the following.

- Gradually increase the eligibility age for Social Security to 70 or more, recognizing that life-spans have increased by nearly 20 years since the program was enacted. Encourage private retirement accounts via generous tax deductions and exemptions.

- For people with sufficient assets to live comfortably without Social Security, who already are receiving Social Security payments, make a one-time, reasonable lump-sum payment and then take them out of the system. The same should be done for Medicare with the money deposited in a medical savings account. I am engaged in self-flagellation here.

- For both Medicare and Medicaid, significantly increase the penalties for fraud and abuse to hard time in prison—that is, provide real and tangible disincentives to those scamming the system. Bank robbers are sent to prison; those defrauding government programs also are robbers.

- Back down major pieces of the idiotic health-care reform endlessly promoted by progressives and passed by congress in 2010. Institute private catastrophe insurance or a government catastrophe insurance pool while allowing people to set up tax-deductible medical savings accounts for routine and mid-level medical problems; businesses can contribute to such accounts along with the individuals. The latter has been done by companies such as Whole Foods and it works. The base-level problem with the 2010 package, aside from its heavy Statist component, is the absence of incentives for people to stop treating medical care as a free good, or nearly so.

- Increase the retirement age for public-sector employees. For jobs taken following retirement, reduce their pension benefits commensurately with earnings received from the post-retirement job. At the very least, prevent state employees who have retired from returning to their old jobs while drawing retirement pay, resulting in double-dipping the system.

- Immediately reduce salaries and fringe benefits for new public-sector em-

ployees, especially the generous and unsustainable retirement benefits.
- If necessary, many municipalities should find a way to declare bankruptcy, pay off the bondholders in full, and have a bankruptcy judge revise all pension promises, where necessary and possible. Outlaw pension-obligation bonds.
- Increase real privatization of education, highways, and other public services.
- Force all states and localities to adopt standard, transparent accounting practices so that honest statements of financial health or financial disorder are available.

Doing nothing more than taking some people off the Social Security, Medicare, and Medicaid rolls, along with providing incentives for people to be selective in their use of medical services and to take better care of their bodies would go a long way toward reduction of government deficits (and hence the national debt). In all such matters, think hard about humans and decision-making. TIAA-CREF retirement systems for college professors, whereby retirement funds cannot be accessed prematurely but yet allow choice of how the money will be invested, is a good example of constraining behavior and forcing a low discount rate being attached to the future while providing the liberty to make personal decisions within the constraints.

Here's an idea that I have not seen anywhere. Each year, states and the federal government should publicize budgets for natural disasters—in the U. S. and abroad—budgets that will not be exceeded, period. Much aid, domestic and foreign, is driven by false compassion and an effort to gain votes or national stature. Example: A few hours after the Haitian earthquake in 2010, President Obama announced a $100 million aid package, followed by a pledge to send a billion dollars more. Why $100 million or a billion? Why not $10 million? Where did the money come from? Why wasn't the $100 million previously available for trade-school and college scholarships for poor American citizens? Because President Obama and politicians before him do not understand scarcity; not everything can be done for everyone, everywhere, all the time, including the distressed citizens of Haiti. Plus, ostensible humaneness can itself become inhumane by creating dependence and depriving others equally deserving of resources, along with the inhumanity of using Americans' tax dollars to bail out those in far away places. If Americans want to make private charitable contributions to Haiti, that is their business. But endless and conspicuous national compassion in the face of limited resources is pure foolishness. A modest budget for such matters should be set and not exceeded. Monies remaining in the disaster relief fund must not be accessible for any other reason and can be carried over from year to year to even out yearly costs.

The above are examples of an incremental approach. For a more detailed strategy see the proposals by Paul Ryan and others that are designed to attack federal deficits over the long- term. Ryan is a member of the House of Representatives from Wisconsin, and he thinks hard about such matters. Plus, he has the Congressional Budget Office as a resource, which I do not.

Here comes a sledgehammer strategy, though the small increments above can be couched within it. As a start, I suggest a three-year program; call it a "Darwinian flush." All government agencies at all levels will have their budgets reduced immediately to 85 percent of current levels. This will have to be taken from staff reductions, removal of duplicative programs, and other expenses, mostly, since entitlements will have to be dismantled piecemeal, as described earlier, though hefty decrements in entitlements must make up substantial pieces of the meal.

Starting in two years, all budgets will be reduced to zero and each agency will be required to justify expenditures line by line for year three, applying Murray's public-goods criteria, with the constraint that its new budget will be no more than 65 percent of the level prior to the initial reduction. This is called zero-based budgeting, and it works when implemented.[4] If agencies whine this is far too much work for them to do, then that indicates the agencies are far too big. Presently, budgets never decline as increases are routinely awarded or, at best, the rate of increase is slowed (which politicians like to call budget cuts).

Concomitantly, special and empowered project teams for all major

---

[4] My 60 percent constraint is more draconian than ordinarily applied, but a figure similar to that or greater is necessary if we are to regain control of our lives and government.

federal government departments will study and identify programmatic changes where federal expenditures can be reduced or agencies eliminated; this will be done in coordination with the zero-based budgeting process. The Department of Agriculture has 198 programs. The Department of Housing and Urban Development has 108 different programs, coupled with the 3,600 pages of regulations for which it is responsible. The Department of Commerce has 53,000 employees and nobody seems to understand exactly what it produces of consequence except the census taken every ten years and the census has become a mismanaged example of government waste—hundreds of millions of dollars spent on handheld computers for the 2010 census, devices which had to be scrapped because of malfunctions. Other departments such as Health and Human Services, Energy, and Education have similar or larger numbers attached to them. The Department of Education can be done away with; it meddles rather than helps. Include congressional staffs in the study; arbitrarily cut the staffs by half to start with. If Air Force One and other government vehicles are used for purely political purposes, all expenses must be paid by campaign contributions and salaries reduced by the amount of time government workers are campaigning rather than working at their jobs, including the president and other elected officials.

Parenthetical note. Notice what is occurring here. Politicians and bureaucrats treat resources as free money, unlike expenditures from their own checkbooks. Once tax or debt dollars enter the political arena, nobody "owns" them and the pool of resources appears virtually unlimited, as with Hardin's commons. My scheme reduces the pot; it enforces scarcity where none appears to exist.

Institute a consumption-based federal income tax or a flat tax; either will create absolute transparency in the tax system and will be cheaper than the present tax system by the several hundred billion dollars per year spent by Americans on compliance with the morass we now have. Only two deductions or exemptions will be allowed: Retirement savings such as individual retirement accounts, in recognition of the never-ending lure of the short-run, and individual medical savings accounts.

Critically, the findings of the task forces will not be open to debate or congressional or presidential meddling; an up-or-down vote will be required in those cases where congress must be involved. The use of outside task forces thus removes most of the congressional tendencies to pick and choose based on the electability criterion and favoritism toward certain constituencies. Plus, the up-or-down vote will clearly distinguish the prudent from the profligate.

The percentage figures I propose are arbitrary as is the time allotted for implementation, which would be true of any such proposal, but one must start somewhere and incremental attempts at government budget reductions have limits because of self-interest and the electability criterion. Furthermore, just as dishonesty among corporate executives has been punished recently by severe prison sentences, politicians and bureaucrats who enrich themselves at taxpayer expense should suffer equally. Frankly, though citizens have a right to petition their representatives, I also would find more strict means of controlling professional lobbying; however, reducing the size of the federal and state budgets, along with a simplified and transparent tax system, would remove much of the incentives for lobbying. Lobbying exists because the bank is large and accessible, and you are allowed to stand in the lobby (and other locations) of the government bank while pleading your case.

Simultaneously, because of the impact on the economy, both individual and corporate taxes should be reduced by an amount that will partially offset declines in spending by the government while still allowing reduction of the federal debt. Decreases in taxes will increase consumer spending, help businesses compete worldwide, and tax decreases will then increase government revenues as wealth is created in the private sector.

By now, you may have thrown the book across the room or are rolling on the floor laughing at my naiveté. And if I am such a proponent of small increments, why even consider oversize tactics? First, the task forces will be working in incremental fashion. Secondly, when one confronts the utter madness of a positive feedback cycle involving such a large creature as the State, sometimes brute force is the only way to subdue it; scalpels are of no use in pounding railroad spikes, sledgehammers are. Moreover, bureaucrats have incentives to preserve or increase the status quo, and forcing them into making hard decisions is the proper course.

Do I really think my proposal would have a lasting effect, given human proclivities? No, but it would allow us breathing space of a generation or three before statist voters and Statists can reinstitute the waste and inefficiencies we presently must contend with. The lure of the short-run and the benefits of being a free-rider are embedded too deep in human affairs to be permanently conquered.

Remark. When the stock market pays no attention to the latest federal government pronouncement or proposal or program, this will be a signal the State has been reduced to a manageable size.

Summary

Figure 14.1 will serve as a précis for much of this chapter. The size of the paper on which we record our ideas limits the size of the ideas. This is such a case and elements have been omitted that easily could have been included. If you have read the entire book thus far, the structural model should be self-explanatory. I have dealt with several of the cycles earlier in this chapter. Note that "Freedom" has been highlighted.

Just to make sure Figure 14.1 is understandable, however, allow me to offer a short guide. The left portion of the diagram is the same as Figure 13.1, showing the self-reinforcing aspect of government growth. A line has been added from "Government Employment" to the element "Government Salaries" and after that to "Total Government Expenditures." The latter element is a summation of salaries, non-salary costs (e.g., equipment, supplies), and general expenses such as recruitment advertising for the military. Total government expenditures must be financed via "Government Borrowing" and "Taxes," which taken together contribute to government debt—higher taxes used to retire government debt lowers debt, while borrowing increases it. The more debt, the greater the service charges, which also is a component of total expenditures shown by the feedback loop. Government debt impacts on overall interest rates, which in turn impact on business and consumer borrowing, both of which impact on economic growth and, hence, employment. At the top of the diagram "Freedom" is severely impacted by laws and regulations (shortened here to "Regulations") and along with taxes impacts on individual freedom.

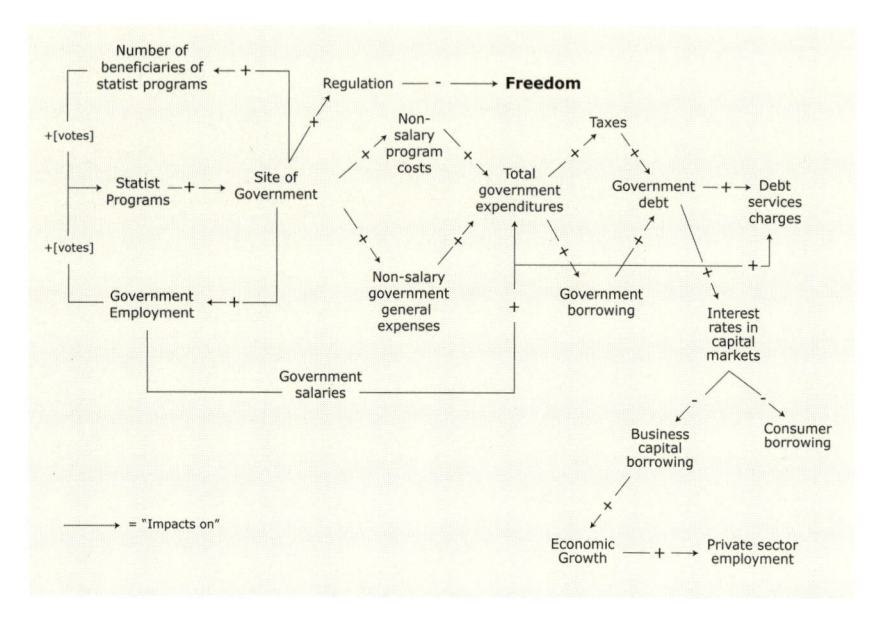

Figure 14.1 Government and Its Impact

PART III: LOOSE ENDS AND RECAPITULATION

Chapter 15

SYNTHESIS

One of several failures in my life has been my inability to convey the following (a failure of exhortation): The necessity of practicing intellectual technologies in the same way you would practice a musical instrument or a golf swing. Take a problem, any problem, and attack it with the ideas laid out in this book. For example, your retirement savings plan or the Greek debt debacle or your body weight (if it is a problem) or the behavior of a politician who purportedly represents you or the failure of many school systems to properly educate children. Drill down and identify decisions, criteria (they may be vague and implicit), expected outcomes and how they are acting as incentives in the both the short- and long-run, how the outcomes are being discounted, and how the alternatives selected may lead to unintended consequences in the form of traps. Do only that a few times—do it on paper, not just in your head—and you will begin to see how the pieces fit together. Such model building will be difficult and frustrating at first, but like golf swings and fly casting, it becomes satisfying as skill increases. That's how you become proficient at making practical use of conceptual tools.

At the beginning, I promised to explain one man's portable theory, a paradigm, for eliminating the great buzzing confusion of modern life. That has been developed in this book at a basic level. To go further would require more than I intend this particular book to be, having omitted such things as probability theory (for decisions involving risk), techniques for handling multiple and conflicting criteria in decision-making, the mathematics of financial and personal discounting, long excursions into micro- and macroeconomics, dynamic systems modeling, game theory, the vast literature on distributive justice and equality, and so forth. Here I review what has been previously said, providing a useful and transportable package for your consideration.

The diagrams with arrows I have been using in the book are mathematical at their core. They are called *structural models* and involve something called graph theory, a branch of mathematics founded on set theory, Boolean algebra, and combinatorics. The beauty of structural models is they are easy to view and understand by everyone, including non-technical people, while preserving the underlying mathematics. I use them constantly in my everyday life for everything from estate planning to investing to visualizing the evening news as it hammers my brain in essentially disorganized fashion. As you read this brief summary chapter, please refer to Figure 15.1, which contains most of the topics covered in the book, to see how the parts fit together. A few topics are omitted in the diagram to keep it relatively simple, e.g., feedback (however, feedback can be thought of as being included in traps). And I note this is not a rigorous structural model but rather a conceptual diagram.

Recapitulation: Decision-Making

Making decisions is what we do. Decisions arise from one of three sources:
- Personal problems or opportunities. Examples: Saving for retirement, which insurance policy to purchase, choosing a job, quitting or avoiding a bad habit, losing weight or preventing weight gain, buying a car, voting.
- Societal events. Examples: Unexpected traffic jams on our normal commuting route, changes in government programs, unsettling economic events, new government policies resulting in tax changes, unforeseen international events.

- Unpredictable natural events such as a tornado.

Some decisions are routine, such as brushing your teeth in the morning, while others are decidedly non-routine, e.g., where to invest retirement savings, whether to have surgery for prostate cancer, whether to change jobs, where to go on vacation.

Decisions involve the following (Chapter 2):

- Alternatives.
- The expected outcomes of alternatives, which act as incentives.
- Discounting—how the present is traded off against the future when calculating outcomes. The discount applied to future outcomes is determined by the time value of expected future outcomes (how far they are in the future), risk, and the lure of the short-run (impatience). See Chapters 1 and 2.
- Criteria. Examples: Maximize retirement income, minimize gasoline consumption while maximizing cargo capacity when considering a car purchase (conflicting criteria), maintain a svelte appearance, environmental sensitivity. See Chapter 2.
- Scarcity. If you (or a society) could have all you wanted of everything, there would be no need for decisions.

If economics is the science of dealing with scarcity, then all decisions are economic decisions. Since the choice of any one alternative requires not choosing one or more other alternatives because of scarcity, then cost or price are always present; the true cost/price of buying a consumer product now is what else could have been purchased with the money, such as a larger retirement fund. The cost/price of time spent watching television is what could have been the best alternative use of that time. The true cost of sending aid to Haiti is what else could have been done with the funds.

Recapitulation: The Value of Small Increments

Life is mostly composed of small increments; a decision here, another one there. Often these are repetitive decisions, as with meal choices. Small increments sum to large consequences, almost unnoticed. The sums amount to happiness or the reverse, to regret at not having seen the future clearly or satisfaction at having done so. At age 72 I take satisfaction in weighing

Loose Ends and Recapitulation

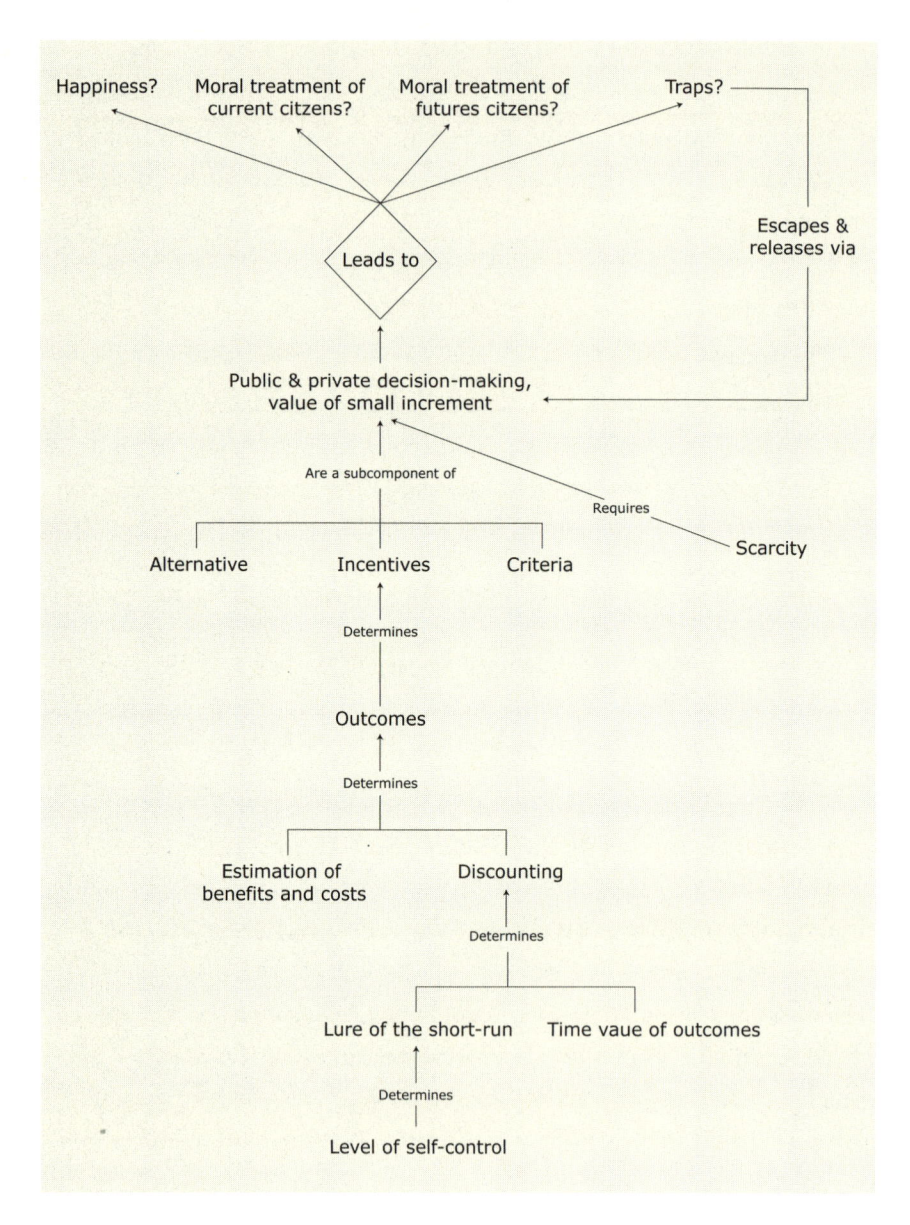

Figure 15.1 Book Summary

exactly what I weighed when I played college basketball, and maintaining that weight over 50 years has been a matter of decisions, day by day, meal by meal, hour after hour on the treadmill and weight machine.

Conversely, I am chagrined by the poor incremental decisions I made along the way that could have provided more financial and personal happiness at the present, for me and others. Most of the bad decisions, I reflect, were the result of the blindfold effect or simple inattention, both of which have been discussed earlier. The good decisions, fortunately, have substantially outweighed the bad ones, the small increments have summed to more than the bare minimum level of happiness.

Recapitulation: Individual and Social Traps
The lure of the short-run driven by incentives is omnipresent: Skip exercise today, skip exercise again tomorrow, the outcomes of the small decisions mounting up. The results of the incremental decisions often work as additional incentives to continue detrimental behavior (sliding reinforcers): Thinking about beginning a new diet when it seems hopeless works against deciding on the new diet. When the results of many decisions are tabulated, traps frequently are the result. Individual traps (Chapter 4) are exemplified by weight gain or poor financial condition in later years or addiction or lack of necessary skills for employment.

When individual traps ensnare others, a social trap is created, with the tragedy of the commons standing as the archetypal social trap (Chapter 5). A simple example is the presence of traffic jams, which are the result of many individual decisions. Voting in a self-interested fashion without regard to the vote's impact on the future results in social traps that enmesh not only present generations but also future ones. Increasing government debt is an example of the latter (Chapters 11-14), as are air and water pollution.

Feedback loops play an important part in traps. See Figure 6.2 involving the dentist-avoidance trap. If the time duration between the harmful outcomes of decisions is long and the velocity of the feedback slow, the necessary incentives to change behavior are not noticeable until the trap is sprung. America presently is entering a number of very nasty financial traps resulting from long feedback loops (Chapter 13).

Recapitulation: Getting Out of Trouble and Avoiding Trouble

Among all the possible solutions to problems or avoiding problems in the first place, two essential elements stand out: Awareness and self-control when dealing with the lure of the short-run. Lectures, laws, and religion offer solutions or trap-avoidance devices but always by constraining choice sets (alternatives), inevitably resulting in a loss of freedom. The use of incentives preserves or expands freedom of choice.

Simple education as a means of trap escapes or trap avoidance is ineffective; knowing the harmful effects of an action does not necessarily change behavior when incentives make the lure of the short-run overwhelming. But education does have a role in creating awareness and awareness is the first stage of self-control. If purely knowing the damaging effects of high government deficits and the consequence of increasing government debt were enough, however, voters and politicians would behave differently, since there is already a good understanding of those effects. Therefore, simply educating people is not enough. Incentives must accompany awareness, with the proper incentives operating as proxies for lack of self-control and/or the inability to visualize futures and work toward those futures. When enough conscientious voters form groups and demand change via the choice of senators and representatives, politicians will respond to the revised electoral incentives and things will begin to turn toward improvement (trap escapes).

Recapitulation: Democracy and Its Failings

Democracy as a form of socio-political organization is particularly susceptible to all we have discussed. Incentives of voters and politicians (Chapters 10-13) lead to short-run decision-making leading to traps. Tocqueville clearly understood this in 1837, even as he admired America, foreseeing exactly the sort of problems we now confront. Edward Gibbon saw it in studying the history of Athens.

Recapitulation: The List, One More Time

So my portable theory, my paradigm, appears as follows:
- Decisions driven by scarcity are unavoidable. When you listen to a newscast or read an article or think about your life, look for decisions

already made or forthcoming. Observe how individual decisions are leading to societal problems or how societal-level decisions stream down to influence individual decisions.

- Incentives and the lure of the short-run can lead to traps when decisions are made. In newscasts and articles or self-introspection, look for incentives driving the decisions.
- Self-control can get us out of traps or avoid them entirely via revised personal discount rates, which change the values of decision outcomes, which change incentives. Also, self-control can be aided by the use of incentives that make self-control easier.

The summer nights never end until they do, and when they end and where they end determine an individual's life and its attributes. The same is true of societies. Good alternatives remain or alternatives are constrained by choices already made.

The future must be given a voice much larger than it presently has if a plodding, gray-hued, parental society is to be avoided, if happy and productive lives are to be led. Life is not easy, happiness is not a birthright. Nobody with a realistic view of people promised they would be. But, still, there is snow on the mountains, the long grass blows in prairie winds, sails are aloft on the waters around us, MRI and CRT machines clank and whirl helping with diagnosis and cures, and serious people are working on the problems before us. All is not lost, nor should it be. But happiness and freedom are not resources to be squandered like the grass of Hardin's commons, and the opportunities for them must also be preserved for future generations.

A Final Note

At the close of Chapter 2, I offered the following: One of the main attractions of a socialist or statist economy has to do with risk tolerance. People, in general, but fortunately not all, have an aversion to losses; they value loss avoidance greater than possible gains. In terms of a society's economic arrangements, and strumming on our fears, the Statist economy seems to promise security versus the risks involved in a market-based economy. Government employees—including teachers and state university professors (along with those in well-endowed private universities)—

have almost ironclad job security, guaranteed (or nearly so) pensions, and decent salaries. Entrepreneurs and capitalists in general, prefer a world of possible high payoffs coupled with the possibility of great loss, especially when they are young. Thus, the choice between a government-run economy and the market system involves the Classic Decision Problem I illustrated in Chapter 2. If risk avoidance becomes a dominant theme in voting, the market system closes down and freedom slips away. Statist academics demand certainty in the form of tenure and yearly salary increases but carp incessantly about the tastes and incomes of the risk-takers who support them.

The Friday discussion group of which I am privileged to be a member is a diverse gathering of intelligent people who pay some attention to events around them, and we are scattered across the political spectrum from classical liberal to middle of the road. The general opinion, though, is an increasing sense of political impotence in the face of government, particularly at the state and national levels. The words "oligarchy" and "aristocracy" are most often used to describe how we view what should be our governments instead of an overweening presence. Who comprises the oligarchy? High-level politicians remaining in office term after term, the administrative branch of the federal government, untouchable bureaucracies such as the Environmental Protection Agency, labor union chieftains, and powerful business interests exerting background influence with money and lobbyists.

How large the American oligarchy might be is indeterminable, but I would estimate it lies near .001 percent, which is about 3,000 people, and that may dramatically overstate the number in terms of functional, policymaking clout. I am not implying that the Friday group is a gaggle of conspiracy theorists. Rather we see the oligarchy as a loosely knit array of people all benefiting from government and communicating via mostly informal understandings, a wink-and-a-nod brotherhood that shares a general aim—to profit by the work of others, those others being citizens. The oligarchy holds the view that citizens are nothing more than taxpayers and voters whose favor is to be curried at certain times, but ignored otherwise. And, besides, when a new air-conditioned wing for tourists was added to the capitol building, Senate Majority Leader Harry Reid applauded, stating how pleased he was because citizen-tourists reeked of body odor, the smell offending him. The aristocracy rules and cannot be moved, and that is the way the aristocracy wants it. My conclusion: Liberal-progressive Statists are autocrats in drag, as are those who profess conservative values but behave otherwise.

It does not foretell a bright future for democracy and freedom when a group such as ours, meeting in a small kitchen on Friday mornings—including a plumber, a classical musician, a businessman, a biologist, a man trained in mathematics and physics, an economist—is frustrated and losing faith in the American political system. In small increments, our freedoms have dissipated and continue to dissipate. Statists intuitively understand the power of small increments, handing out blessings a little at a time, constantly seducing us toward their aims. Rossiter (2006, 30) agrees that, "…the decline in citizens' freedom is gradual enough to avoid alarming them." Levin (2009, 9) underscores this point: The Statist "…marches in incremental steps, adjusting his pace as circumstances dictate. Today his pace is more rapid, for resistance has slowed." Norman Thomas, the longtime American socialist, believed in the power of small increments as evidenced by the quote at the beginning of Chapter 13.

I lived in apartments ranging from decrepit to passable for 26 of my first 31 years. The other five years were spent in a worse-for-the-wear boyhood home of 1,200 square feet. My mother left her semi-impoverished family and one-room rural school after eighth grade to find work in a nearby town. My father graduated from high school and opened a small produce business supplying eggs and poultry to various wholesalers. It was not Lincoln-esque, replete with oil lamps and a drafty log cabin, but the circumstances were modest by any definition, similar to how most other folks lived in 1950s rural Iowa. Yet, it was America and dreams were possible, the fulfillment of them dependent on working hard, working smart, being patient, and perhaps getting a bit of luck along the way.[1] I wrote an essay years ago

---

[1] Luck is a tricky concept to use as an input to achievement. Among other things, in a vast world of ideas and products, assignment of luck as a factor in success is difficult to pinpoint. In lotteries, luck is obvious. In making the most of one's abilities and profiting thereby, it is not so obvious.

titled, "One Good Road Is Enough," where I talked about the dreams of a small-town kid, a town that had a blacktop road connecting it with a highway 7 miles distant (the other roads out of town were gravel).

In 1983, occupying a window seat on Air India, I looked down at the beige terrain passing miles below me when the pilot announced we were passing over Baghdad and would arrive in Bombay in a few hours. In the space next to my feet was a briefcase crammed with lecture notes on computer modeling of human decisions. Tears came into my eyes at that moment; one good road had been enough. I have a growing fear the roads I traveled from Rockford, Iowa to the larger world are closing, one by one, in small increments hardly noticeable. And that is why I experience disquietude and sadness. As I count the butcher's bill of freedoms lost, my deep affection for democracy is akin to how one must feel about a careless and unfaithful lover: The love remains but is mingled with sorrow at failings so easily seen and flaunted.

The parental State creates safety nets, institutes rescues and bailouts, and with tender mercy asks nothing from its citizens except votes, taxes, and obedience. A cycle thusly forms: The nanny state rescues, moral hazard disappears, and self-responsibility declines, leading to more rescues and . . . when the freedom they wished for was freedom from responsibility, then Athens ceased to be free.

Epilogue

WHAT THE RIVERS TAUGHT ME

I will begin with a verse and the chorus from a song I wrote some 30 years ago. The song is called "Some Play the Hornpipes," a hornpipe being an instrument to accompany a lively dance with the same name, originating in the 18th century. The first verse and chorus run like this:

> *I guess I lay beneath*
> *Every tree in my home county,*
> *Watching what the autumn does*
> *To leaves and butterflies,*
> *Hearing ancient melodies*
>   *And winnowing down the words*
> *Of those who brought me promises*
>   *And those who told me lies.*
> *(cho.)*
> *Aye, some play the hornpipes, others play the reels.*
> *Some may play a waltz*

or another dancing tune.

But I... I am bound to follow

the Wizard as he runs

In ever-growing circles...

... tracing rings around the moon.

After all these years, the images are crystalline, a mental film clip of what occurred on one of those high, hot, late-summer mornings common to the Middle West in July, on the trailing edge of my 11th year. And just what occurred? The opening idea to an epiphany of sorts, something that has stayed with me for more than 60 years, has guided me, and gives me a measured lightness here at age 72.

A Sunday it was, back then. My father had trundled us off to early Mass at Holy Name Catholic Church a few blocks from our small, one-and-a half-story house with a dangerously sagging front porch and an overall condition best described as a handyman's special. Finally released from what seemed to be interminable directives regarding the true path to eternal salvation and then forgetting quickly the sound of the choir but with the waft of incense still, sharp and clear in my head, I grabbed my fishing gear and headed for the rivers, pursuing salvation of a more immediate kind.

There were and are two lovely rivers flowing through 900-person Rockford, Iowa, two places of streaming change that became my friends and my teachers. One river was little over a hundred yards from our front door, the other a quarter mile from the back. A river rat's Valhalla, in other words.

On this Sunday I was headed for a good fishing place, the confluence of the two rivers about a mile below town. South along a dirt road, across the Rock Island Railroad tracks, past Billy Briggs's red barn, and farther south across a pasture and then through a small cornfield redolent of things green and growing. Down to where the rivers joined and the Wizard lived. If the wind was a north one, you could sometimes hear the tintinnabulation of the Lutheran church bells far upstream.

It was quiet. Understand, for every two people in America now, there was one in that distant time. No televisions or iPads or cellular phones. Fewer people had cars—one at most if they had a car—and often could not afford to drive them much or very far. Jet contrails were infrequent enough to be things of wonder and, in fact, so were commercial airplanes. How quiet the world seemed, how very quiet and subdued; I clearly remember that from my boyhood, the near-silence of my surroundings.

Sitting there on the upturned, external section of my minnow bucket, looking around and listening to the soft gurgle and slosh of two rivers conducting their marriage rites, I made the following observation: Let's see, minnows eat algae, bass eat minnows, and I eat the bass. Then what? I looked at the water, the sky, at everything around me. The Wizard began to speak, distant and almost unintelligible in the lightness of his voice. His was the voice of capricious wind, of trees bending and fish swimming, of rivers running far and fast, of clouds and sun, and stars that would appear later on. He operated then and still does at the nexus where reason and magic unite.

The idea slowly formed: Algae to minnows to bass to Bobby. It then occurred to me that Bobby likely was not at the top of the food chain. What was? What if there wasn't any top of any food chain? What? What? More whats and what-ifs and wheres and hows. The Wizard now was smiling, and nodding, but understanding that a boy of 11 was not ready for such heavy abstractions. Though excitable, he also was patient (I visualized him then, and still do, as about 3-feet tall, wearing an ankle-length black gown with gold salamanders sewn upon it, scuffed high-top shoes, and a worn, 1906 Brooklyn Dodgers ball cap some fisherman had lost to an April breeze years before).

Eventually I found language to express what I felt that day, that hot summer day 60 years back, and said as much in my novel *Border Music*. My protagonist in that story, a semi-wild fellow named Texas Jack Carmine, who long has served as my alter ego, is asked by his traveling partner Bobby McGregor about his view of life. When writing the story, the words came unbidden, without effort, and I then understood completely what had occurred by two rivers all those years ago. Texas Jack Carmine, a small-time rancher who rode wheat combines north to Canada during the summer, and a player of only one harmonica song, for that is the only one he knew, said this: "We come, we do, we go . . . nothin' more, and that's about as serious as we ought to take ourselves."

After typing that sentence, I breathed long, leaned back and took a sip of coffee. I read the sentence again, and then once more. And I grinned, a big grin, knowing finally I had put into words what I had sensed on a far-back Sunday morning where two rivers come together. Somewhere the Wizard was smiling too, maybe dancing through long meadow grass of a summer evening, waving his Brooklyn Dodgers cap.

We come, we do, we go...nothing more, and that's about as serious as we ought to take ourselves

Some people may find that outlook irreligious, and I have been so-accused. They should not, for the words of Texas Jack Carmine imply exactly the opposite of a skeptic's attitude, and a bit of reflection will make that clear. Only those who define religion *religiously* in terms of institutions, books, and physical structures will find it troubling. If, in fact, people who proclaim to be of great religious faith were to live by Jack Carmine's humble take on things, religion would be far more meaningful to far more people, and much of the religious strife stalking the earth would dissipate.

Understand then, for me an appreciation of the infinite and of existence is not a matter of foot-shuffling, head-bowed piety or people lifting reverent arms, beatific visions on their faces while music plays. Confronted by the near-mystical size and complexity of the universe I inhabit, I need something I can grasp and hold, something that brings infinity back to a level I can make sense of and use as a guide to living.

So my personal dictum—we come, we do, we go—functions as an unabashed approach to a happy and productive life, and as preparation for the end of that life. Take your work seriously, take the recipients of your work seriously, but when it comes to yourself, at least a modicum of humility is in order. It is a liberating, workable approach to day-by-day living and loving.

There have been times in my life when I did not keep that idea in mind, when it got lost in all the doing and perhaps obscured by that human failing called hubris, but I always have come back to it, to the idea, even before

I found the language to express what I believed. *Always*. And I keep it in mind as I write or lecture, taking my audience seriously, taking the ideas seriously, but not myself, for how can we take ourselves seriously in a seemingly infinite universe when our individual lives are nothing but an infinitely small and transient speck in the great sweep of time and space?

We come, we do, we go is a useful turn of mind, I think. It is not puffy moral exhortation, not as interminable as a Sunday sermon, and is easy to remember. I keep a list of things I call "Dumb-Bobs," idiotic behaviors I have periodically launched, and when I am tempted to think too well of myself, that list serves as a reminder to once more repeat, "We come, we do, we go." And the doing can be a rather grand voyage if you don't panic and if you believe, as I believe, not just in the calculus of Newton or the brilliance of Adam Smith, but also in magic and imagination and...yes, wizards who live along quiet country rivers.

So it was, the two rivers and I were friends. They were teachers without lesson plans or blackboards or PowerPoint. I will return to them following my death and cremation. I go to rivers now not so much to fly-fish as to be by and in running water. As for the rivers and what they taught me, Albert Camus captured it well:

...a man's work is nothing but a long journey to recover through the detours of art the two or three simple and great images which first gained access to his heart.[1]

And so it was for me, minnows to bass to Bobby to whatever lies at the top of the great food chain leading to some distant forever.

Architect Sir Henry Wotton is famously quoted (the idea originally came from the Roman architect Vitruvius) as saying a structure must have three qualities, those being commodity, firmness, and delight. Perhaps a life should be structured that way; that is, *useful, strong* and *durable*, and in

---

[1] At the turn of my 47th year, I made an eight-day solo canoe trip down those rivers. The object was to reconstitute the images of which Camus speaks. I subsequently wrote a long essay, "Going Soft Upon the Land and Down Along the Rivers," which was published in eight parts by the Des Moines Register. Later, the essay was included in a collection titled Just Beyond the Firelight. The rivers? They were as I remembered them: Good friends and gentle teachers.

one fashion or another, have an element of beauty that causes delight for oneself and for others. While you are involved in the doing, that's not a bad recipe for a good life.

For 20 years I had an old Zen expression pasted above my desk: "*To obtain a thing you must first stop wanting it.*" That seems enigmatic at first reading, but contains a basic truth about living well—passion begets both accomplishment and goodness. I learned to seek small universes with endless frontiers, diminutive worlds to explore within the context of an infinity beyond my comprehension—from long-range jump shots to three-cushion billiards to writing to economics and mathematics, to the subtleties possible on the fingerboard of a guitar or the many ways to interpret a lyrical song. It has been a place of adventure, physically and mentally, with moments of grandeur but grandeur restrained, where limits on my abilities are accepted, boundaries are recognized, and not taking myself too seriously.

I once wrote a song about my boyhood with the following snatch of words: "My world was circumscribed by the distance I could walk and still be home for suppertime." Nothing much has changed, it turns out; I have been to the rivers and now, at 72, I am turning for home with smell of my mother's cooking, like incense, still sharp and clear from 60 years ago.

Some nights I fix vegetable soup, and after supper walk outside and look at the sky. It is permissible to feel small and humbled by what you see—and I do. Some day the subatomic pieces of you might be part of those swirling galaxies, and that should be a happy thought, one of being a universal traveler. My dog Jack the Border collie and my old buddy Roadcat will all be specks whirling about out there; maybe we will bump into one another at some point, equal as always, riding together on Eddington's great arrow of time. Now that will be a grand adventure.

In writing about calculus, Bishop Berkeley described infinitesimals as the "ghosts of departed quantities." And we shall all be that one day. As you look out toward the universe, try saying quietly to yourself, we come, we do, we go, and that's about as important as I ought to take myself. I hope you will smile then, for that level of humility is liberating and also useful in dealing with the complex problems of life and society.

Measured against boundless infinity, the watermarks we leave will be infinitely small, no matter what our accomplishments—a matter of all things passing and the small increments we call our lives, and that is what the rivers taught me.

Eventually, wisdom emerges and you learn the niche of your organism—its biological job description—is to seek truth and not applause. Lamentably, so very regrettable, many of the best-known public figures affecting our lives have never progressed beyond the applause.

And so I still go to rivers, their ever-changing runs and riffles talking to me as they always have done, their voices composed of quickly passing, almost human sounds caused by random variations in current over rocks or transient changes in amplitude. The rivers spoke to me as a boy, they still speak to me as a man, reminding me of something I once wrote, "Old men and old rivers—it's gravity that does them both in." The rivers and I cannot thwart gravity no matter how much we resist it, and thus we come, we do, and finally we go.

The following is an entry from one of my notebooks. The relation to what I have said thus far is unmistakable.

Notebook entry, March 1990:

South India, busy village

Mid-afternoon, driver's tea-stop

Buy oranges, give most to children

Back in car, checking cameras

(Damn, it's hot)

Woman leans in window

 hand outstretched

  murmuring a beggar's cant

Dig in pocket, give her rupees

One click of the Nikon as she backs away

Then down the road

 toward Pondicherry

And thinking:

Epilogue

The distance between
God and beggars
is a matter of time
not of oranges
or rupees
But that preachy ice
melts quick in the mind
When the sun is a hammer
And heaven is a lifetime away

So it is, we come, we do, we go, and I have a distinct but reasonably tranquil sense the going is getting much closer, as gravity has its way with me, a relentless pull rivers understand all too well. Incidentally, I do not welcome the going, quite the opposite: I am having too much fun.

Thank you again for traveling with me through these pages. Time is a scarce resource, and I hope the benefit gained from your journey exceeds the cost.

I wish you adventure and success accompanied by a bit of humility, maybe with the help of a friendly wizard along the way. Though . . . a warning: If I begin talking about my wizard in polite company, people edge their children away from me, looking over their shoulders to be certain I am not wearing an old Brooklyn Dodgers ball cap and dancing a hornpipe.

I leave you with this, something I wrote during the ten years I lived on a remote, high-desert mountain ranch:

Wearing a floppy hat, the summer ran,
Afraid I might try to catch it one more time.
The Border collie and I,
By the south fence,
Smiled at such innocence,
And along with the mountain
Put on our winter clothes.

Appendix

FINANCIAL VERSUS PERSONAL DISCOUNTING
(OPTIONAL READING)

Here I explain discounting a bit more, avoiding complex mathematics and calculations. I think you will find it useful.

Case 1: No Risk

Suppose you have $5,000 to invest and decide to buy a one-year CD (certificate of deposit) paying 5 percent from a reputable bank. At the end of the year you will have $5,250, a no-risk, low-reward venture, given normal interest-rate levels. If you discount the $5,250 at 5 percent, it will be worth exactly $5,000, your original investment. To understand why $5,000 is the present value, simply multiply $5,000 by 1.05, with the result being $5,250. It is called the *present value* because $5,000 invested presently at 5 percent returns $5,250, the *future value* of money invested today.

This is straight, no-risk *financial discounting*. It involves only the time value of money and nothing else.

Case 2: Incorporating Risk

Suppose instead of purchasing a CD, a friend wants to borrow the $5,000 from you for one year. Your buddy has a spotty credit rating and needs the

Appendix

$5,000 to pay off one of six credit cards he uses. If you decide to loan him the money, you naturally want somehow to account for the risk. You can get 5 percent from the bank with no risk, so you offer to loan your friend the money for one year at 11 percent. If he repays the principle plus interest, you have $5,550 at year's end.

Incorporating a *risk premium* into interest rates is a standard way of accounting for risk. The risk premium here is 6 percent, added to the simple time value of money of 5 percent. Risk is why certain people have to pay more for "renting" money than others with better credit ratings. Banks unfairly are charged with discrimination when they demand higher interest rates on loans to people with less than sterling credit histories, but they have sound reasons for doing so. The higher the risk, the higher the reward must be, so runs the old adage, reminding us to be especially careful of too-good-to-be-true opportunities. So lenders incorporate a risk premium into their calculations in addition to the time value of money.

By the way, never loan money to friends or family. If you do, privately treat it as a gift, expecting never to get it back. Such loans are a good way to lose friends and cause strained familial relations. Uncle Ed will treat you differently than he would a bank or credit card company. Years ago I stopped loaning out my tools, as well, for many of the same reasons.

Case 3: Risk Plus Impatience

It may seem the time value of money incorporates behavioral impatience. You can make it do that by adding yet another premium onto the base rate of 5 percent used above, but then interest rates start to get fuzzy: how much is due to time, how much to risk, how much to sheer impatience? I prefer to partition these factors into their separate parts instead of commingling them into one interest rate that becomes obscure in its origins.

That is, let T represent Time, R represent Risk, and I represent impatience (impatience is sometimes called "present bias" in behavioral economics, a good general term). Let's return to Jimmy and Julia from Chapters 1 and 2. Jimmy discounted the investment of $1,000 for one year at 45 percent so that the $1,200 at the end of the year was worth only $828 in present terms, less than the $1,000 value of spending the money now.

Julia, on the other hand, used a discount rate of only 5 percent, resulting in a present value to her of $1,143. If 20 percent included both the financial and personal discount rates, the present value would be $1,000 and both Jimmy and Julia would be indifferent toward investing the $1,000 or spending the money now.

Thus, the value of *I* is critical in how people value the future. Jimmy unconsciously (well, almost) computed his discount rate at 20 percent + 25 percent = 45 percent, where the 25 percent is level of impatience added on to the time value of money of 20 percent. Julia, valuing the future highly and exhibiting *negative present bias*, subtracted 15 percent from the time value and discounted at 5 percent. So the *I factor* in decision-making is important.

If return of the $1,000 plus interest had risk attached to it, both Jimmy and Julia would want to account for the risk. Suppose each judge the likelihood of getting the principal plus interest back at .8, implying a risk factor of .2. Then Jimmy would multiply his discounted value of $828 times .8 and judge the investment to be worth only $662 (.8 x $828). Julia would value the investment at $1,143 x .8 = $914 and she, too, would not make the investment.

Handling the discounting in this fashion makes clear how much each element—*T, R, I*—is contributing to the discounting. Think of it this way:

- Compute the time value of money in the investment, *T*, ignoring *R* and *I*.
- Add/subtract to the pure time-value-of-money interest rate the impatience factor, *I*, and recalculate.
- Multiply the above result by the likelihood of obtaining the reward.

Alternatively, you can multiply the likelihood of receiving the money times the original outcome before discounting then take *T* and *I* into account. The answer will be the same. This is all handled somewhat differently in formal treatments in behavioral economics, but the results are equivalent. To show the behavioral economics formulations, I would have to develop a fair amount of notation and get into the underlying mathematics, though the mathematics is not unduly hard.

People do not ordinarily do these computations, instead relying on their intuition, commonly called "gut-feel," in making their decisions. But I find it a useful way of thinking about life in general, not just monetary investments. And it makes clear how risk and impatience influence decision-making.

Perhaps you have seen television advertisements for converting certain assets involving a stream of payments, such as an annuity from an inheritance or a lottery payout over time, into cash. "It's my money and I want it now!" abrasively shout the people in the ads. This is an appeal to the *I* factor inherent in people. The company offering the conversion will compute the settlement based on *T* and *R*, providing the shouters with a good deal less cash than the stream of payments would amount to over time even with *T* and *R* taken into account. Nothing illegal about any of that, but it an interesting example of the I factor being separated from time and risk.

References

Barrs, B. and Gage, N. 2007. *Cognition, Brain, and Consciousness*. London: Academic Press.

Baumeiser, R. and Vohs, K. 2003. In Lowenstein, G.; Read, D.; and Baumeister, R. (eds.) *Time and Decision*. New York: Russell Sage Foundation.

Biggs, A. 2010. "Public Pension Deficits Are Worse Than You Think." *The Wall Street Journal* (online edition), March 22.

Caplan, B. 2007. *The Myth of the Rational Voter*. Princeton, NJ: Princeton University Press.

Cross, J. and Guyer, M. *Social Traps*. Ann Arbor: The University of Michigan Press, 1980.

Evans, D. 2009. "Hidden Pension Fiasco May Foment Another $1 Trillion Bailout." Bloomberg.com. March 3.

Friedman, M. and Friedman, R. 1979. *Free to Choose*. New York: Harcourt, Inc.

Goldberg, J. 2009. "Democrats and Businessmen, Sitting in a Tree." *National Review*. May.

References

Goodman, J. 2009. "Three Strikes." *National Review*, August 14.

Hardin, G. 1968. "The Tragedy of the Commons." Science 162, 1243-1248. This article is widely available from a number of sources.

Hardin, G. 1995. *The Immigration Dilemma*. Washington, D.C.: Federation for American Immigration Reform, p. 40.

Hodge, S. 2009. "Accounting for What Families Pay in Taxes and What They Receive in Government Spending." Tax Foundation (online), September 21.

Kirk, R. 1997. *Edmund Burke: A Genius Reconsidered*. Wilmington, Delaware: Intercollegiate Studies Institute.

Konow, James. 2003. "Which is the Fairest One of All? A Positive Analysis of Justice Theories." *Journal of Economic Literature*, Volume XLI, December 2003, 1188-1239.

Levin, M. 2009. *Liberty and Tyranny*. New York: Simon & Schuster, Inc.

Levitt, S. and S. Dubner. 2005. *Freakonomics*. New York: HarperCollins.

McGurn, W. 2009. "My Big Fat Government Takeover." *The Wall Street Journal*. December 7.

McKenzie, R. 2008. "Dieting for Dollars." *Wall Street Journal*, January 4, 2008, p. Wll.

Murray, C. 1997. *What It Means to be a Libertarian*. New York: Broadway Books. Note: Murray is not a strict libertarian, but rather a classical nineteenth-century liberal. He explains his reasons for using the label libertarian in the introduction to the book.

Obrian, P. 1992. *The Letter of Marque*. New York: W. W. Norton & Company, Inc. (Originally published in 1988 by William Collins & Company, Ltd.)

Rahe, P. 2009. *Soft Despotism, Democracy's Drift*. New Haven, CT: Yale University Press.

Rawls, J. 2001. *Justice as Fairness*. Cambridge, MA: Belknap Press.

Read, L. December 1958. "I, Pencil." *The Freeman*. The essay can be easily found on the internet, as well.

Rossiter, L. 2006. *The Liberal Mind.* St. Charles, IL: Free World Books, LLC.

Rothbard, M. 2000. "Egalitarianism as a Revolt Against Nature." *Egalitarianism as a Revolt Against Nature and Other Essays.* Auburn, AL: The Ludwig von Mises Institute.

Rothbard, M. 2006. "Origins of the Welfare State in America." *Mises Daily,* Ludwig von Mises Institute. August 11.

Schelling, T. 1960. *Choice and Consequence.* Cambridge, MA: Harvard U. Press, p. 62.

Singer, P. 1993. *Practical Ethics* (2nd edition). New York: Cambridge University Press.

Sowell, T. 2007. *A Conflict of Visions.* New York: Basic Books. The original version of this book was published in 1987.

Staib, E. 2009. "Is Emergency Room Care a Failed Market?" *Mises Daily,* Ludwig von Mises Institute. September 24.

Thaler, R. and Sunstein, C. 2008. *Nudge.* New Haven: Yale University Press.

Unruh, B. 2010. "Taxpayers pay $101,000 for Pelosi's in-flight 'food, booze.'" *World Net Daily.* Original data from the article was obtained from Judicial Watch, which requested the data through the Freedom of Information Act.

Waller, R. 1990. "The Trials of Hunter Rawlins." *One Good Road Is Enough.* Ames, IA: Iowa State University Press.

White, Eugene. 2010. "The Poor Are Better Off Renting." *The Wall Street Journal* (online edition), February 10.